NEIGHBORS, STRANGERS, WITCHES, AND CULTURE-HEROES

Ritual Powers of Smith/Artisans in Tuareg Society and Beyond

Susan Rasmussen

University Press of America,® Inc.
Lanham · Boulder · New York · Toronto · Plymouth, UK

Copyright © 2013 by
University Press of America,® Inc.
4501 Forbes Boulevard
Suite 200
Lanham, Maryland 20706
UPA Acquisitions Department (301) 459-3366

10 Thornbury Road
Plymouth PL6 7PP
United Kingdom

Library of Congress Control Number: 2013938014
ISBN: 978-0-7618-6148-5 (clothbound : alk. paper)
eISBN: 978-0-7618-6149-2

Cover photo by the author.

⊖™ The paper used in this publication meets the minimum
requirements of American National Standard for Information
Sciences—Permanence of Paper for Printed Library Materials,
ANSI Z39.48-1992

CONTENTS

PREFACE

NEIGHBORS OR STRANGERS? ALLEGEDLY "MYSTIC" POWERS, MARGINALITY, AND IDENTITY AMONG SMITH/ARTISANS

During my research in Tuareg communities of Niger and Mali, friends often warned me to never refuse anything a smith/artisan requested. Otherwise, many insisted, some mayhem would follow—expressed in the local idiom as anger "flying" from the heart of the offended artisan toward the offender, his/her kin, or property. Local residents called this force *tezma* in Tamajaq, their Berber (Amazigh) language in northern Niger and Mali. Regardless of whether or not this force "really existed" in my own cultural logic, I took this warning very seriously. Overwhelmingly, most local residents, including smith/artisans called *inaden,* treated me with kindness and hospitality, and were concerned about protecting my welfare. Still, I pondered what this advice meant, what sort of power was involved, and why it was so important to recognize it. I tried to comply with these injunctions myself, and observed cases of *tezma* accusations which often followed infractions of this rule. Even minor and inadvertent infractions did, in fact, result in misfortunes, or at least reactions from smiths, though such episodes were usually temporary and mild.

Anthropologists often study and write about so-called "mystic" or ritual powers glossed in English as alternately "witchcraft," "sorcery," "evil eye," more generally associated with concepts of evil and pollution (Douglas, 1966; Parkin, 1985). Some have attempted to explain them in terms of "western" or Euro-American logical categories (Evans-Pritchard, 1937,1950), intending to show the connections between "magic," science, and religion. Others have acknowledged the problematic implications of this approach, preferring instead to place these beliefs and practices in local contexts and explanatory idioms (McNaughton, 1988; Stoller, 1987,1989; West, 2007) or to accept that their significance is perhaps unknowable. I take a middle-ground on this issue. On the one hand, I eschew efforts to force local systems of thought—globalization and nation-state influences notwithstanding—into the anthropologist's own logical categories, implicitly assuming that everyone must be exactly alike—i.e., "others" must be "like us," in order to make sense as rational human beings. On the other hand, I consider it imperative to ground so-called "witch-like" and other ritual powers in social and historical contexts, and convey them, in so far as possible, as represented by local viewpoints and voices. The anthropologist must alternately saturate him/herself with these powers and stand back from them at a distance in order to appreciate their complex meanings .

This book is about the allegedly superhuman powers and social predicaments of skilled specialists usually called in English "smith/artisans" or "blacksmiths," though their roles in some communities—particularly in Africa— are much broader, encompassing not solely material visual art production, but also sociopolitical and spiritual reproduction. The primary focus here is upon their ritual roles and their social and economic relationships to non-smiths.

First, I analyze primary data from my long-term , approximately thirty years of ethnographic field research in rural and urban Tuareg communities of Niger and more recently, Mali. Next, I conduct a cross-cultural comparison: I re-analyze secondary social-historical and ethnographic data from several other African societies: the Amhara in Ethiopia, the Bidan (Moors) in Mauritania, the Kapsiki in Cameroon, and the Mande peoples in southern Mali. In Tuareg society and beyond, smith/artisans' alleged powers and statuses and their relationships with traditional, often aristocratic patrons and other non-smiths have played important roles in shaping local and "neighboring" identities of self and "other." More broadly,the goal of this book is to contribute to current efforts in anthropology and African Studies to explore instrumental and social constructionist, rather than primordial or essentialist aspects of identity and difference (Grinker and Steiner, 1997).

Smith/artisans' ritual powers and social relationships have received some attention in the literature, but not in terms of the broad anthropology of religion framework I pursue in the present book: namely, a post-structural approach to ritual powers that draws on, but also critically refines classical perspectives pioneered by Mary Douglas (1966), thereby enriching recent anthropological explanations of so-called "witch figures," "evil eye," and "pollution beliefs," which tend, with few exceptions, to inadvertently convey the discourses and viewpoints of the accusers and oppressors, and to emphasize static structural positions and official ideology and history. For example, despite the richness of recent and current studies of powers resembling witchcraft and evil eye, even those works concerned with modernity and globalization tend to echo more classical studies' emphases upon witch-hunting and scapegoating as having positive consequences in the old functionalist manner of searching for ultimate harmony over long-term—as either leveling mechanisms in times of socioeconomic and political upheaval (Comaroff and Comaroff , 1993; Englund, 1996; Greschiere, 1997; Sanders and Moore, 2001), or as fostering internal cohesion of the group in times of threats to it (Auslander in Comaroff and Comaroff, 1993; Douglas,1992; Douglas and Wildavsky, 1982). By implication, these perspectives in their unintended consequences tend to blame the accused "witches," rather than their accusing aggressors. In other words, there is the need to stop inadvertently blaming the accused "witches" in anthropology of witchcraft studies, and to include more intimate viewpoints of the supposed "witches" themselves.

The present study of ritual powers is inspired by valuable pioneering studies of smith/artisans' conversion of natural substances into cultural and material artifacts (Herbert, 1993; McNaughton, 1988), but this book emphasizes the social construction of these powers as alternately empowering and endangering to those alleged to possess them. The goal of this book, in its first sections ethnographic, and in its remaining sections comparative, historical, and theoretical, is to reclaim the positive in those powers conventionally glossed as "witchcraft," "pollution," or "evil eye" in anthropology, and more broadly, to recast accusations of apparently "witch-like" powers as related to the larger concepts of other and "strangeness" (Berland and Rao, 2004; Simmel, 1950) but in terms that are dynamic and fluid, thereby shifting the locus of malevolence away from those accused of ritual powers toward the structural and relational conditions of accusation. More broadly, the book analyzes the social constructions of fear and ambivalence, as illustrated in the ambiguous, changing powers of these skilled ritual specialists and culture-heroes within larger religious, socioeconomic, and political contexts, but also in intimate social contexts that give them greater voice in their own representation. In this endeavor, I draw on theories and concepts more akin to social constructions of exclusionary projects than to narrower foci upon "witches," although some witchcraft theories are also relevant to my data and argument. Hopefully, these efforts will counterbalance some tendencies in the literature to echo the official authoritative representations of superhuman powers.

Smith/artisans and their alleged powers are entangled in religious and socioeconomic forces beyond accuser and accused. While there is generalized fear of smith/artisans and their powers that enable them to transform nature into culture in many societies, this fear, I show, is expressed differently and has varying consequences, in different social contexts. The imagery surrounding these specialists suggests alternating perceptions of them as neighbors, strangers, witches, and culture heroes. These chameleon-like transformations and their consequences emerge from two kinds of encounters: collisions between "official" (i.e., textual/scriptural and state-sponsored) religions and indigenous "traditional" religions, on the one hand, and between longstanding and changing socio-economic orders, on the other.

In Tuareg ethnographies, there is only brief mention of smith/artisans (Bernus, 2006; Casajus, 2000; Rasmussen, 1995,1997,2001,2006) in relation to *tezma* power, which they are often accused of activating. Here I emphasize Tuareg smiths' ritual and socioeconomic roles, their oral art in mythico-historical memory and performance, and their social relationships more than their finished visual art objects; for these objects, particularly the silver jewelry, have already been vividly described (Bernus, 2006; Gabus, 1970; Gardi, 1977; Loughran ,1990; Loughan and Seligman, 2006; Nicolaisen, 1997; Saenz, 1980). Thus my own emphasis is intended to complement and augment these other rich works, and I refer to the Tuareg smiths' material visual arts only when relevant to their ritual and social roles.. Likewise, in re-analyzing the secondary data on smith/artisans and their alleged powers in four other African societies, I also emphasize their ritual and social roles, rather than their material visual arts.

APPROACH, ARGUMENT, THEORETICAL FRAMEWORK, AND ORGANIZATION OF BOOK

In anthropology, there is the need to re-frame ritual powers beyond narrow theories of anomaly, pollution, (Douglas, 1966) and "witchcraft," to analyze more fully ambivalence and mixed sentiments toward those with ambiguous, continually re-defined powers, and include diverse viewpoints and "voices." These powers, I argue, cannot be explained in terms of either functionalist-inspired social integration and solidarity, or in terms of structuralist-inspired reified classification and contrast. Instead, when these powers are analyzed in post-structural terms situating them in context, they come to light as alternately exclusionary (Bunzl, 2004), resulting in "abject" status for those at the confluence of conflicting forces (Butler, 1993) and celebratory, recognizing the heroic cultural reproduction of specialists who are needed, yet feared for the uncertain sources and uses of their powers. Smith/artisans in Tuareg society and in some other African societies, I show, stand at a nexus of organized religion and more longstanding "traditional" or indigenous local religions, which, in some contexts, interweave, and in other contexts collide and compete with each other. As close neighbors but also strangers from outside with ambiguous origins, these skilled specialists become mediators and culture-heroes, but in other contexts they become the focus of ambivalence. Perceptions of them as alternately neighbors, strangers, witches, and culture-heroes reflect the ambiguity and indeterminacy of their alleged powers, as well as the wider fears of the unknown and the uncontrollable, which emerge from overlapping and competing religious traditions and changing socioeconomic predicaments in their societies. Many smith/artisans are simultaneously like journalists and diplomats, and this complex role requires delicate balancing since one enables verbal freedom, and the other demands discretion.

In the first portion of this book, the primary focus is upon *tezma* power primarily associated with smith/artisans by many Tuareg (sometimes called Kel Tamajaq, after their language), whose communities today straddle the central Sahara and its Sahelian fringes, regions with cultural influences from north and south of the Sahara. Today, most Tuareg reside in the nation-states of Niger, Mali, Algeria, Libya, and Burkina Faso, are nominally Muslim, socially stratified, and practice semi-nomadic stockbreeding. Many have suffered from recurrent ecological crises (droughts) and political violence (wars) in their regions. In the opening sections of this book, there is presented an ethnographic background of the Tuareg of Niger and Mali, a description of the *inaden* smith/artisans, their alleged superhuman ritual power, with cases and discourses from the perspectives of both smiths and non-smiths, whose pre-colonial roles and relationships are changing to varying degrees in rural and urban settings.

Next, I contextualize this power in *inaden* accounts of their origins and history, and details of their social, economic, and ritual roles and relationships to their formerly inherited aristocratic patron families, as well as other non-smith customers in their increasingly more flexible client-patron arrangements. At intervals, I pause to engage broader theories on ritual powers, witchcraft, exclusionary projects, and self-other relationships more generally. In this I am inspired by, but also critique and refine, the analytical devices of "peripatetics" and Simmel's concept of the "stranger" (Berland and Rao, 2004; Simmel, 1950) for understanding smiths' alleged superhuman powers.

In the second portion of this book, I interweave secondary social historical and ethnographic data on ritual powers and social relationships of smith/artisans in Amhara, Bidan, Kapsiki, and Mande societies with my own re-analysis of them, and compare and contrast the roles of these specialists and their alleged powers in these societies to those in Tuareg society. Specifically, in these latter chapters, I focus on the following alleged ritual powers: namely: *qalb* attributed to *buda* people conventionally translated as "people of the evil eye," who tend to be predominantly smith/artisans, among the Amhara in Ethiopia (Freeman, 2003; Reminick, 1974; Mains, 2007), *echar*, widely attributed to *m'allemin* smith/artisans among the Bidan (Moors) in Mauritania (Cervello, 2004), *beshengu* associated with a strong aroma, attributed to the *rerhe* smiths among the Kapsiki people in Cameroon (Van Beek, 1992), and the power called *nyama* attributed to smith/artisans within the *nyamakala* social stratum among the Mande-speaking people in southern Mali (McNaughton, 1988). I juxtapose and interweave these secondary data with the Tuareg data, "tacking" back and forth between these cases for their comparative significance and more general theoretical implications. All these specialists share the following features in common: in general, like Tuareg *inaden*, they tend to practice smithing and also sometimes, additional ritual specialisms—for example, in healing, rites of passage, and verbal art performance for patrons; they define themselves (and are defined by others) as having originated from outside the community; they are widely believed to hold ambiguous powers which may be used in diverse ways; and in rural communities, they practice (or have until very recently practiced) client-patron relationships with their inherited dominant, higher status (often aristocratic) neighbors, in which there are some tensions, but also—to varying degrees in these societies—some mutual dependencies, fictive kinship affection, and even hints of awe. Yet there are also some contrasts between these powers, their practitioners, and their different ritual, social, cultural, and economic contexts. In some respects, these conditions confirm Simmel's concept of the "stranger" as a mediator, but in others they modify or refute this interpretation of smiths' roles, thereby revealing the value of opening up these analytical odd-job concepts to include fluid dynamics of smith and non-smith relationships.

In the more comparative and theoretical sections, I critically assess the varying degrees to which, and how, smiths' identities and powers in the social and ritual spheres have been modified and redefined—to their advantage or disadvantage, depending upon the context—by dominant official state and scriptural religions, on the one hand, and by changing socioeconomic circumstances, on the other. Particularly significant in shaping definitions of smiths' powers, I show, are the relative degrees of influence of organized ("official" or scriptural) and indigenous ("traditional" local African) religions pre-dating Islam or Christianity. Powerful in shaping attitudes toward smith/artisans' powers, for example, is the marked influence of Christianity among the Amhara, as contrasted to its much lesser influence, and, conversely, the marked persistence of "traditional" African ritual and cosmology that remains much stronger in the Kapsiki communities. I show how the powerful influence of Islam among the Bidan (Moors) and among the Tuareg impart both positive and negative attitudes toward these specialists' ritual powers and social roles, but in the Tuareg case, there is also a greater interweaving, at times harmonious and at times conflictual, of Islam with pre-Islamic local religious and cultural influences. In other words, there are powerful local Tuareg cultural interpretations of Islam that mitigate some of the ambivalence toward smith/artisans despite the ambiguous position of these specialists (in their own, as well as others' viewpoint) within "official" (Qur'anic) Islam. By contrast, there is much less official Qur'anic Islamic influence upon smiths' ritual roles, despite some presence of Islam and to a lesser extent also of Christianity, among the Mande, and these specialists, like those among the Kapsiki, tend to suffer less scapegoating, their power tends to be less negatively defined, and they tend to enjoy greater social integration with non-smiths (notwithstanding their officially "low" or at least ambiguous status and endogamous marriage patterns).

Also relevant to attitudes toward smiths' powers, I show, are property relations. In cases of greater tensions over ownership of land and other property, particularly in sedentary farming communities and those communities undergoing transitions to settled lifestyles and farming occupations, and where there are land shortages and other changes threatening the social prestige and economic security of former pre-colonial (and current post-colonial) aristocrat/patrons of smith/artisan clients, the latters' ritual powers tend to become more negatively defined, and there tends to be greater scapegoating of them.

Yet despite the importance of economics— a powerful factor in many recent and current studies of the connections between contemporary "witchhunts" and globalization (Comaroff and Comaroff , 1993), witchcraft accusations in general, and allegations of smith/artisans' ritual powers more specifically, have existed in many societies even before globalization and also, in many cases, have emerged in times of relative economic and political calm, as well as in upheaval. Thus while I do not ignore economic processes here, nonetheless, I argue that, in many respects, also fundamental to understanding so-called "witch-like" powers, is the play of moral and political powers, which sometimes, but not always, produce exclusionary projects (Bunzl, 2004). In fact, such mediators as culture-heroes may become celebrated. Why, then, the cultural need to classify certain powers in one way or another regardless of more generalized economic forces? Envy, for example, may occur in societies during times of relative prosperity, as well as times of deprivation, (Epstein, 2004), although this may become intensified in times of turmoil.

The basis for the construction of power is not so much the "witch-like" figure's static identity as pollution, anomaly, or stranger/mediator, but rather, the accuser's reiterated ambivalence toward the accused, which can respond differently according to their predicament. These different predicaments and uncertain outcomes suggest that smith/artisans stand at a nexus of shifting philosophical, cosmological, mythical, and socio-political forces that can alternately empower and disenfranchise them in their relations with patrons. They also suggest that some aspects of smith/non-smith relations—particularly in socioeconomic property concerns—do indeed recall some conventional "witchcraft" and "evil eye" concepts and practices elsewhere, much analyzed in anthropology. But additional, more complex nuances emerge here in their relation to the wider problem of exclusionary projects, concepts of "other," stranger, and evil, and abject status. In contexts of religious pluralism and tolerance, with strong persistence of local or "indigenous" or "traditional" religions, and where there are fewer insecurities over socioeconomic hierarchies, I show, smiths' powers tend to be perceived as less threatening, somewhat like those of a neighbor close by, with whom one enjoys mutual assistance and sociability, and even, at times, a culture-hero who protects the community from harm. But to do this, smiths must also protect themselves and their esoteric special cultural knowledge and skills. In contexts where smiths' powers compete with specialists in organized (textual/scriptural) religion, and where there are challenges and ambiguities to older hierarchies and tensions over property—particularly land—smiths' powers tend to be perceived as much more threatening.

I conclude with a discussion of more general implications of these findings for anthropological understandings of power, belonging, and distinction. Hopefully, the present book offers ethnographic, social historical, and comparative perspectives which engage and contribute to wider theoretical issues in so-called "witchcraft" studies, especially in continental Africa. Widely-held beliefs in smiths' ritual powers therefore have a double-face of positive and negative consequences for these specialists' predicament. Valuable studies have illustrated the material creativity of these specialists, who convert natural substances into cultural artifacts (McNaughton, 1988; Herbert,1993). In this book, I take this process to another level, previously less explored: I show how smith's powers and their social constructions illustrate the ways in which societies and individuals situate themselves vis-à-vis their neighbors—otherness is highly subjective and relative—and the imagined philosophical, social, and material worlds in which they live. Concepts of ritual powers of smith/artisans reveal how some are included and how "others" are excluded, in the play of hegemony and resistance, and how allegedly "superhuman" powers are manipulated to advantage and disadvantage in aggressive, but also protective strategies—I show, for example, how some local typifications and stereotypes are also used by Tuareg smith/artisans as "weapons of the weak" (Scott, 1992).

In these formulations of identity and power, smith/artisans can be simultaneously local and other, neighbor and witch. They are culture heroes mediating between different worlds, but in that process, I argue, we should remember that such persons are vulnerable as well as powerful; for these worlds may regard their status ambivalently precisely because of their flexibility. This book is important more broadly in its human rights implications, in its implied appeal to support all those falsely accused of witchcraft or otherwise scapegoated. The concept of marginality is very subjective and relative. Anthropology needs to be more explicit concerning the vulnerability, as well as the protective (not solely aggressive or harmful) powers of ritual specialists—whether defined by the gloss of "witch" or not (Crick, 1976). The book also draws attention to a larger issue for anthropology and ethnography: how does one represent local stereotyping (very real in all cultural settings, including our own) (Herzfeld, 2004) without reproducing those stereotypes? How do anthropologists celebrate the rich diversity of humanity without reproducing exoticism and hierarchy? As Arens and Karp (1989) point out, anthropologists should view ritual powers from a perspective outside western cultural concepts of official political power; only then can one appreciate their regenerative and regenerating capacity. I undertake this task here, beginning with the Tuareg case.

ACKNOWLEDGMENTS

It would be impossible to thank all those persons in Niger, Mali, France, and the United States who over many years have made this study and other studies in my longitudinal research possible. I use pseudonyms throughout the main body of this book for those who are the research subjects, friends, assistant/consultants, and colleagues in Niger and Mali, in order to protect their identities. I express my deepest gratitude to them , many of whom reside in rural areas and regional towns, as well as to the directors of the l'Institut de recherches en sciences humaines in Niamey, Niger and of the Centre National de recherches scientifiques et techniques in Bamako, Mali, for their kind generosity, hospitality, and assistance in explaining to me the nuances of the Tamajaq language and Tuareg culture and society. Likewise, I change or omit the names of small oasis villages and nomadic camps. Only names of large towns and regions are specified. In this project, originally a comparative study of rural and urban Tuareg smith/artisans, as well as other research projects enabling me to continually return to Tuareg communities in many residences and visits between 1983 and 2012, I gratefully acknowledge support from Fulbright Hays, Wenner-Gren Foundation, Social Science Research Council, National Geographic Committee for Research and Exploration, Indiana University, and University of Houston. I am also grateful to a number of scholars, colleagues and friends in France and the United States for their intellectual inspiration in my work, as well as their kind encouragement and advice, at various times. In France, they include Andre Bourgeot, Dominique Casajus, Helene Claudot-Hawad, Hawad Mahmoudan, Alhassane Ag Solimane, and Mohammed Ag Erless. In the United States, these persons include long-term inspirations for my research interests in anthropology of religion, medico-ritual healing and healers, aging and the life course/cycle, gender, verbal art performance, and African Humanities, namely: Mary Jo Arnoldi, Charles Bird, John Johnson, Johannes Fabian, Thomas Hale, Michael Herzfeld, Roy Wagner, Robert Levine, Leonard Plotnicov, Thomas Seligman, Paul Stoller, Jaan Valsiner, and last but not least, the late Ivan Karp. Finally, I am also infinitely grateful to my family, particularly my husband Manuel, for encouragement and moral support in all my endeavors, as well as our shared concerns for social justice. As for my personal connections to this topic, my family does not include blacksmiths in its recent, known history, though a sister makes beautiful beaded jewelry. Others who inspire me to explore powers and dangers and their human rights implications include a great-grandfather who was a tailor, socialist, and activist in labor rights, a cousin who fought the Nazis and was imprisoned during that war, and numerous other friends, neighbors, relatives, and teachers whose humanity I have greatly admired.

INTRODUCTION

Power, danger, and protection are intertwined in human experience. In many African and other societies, including Tuareg communities of northern Niger and Mali, smith/artisans, called *inaden*, are surrounded by paradox and contradiction. As social mediators, technicians, and artists, these specialists are needed, yet feared. Many local residents—smiths and non-smiths alike—allege that these specialists have outside, ambiguous origins, but their separate origins often have close connections to those of non-smiths in the communities where they continue longstanding, albeit modified, client-patron relationships. More broadly, specialists as far-flung as smiths in Africa and the Middle East, tinkers in Ireland, and Roma in eastern Europe are believed to possess superhuman ritual powers sometimes defined by others (and occasionally, also by these specialists themselves) as dangerous, potentially even "malevolent," and can be activated unconsciously or consciously, depending upon the context. Among the Tuareg, I first encountered this power in the Air Mountain region of northern Niger.[1]

One blistering hot June morning, during the season preceding the sparse and uncertain annual rains, in rural Tuareg communities of semi-nomadic, Muslim, socially stratified herders, oasis gardeners, smith/artisans, and Islamic scholars, I awoke after sleeping fitfully—shaking violently with chills, fever, respiratory distress, and stomach queasiness that I attributed to a "cold," "the flu," or possibly malaria. Yet I also experienced more alarming, less explicable symptoms I did not usually associate with these illnesses, or believe I could feel altogether at the same time: all night long, I had smelled a powerful, yet indefinable aroma emanating from my surroundings, gradually approaching me and penetrating deep within my sleeping-bag. There had also been strange rustling noises I could not identify. But these symptoms, though intense, were brief. Eventually, all of them subsided, including the odor (which curiously, remained for a while, highly concentrated inside my sleeping-bag!), but left me exhausted. After another day, these symptoms left suddenly overnight (I perspired heavily, smelled the same odor much nearer, but curiously, then woke up without the illness).

Friends in that small semi-nomadic camp, where several closely-related families of noble descent clustered their mat and hide tents and small adobe houses into a few compounds, herding a few scrawny animals left over from droughts and seeking additional livelihood in erratic oasis gardens and labor migration of younger male kin, offered an explanation to me upon hearing about my experience. They instantly sat up, startled, but with an air of certitude, declared, "You caught *tezma* from Bidi (pseudonym), the old smith/artisan man (you visited the other day) in that smith village over there," (gesturing toward the small smith/artisan village—relatively prosperous from their widely admired leather and silver works, just over the hill). Earlier, upon my visit there, I had gently and reluctantly refused an old smith man's request for eye ointment, explaining to him that I had left it behind me in another larger village where I stayed longterm with my host family during my field residence. Later, upon his visit to the noble household where I had spent that night in great distress, I had given him food. Following my food gift to him, my strange symptoms had departed. Although I was aware of local theories of illness and misfortune including allegedly "malevolent" powers from smiths, I had not made any causal connections between these events until discussing these events with friends.

Of course, not all Tuareg believe in this power, but many do, and it is a frequent topic of discussion among diverse residents in Tuareg communities. Families of aristocratic background—the traditional patrons of smith/artisans, once controlled the Saharan caravan trade, monopolized large livestock and weapons, and collected tribute and labor from subordinates in the hierarchical pre-colonial system in exchange for protecting them militarily. Many persons of aristocratic or "noble" origins are now impoverished in the wake of ecological disasters and political violence in their region. Yet despite some shared viewpoints and common experiences, even these noble families disagreed on the causes, effects, and symptoms of this power. For example, during our conversations the next day, a woman who frequently did business with the smith/artisans insisted that what I had caught was not *tezma,* asserting to me, "only stomach and molar tooth aches can be caused by *tezma.*" She did, however, strongly believe in that power, and related several cases of it to me: for example, how once when she traveled to that nearby smith/artisan village, she did not have a pleasant experience there. After ordering work from a male smith renowned for his work and bargaining with him over prices, she claimed that he gave her *karambaza* (a stomach ache specifically from *tezma).*

During conversation over tea as we listened to local song recordings, the same woman also related another case of *tezma,* allegedly from a smith who resided in her own village. [*Inaden* do not all invariably reside in separate villages or camps, but tend, in both rural and urban areas, to reside in their own neighborhoods.] This power was cast on a mutual acquaintance: the nephew of an older woman, while he was a child. Concerned about his welfare because *tezma* can allegedly kill small children and livestock, I inquired about the outcome. She explained: "To undo this, the accused smith had to jump three times over the child, while the latter was stretched out on the ground." She added that the smith/artisan had seen wheat in that family's garden, and had gone to the noble's home. Yet the smith had not actually asked for the wheat; he merely had wanted or coveted it; "...and that," she insisted, " is sufficient to activate and cast the *tezma.*"

During the same conversation, another person, a man who often assisted me with oral art transcriptions, confirmed that my illness was indeed *tezma,* cast or sent from the same elderly smith man who had requested eye medication from me, but whom, recall, I had to refuse because I had left it elsewhere. Indeed, he declared that even he had caught some degree of *tezma* from the same smith/artisan, who attacked him in his molar tooth. "The reason," he explained, "was because I accompanied you over there." This power can be activated against the accomplices, as well as the violators of the taboo against denying smiths what they request. He also asserted that "elderly smiths, especially, have very strong *tezma*."

Many smith/artisans with whom I discussed this power acknowledged its existence, but asserted that "anyone can practice *tezma*...although our nobles say we do (activate) this (power) more often." Indeed, even some persons of aristocratic background acknowledged this, but added cryptically, "nobles rarely practice *tezma*, but when we do, it is really strong!"

Regardless of some disagreements over the precise causes and symptoms of *tezma*, its association with smith/artisans was prevalent. Everyone anxiously urged me to give to smith/artisans. Yet seemingly paradoxically, Tuareg smith/artisans are ideally supposed to be poor, in their own as well as noble typifications, notwithstanding the increasing prosperity of some *inaden* in their specialized work as jewelers in tourist art and international itinerant trade of their art objects. These preliminary observations prompted me to reflect on the significance of this alleged power and others resembling it.

THE ISSUES AND QUESTIONS

In this analysis, I ask first, what exactly is superhuman or "mystical" power in general, and in particular, what part does it play in identifying Tuareg and other smith/artisans and related groups some scholars call "peripatetic" (Berland and Rao, 2004) or "marginal" yet who also occupy centrally important mediatory roles, in many cultural settings, especially in Africa? I take this question a bit farther, however, in asking also what are their socioeconomic roles and relations to non-smiths, in not solely the latters' viewpoints, but also in smith/artisans' own viewpoints.

Why are skilled specialists sometimes scapegoated, rather than rewarded? To what extent, and in what circumstances, do widely-held beliefs in the superhuman ritual powers of Tuareg and other African smith/artisans result in lauding them as culture heroes, and to what extent, and in what circumstances, do these beliefs result in oppressing them, in exclusionary projects conferring abject status? The foregoing vignettes hint of envy, a prominent theme in the literature on "witchcraft" and "evil eye" in anthropology (Moore and Sanders, 2003; Stewart and Strathern, 2004). Yet on closer scrutiny, there emerge additional, more complex, even contradictory themes in these dynamics. For example, although in standard local typifications, *inaden* are ideally supposed to be poor, and non-smiths, in particular those of aristocratic origin (called *imajeghen*) , should give generously to smith/artisans, many nobles asserted that "*inaden* are now rich." In fact, not all *inaden* were wealthy, though some were becoming prosperous from the tourist trade. On the other hand, persons of noble origin have always been obliged to give to smith/artisans, whatever the socioeconomic status of either party, in the past or in the present, and all Tuareg have suffered intermittently from wars, droughts, and other upheavals in French colonial and post-colonial eras, thereby suggesting the need for caution in concluding that *inaden* upward socioeconomic mobility is the sole "culprit" in cases of envy and scapegoating.

Most Tuareg are Muslim, and practice bilateral descent, inheritance, and succession , retaining some local matrilineal cultural, legal, and medico-ritual institutions pre-dating the more recent patrilineal institutions introduced by nation-state, Arab, and Qur'anic influences. Most Tuareg converted to Islam between the eighth and eleventh centuries C.E. (Norris, 1975,1990).[2] Today most are predominantly semi-nomadic, and many persons of diverse social origins combine livestock herding with additional occupations such as oasis gardening.[3] Most reside in the rural Saharan and Sahelian regions of Niger, Mali, Algeria, Libya, and Burkina Faso, though some also live in multi-ethnic towns. Their complex, hierarchical but flexible and negotiable social relationships, particularly in the countryside, still remain salient in ideology and practice: these include longstanding but changing hereditary stratification of aristocratic, tributary, and maraboutique (Islamic scholar) descent groups, former slaves in varying degrees of clientage and servitude and their descendants, and smith/artisans.[3]All these groups are organized into larger regional confederations, each headed by a traditional leader called an *amenukal*, who were absorbed into first, French West Africa (or some groups, into Algeria) and later, the independent nation-states, with modified powers (Bernus, 1981; Claudot-Hawad, 1993; Nicolaisen and Nicolaisen, 1997). In many groups in Niger and Mali, this *amenukal* is still elected by representative noble clans, but this leader's powers have been much modified by the French colonial, and more recently, backed by military force of the independent state governments.[4]

In tezma, Tuareg smiths' and nobles' self and mutual perceptions emerge. That force, which is called *ettama* in some regions and dialects of Tamajaq, in some respects approaches classical anthropological definitions of "witchcraft," "evil eye" and pollution (Douglas, 1966,1992; Marwick, 1962). Most residents explain that *tezma* refers to a force unintentionally activated most often when a smith's request for a gift, compensation, or pay is rejected. In the countryside, this force is most often cited as a cause of grievances in rural areas, and usually involves conflict between a smith/artisan and a person of aristocratic origin (sing. *amajagh,* or *imoujagh*, plural *imajeghen*, Tamajaq terms also related to terms for "Tuareg" and Berber, i.e., Amazigh). Tezma is said to "fly" from a client smith/artisan's "angry heart" toward his/her patron noble or non-smith customer, upon the latter's refusal to comply with the former's request. Te*zma* is usually class-specific, usually emanating from *inaden*, and is believed to cause primarily misfortune and ill luck. Only occasionally may persons of noble origins activate this power, and in these instances, nobles claim that their own *tezma* is more powerful than that of smiths. But all my observed ethnographic cases involved *inaden* accused of *tezma*, never *imajeghen* nobles or other non-smiths.

How many Tuareg smith/artisans are there? Surveys have shown their number to be relatively stable within each political unit (confederation). Among the Kel Geres confederation in southern Niger, they represent 3 to 4 percent of the whole population (Bonte, 1976:144). Among the Iwellemmeden Kel Denneg, they make up 3.9 and 3.6 percent of several different groups, and among Tingeregedech of Bankilare (Tera region), they make up 3.8 percent (Bernus, 1993:358,394).

The smith/artisans, as already noted, are called *inaden* in the plural; (*ened*, masc. singular; *tenet*, fem. singular, *tchinaden*, fem. plural), and many still serve aristocratic (*imajeghen*) and tributary (*imghad*) families in the countryside, although these relationships are changing, and many *inaden* are also active in the tourist trade, especially in the towns. Relations with patrons in the towns, though attenuated, have not, however, completely broken down or become forgotten.

Neither "smith" nor "artisan" is adequate as a translation in conveying the precise significance of this Tamajaq term, or for that matter, of the other language terms for these specialists in the other societies I examine presently. Thus throughout this book, I sometimes use the English language terms "smith" and "artisan" interchangeably or combined together, always aware of their limitations for conveying the rich complexity of these skilled specialists' roles. I also, therefore, often use the local language terminologies to designate these specialists to do them justice.

I am much more stringent about using the local language terms for these specialists' alleged powers, and although it is impossible to avoid using, at some points, "witchcraft" or "evil eye,"—particularly in the book's later cross-cultural sections, where the scholars I cite use these terms in describing those powers — nonetheless, I hope in my re-analysis of their data to critically assess the limitations, as well as the uses, of these designations of ritual power here; for I argue here for re-framing these powers analytically in more nuanced terms which include their positive, as well as negative, dimensions. This is particularly important in light of my argument that some elements—some early European travelers and also local organized religion and property concerns, in particular—have in effect, "twisted" these powers into configurations that appear more negative, thereby threatening smith/artisans' heretofore protected status in African religions pre-dating Christianity and Islam.

Most Tuareg, as well as ethnographers who have worked in their communities, tend to use *inaden* as a gloss, usually to refer to the metalworkers, because of the local cultural emphasis on their transformation of metal as crucial to their art and technology, though many *inaden* also work in wood, leather, and in a few regions, clay and stone (soapstone and gypsum). Many in the Air Mountains near Mt. Bagzan, who are attached to aristocratic families of the Kel Ewey Tuareg and to smaller clans of Kel Igurmaden, Kel Chimilan, Kel Timia, and Kel Nabarro in that region, also act as oral historians, and sing at noble rites of passage, performing roles akin to those of griots in neighboring African, including some other Tuareg, communities(Nicolaisen, 1997; Casajus, 2000; Rasmussen, 1995).

Traditionally, in many rural Tuareg rural communities, a smith works for the daughter of the noble woman his/her family is attached to through the generations, i.e., then for the granddaughter of that patron woman, etc., in a pattern of inheritance resembling the matrilineal *akh huderan* "living milk" property, in which livestock herds and date palms are passed through women and retained upon marriage.[5] Thus when a man marries, he gains access to the labor of his wife's attached smith family. For example, the daughter of a local chief of the Kel Igurmaden descent group, in principle inherited the *inaden* family of her mother, but the son of the chief did not; he uses the smith family of his own wife. However, since this is family of the chief, all village smiths should help with this family's rites of passage and with manufacture of their household tools and jewelry. Reciprocity is not completely consistent or symmetrical, however: nobles sing *Iuraran,* special praise-songs sung by noble patrons, at the marriage of smiths, but do not manufacture jewelry or tools for the smiths; whereas, recall, smiths attached to a noble family make jewelry and tools for them, especially for the bride at the wedding, a visual counterpart of smiths' role in helping negotiate bridewealth for noble marriages.

In this context—of these longstanding, very personal and inherited relationships—*inaden* are called "our smiths" or *inadan nena* , and nobles are called "our nobles of the forge," *imachaghalen nena win innoudou*. In the rural Air Mountain Mountain region of northern Niger, this traditionally inherited client-patron relationship remains most important at rites of passage and in women's hairstyling. The chief of the smiths is called upon to organize smiths' participation by the chief of the dominant descent group or *tawsit* there in village-wide ceremonies. Outside these contexts, however, even in the countryside, there is greater flexibility nowadays; for other services, such as manufacture of household tools and jewelry, non-smiths may choose to commission/hire "their" *inaden* or not, that is, they may engage others not inherited by the family for these tasks. But in principle—whether inherited or not, some smith/artisans must be hired, not "bypassed" or "imitated"—these latter acts remain taboo for most people thus far, except for exceptional cases of a few nobles who have taken up the work of the forge (still extremely rare); for *inaden* did not enact a fine or perform their mocking mumming rites called *ilbourousan* (sing. *albourousa*) against these rare nobles who dared to do this recently, as smiths would have done previously in order to express their disapproval of this "imitation" of their protected skills.

Thus the inheritance of *inaden* by families of aristocratic origin in its ideal pattern operates somewhat like the wedding dowry (*tagalt*), and also, like the past inheritance of servile persons: each noble woman brings a smith to her marriage, along with her nuptial tent and (in the past, until the abolition of slavery at mid-century), she also brought a domestic slave. This inheritance and attachment to smith/artisans remains strong in many rural memories despite the modifications and flexibility in this relationship. Recently, Tuareg political leaders have exhorted everyone to forget the old inherited social categories, emphasizing that all Tuareg are equal, and have encouraged everyone to unite on the basis of the Tamajaq language, proclaiming that everyone is under one tent. Moreover, there are new socioeconomic classes, and new sources of wealth, status, and prestige emerging in the modern infrastructure offered by education and jobs. But not all Tuareg have equal access to these benefits, and until recently, many have been marginal within their nation-states, whose French colonial administrations tended to favor the southern farming peoples and neglect the northern more nomadic residents after subjugating them. Also, many residents remain aware of the social stratum origin of each family in smaller communities, and tend to identify themselves and others on that basis in many contexts, such as preferences by parents, in arranging their children's first marriages, for social stratum endogamy—though youths increasingly resist this.

In the towns, there is greater breakdown of the old inherited client-patron relationship, but in Agadez, Niger and Kidal, Mali and other towns where Tamajaq-speakers and Tuareg culture and arts are prominent, *inaden* remain a distinctive social stratum, predominantly still endogamous, and continue to be strongly identified with their separate origins and their ritual and social, as well as artisan, roles. But their old inherited ties to their aristocratic families have declined, and only older *inaden* there remember which aristocratic families they were originally attached to. Also, younger persons in the towns do not know what *albourusa* refers to, and when this mumming practice shaming nobles who break taboos is explained to them, young urban smith/artisans and non-smiths alike deny that this still occurs; whereas in the countryside, though on the decline, I observed that *albourusa* rituals continue and are widely-recognized.

I found much flexibility in some domains of even rural smith/noble relations; for example, in their own interpretation of the nature of their attachment to their old patron families. Some assert that they belong to a *tawsit* (descent group) of exclusively smiths; others identify with, and serve nobles in a given *tawsit*, but explain that they are apart from, or outside (i.e., unrelated by kinship ties to) that *tawsit*; and others freely serve and sell objects to different aristocratic and other non-smith families from diverse *tawsiten* or descent groups, conducting these transactions more commercially and less as client-patron relationships, but rather according to convenience, personal rapports and preferences, and geographic proximity.

Discourses and practices relating to *tezma* reveal, not surprisingly, tensions in these social relations between Tuareg smiths and non-smiths. What is more surprising, in the light of the currently greater flexibility in smith-noble relations, is their tenacity in the face of intra-smith competition for old and new patrons. Indeed, many Tuareg non-smiths also assert that nobles and smiths "are like brothers" or "cousins." Early in my research, many also described smiths as "like women...also like cousins (who practice a joking relationship and also my potentially marry)...you must not get angry at them, but (rather) joke with them." Although they also still refer reciprocally to each other with the Tamajaq possessive pronoun in the first person plural, *nena,* or first person singular, *in*, *inaden* in fact tend to do this more often, and with greater affection than nobles, thus suggesting some asymmetry and tension here, but not necessarily smiths' marginality. Many *tchinaden* female smiths, for example, would state, "I am going to dress the hair of my nobles (*timajeghen in*) now," upon leaving for their patrons' residence to do this task, using the possessive pronoun.

Although many *tezma* accusations are indeed linked to the stresses of "modernity," many others are longstanding, widespread, and are linked to non-modernist predicaments. In fact, these anthropological categories of time and space—of Euroamerican philosophical origins—are not so easily separated, but are in local thought and practice, merged in social memory-related discourses (reminiscences) and practices of identity formation. Indeed, local cosmology, philosophy, mythico-histories, social typifications and practices reveal the problem of Euroamerican bias in some anthropological portrayals of "modernity" as a gloss for what are actually very diverse temporal and spatial processes. Moreover, there are some disagreements within nobles' discourse, as well as differences between nobles' and smith/artisans' discourses. Unraveling the nuanced significance of *tezma* therefore requires examining both discourse and practice, in case studies, vignettes, and also distinguishing between nobles' and smiths' own perspectives of this force.

NOTES

1. The Tuareg data in this book are based on nearly thirty years of longterm residence, beginning in the 1970's initially as a Peace Corps volunteer and teacher, and since then, between 1983 and 2012, as an anthropologist in social/cultural anthropological field research, predominantly in northern Niger, and more recently, also northern Mali, in both rural and urban settings, and more briefly, among expatriates in France and the United States. My projects have focused on the following topics: spirit possession and other medico-ritual forms of healing, aging and the life course, diviners, mediums and herbalists, rural and urban smith/artisans, gender constructs, verbal art performance, and youth cultures. In these projects, I gratefully acknowledge support from Fulbright Hays, Wenner-Gren Foundation for Anthropological

Research, Social Science Research Council, National Geographic, Indiana University, and the University of Houston.

2. The major challenge in converting to Islam was two-fold: for Tuareg and other Berber peoples had to reconcile the Islamic emphasis upon the equality of all believers with local social hierarchies, on the one hand, and on the other, they also had to integrate, to varying degrees, Qur'anic and Arab patrilineal with local matrilineal legal institutions, for example, the latter including ancient Berber queens and warriors, women's right to initiate divorce, and property endowments reserved for sisters and nieces, and gender constructs, such as relatively free social interaction between the sexes, lack of seclusion for women, and women's prominence in education of children.

3. The pre-colonial Tuareg social hierarchy consisted of stratified, endogamous specialist groups with inherited occupations and some mild "pollution" beliefs, but they only approximately resembled other stratified systems, such as the Hindu caste system and the medieval European feudal system. Recent ethnographies of the Tuareg, as in anthropology and ethnography more generally (Asad, 1986), have critically addressed the problems of translating local concepts and categories into European and other languages (Claudot-Hawad, 1993,1996; Kohl, 2007; Rasmussen, 2001a,2006). The principal social stratum divisions in pre-colonial Tuareg society, though experiencing much transformation in their roles and relationships, remain salient in identities today in some contexts and in some settings, especially in rural areas. *Imajeghen* (usually translated as aristocrats or "nobles") until recently monopolized large animals, weapons, and controlled the Saharan caravan trade and asserted military dominance over subordinates such as *imghad* (formerly translated as "vassals", and now as "tributaries"), who raided, traded, and collected tithes for them, *ighawalen* (long-freed clients, who performed work in herding and gardening and paid a portion of their harvest to overlords), and *iklan* (recently-captured slaves who performed domestic, herding, and gardening and caravanning work for owners, now freed, and popularly called Buzu in Niger and Bella in Mali). Islamic scholars (*ineslemen,* popularly called marabouts throughout Niger and Mali), not always a separate social stratum (often, though not always, intermarrying with *imajeghen*) interpreted Qur'anic law and conducted Qur'anic healing and counseling. The *inaden* smith/artisans, as observed in the present book, manufactured jewelry, weapons, tools, and other items for aristocratic patron families and also much more: they acted as go-betweens, ambassadors, poets, and in some regions, for example, in Kel Ewey Tuareg communities of the Bagzan Massif in the Air region of Niger where I conducted much of the research for the present book, approximated the role of *griots* or oral historians and performed praise-singing at their noble patrons' rites of passage. For detailed descriptions of pre-colonial and changing Tuareg social organization and relationships, see Bernus 1981, Nicolaisen and Nicolaisen 1997, Casajus 1987, Claudot-Hawad 1993,1996.

4. There are eight regional confederations, whose major descent group was each headed by an *amenukal* or "Sultan," whose powers have become much modified by first, the French colonial administrations and later, by central state governments. Traditionally, these leaders were elected by aristocratic

clans of their respective regions, ruled by respect rather than force, and mediated between the warring descent groups and confederations, keeping the peace in the caravan trade. Smaller descent groups and clans have been presided over by local-level traditional "chiefs," consisting of an elder (*amghar*) at the camp, and in some places with French sedentarizing policies, village, levels. Councils of marabouts also assert great influence in some regions. Nation-state governments have in recent years backed up powers of the *amenukal* with military force, in for example, tax-collection.

5. These "living milk" matrilineal property endowments, intended to compensate women for the male bias of Qur'anic inheritance favoring males (who receive twice the amount female heirs receive), consist of herds, date palms, and occasionally, houses, endures today unevenly among the different Tuareg groups. Some breakdown of this custom has occurred from the impact of droughts (men, not women, tend to more often own gardens, which are more easily reconstituted after droughts), wars, Islamic scholars' requirements of written wills, and nation-state laws. See Rasmussen, 1997. Smith/artisans and (in the past) slaves formed part of the marrying woman's dowry, consisting also of the nuptial tent, built by the bride's elderly female relatives and retained by her, even upon divorce.

CHAPTER ONE

TEZMA POWER AND TUAREG *INADEN* SMITH/ARTISANS

ETIOLOGIES AND ACCUSATIONS

Tezma attacks a region of the stomach through the orifices, and is usually manifested by a swelling of the stomach among children and animals. This force is locally contrasted to sorcery (*ark echaghel,* literally "bad work") in that, rather than premeditated, it is widely believed to be spontaneous and activated automatically.[1] There are certain points of similarity between local concepts of evil mouth or eye and *tezma.* According to many rural persons of noble origin, the force of evil mouth or eye—called *togerchet, imigurcha* or *tehot* in various Tamajaq regional dialects—comes primarily from envy, coveting, or desire; in their viewpoint, the force of *tezma* has its roots in the idea that one will be punished if one does not give one's surplus or justly compensate someone, primarily a smith/artisan, for services or goods rendered, but it may also become active more generally, if one does not give anything to a smith who asks for something upon demand at any time, even outside formal client-patron rituals and technical work transactions. In the Air countryside around Mount Bagzan in northern Niger, despite the flexibility in contemporary client-patron relations, nonetheless *inaden* may still ask their inherited patrons for something on demand, and these nobles must, in principle, give on these occasions in addition to paying smiths regular remuneration for their specific goods and services. These latter predicaments have become more frequent for nobles. Yet the slipperiness, indeterminacy, and unpredictability in client-patron relationships is both longstanding and recent.

Several questions arise here: given the longstanding negotiability of even "traditional" client-patron relations, smiths' increased independence, and non-smiths' increased ability to choose a smith nowadays, (except for client-patron ties still followed at rites of passage and hairdressing), and given the presumably competitive rivals this freedom of choice would produce among *inaden,* then why do predominantly non-smiths still accuse almost exclusively *inaden* of activating this force? Also, why do *inaden* themselves, when conflicting with eachother in rivalry for patrons and customers, almost never accuse one another of activating *tezma,* but instead accuse one another of activating another malevolent force, such as *togerchet (tehot)* or *ark achaghel*?

Some Tuareg smith/artisans in Niamey, the capital city, are now selling their works abroad and also working for French entrepreneurs in artisan workshops; in these situations, internal tensions and rivalries arise, but there is a re-definition of the force activated. In these predicaments, some tensions are revealed between *inaden,* as well as between *inaden* and others, in coping with not solely socioeconomic challenges, but also success. For example, there are problems of maintaining social reciprocity and balance upon smith/artisans' acquiring of new wealth abroad, in competition and rivalries between *inaden*. Consider the case of two smith/artisan partners I knew who frequently traveled together to France and the United States to sell their jewelry. On one occasion, one of these men remained behind and sent the other to the US., with some of the former's jewelry to sell in New York City. But the latter returned to Niger with neither his smith/artisan partner's jewelry nor his money. The "duped" man assured me, "We are still friends, but nevertheless, I am a little angry with him, and we are no longer (business) partners."

Later, in the capital city at his workshop, the partner who had failed to bring back the money or the merchandize to his former partner experienced sudden difficulties in creating his heretofore innovative silver jewelry designs. This was particularly alarming, since one of his creations, a beautiful necklace, had won a coveted prize. He saw an Islamic scholar to diagnose the cause of his sudden misfortune. The Islamic scholar or "marabout" divined for him by Qur'anic techniques, and indicated that the cause of his troubles was the evil gossip *(togerchet)* coming from other smiths who were jealous of his success. Many persons also believed that the partner's creative problems were caused by sorcery, *ark echaghel*, in Tamajaq literally "bad work" (Rasmussen, 2001b), though sent via the channel of spiteful gossip from other *inaden* who were jealous and resentful over that man's success. The victim underwent more treatment by an Islamic scholar from his home rural region, and subsequently claimed he was cured, and his artistry and business again went well.

What is interesting in this case of "smith-on-smith" rivalry, however, is that the partner's new misfortune (in what many English-speakers in the west would term a "mental block"), although attributed to an outside malevolent power, was not attributed to another smith/artisan or to that power of *tezma*. *Tezma* between smith/artisans appears to be taboo in an almost incestuous sense, akin to too close marriage (endogamy notwithstanding) or at minimum, disloyalty in misuse of this power. Significantly, the purpose of *tezma* in *inaden* viewpoint, is to protect, somewhat like controlled weapons (guns, nuclear power) that should not be used casually or carelessly, nor against close persons. This power also figures in protecting their profession and its esoteric knowledge. In other words, *inaden*—as close kin—should maintain internal solidarity. When they do not, the malevolent force is defined as either "Bad work"/sorcery or "evil mouth"/gossip or both, but not *tezma,* in this light a precious resource fallen back on only, ideally, to guard from other dangers threatening *inaden*. From the smith's perception, therefore, *tezma* is not witchcraft; for it is not activated from within the smith community; whereas *ark echaghel* and *togerchet* are.

Thus *inaden* are frequently forced into competition, not solely over noble patrons in their more flexible client-patron relationships, but also over outside customers such as tourists and functionaries, including many abroad in transcultural borderland interactions, but smith-on-smith accusations of malevolence tend not to involve *tezma* force.

Tezma, despite its malevolence, is believed to be usually less dangerous to adults than *ark echaghel* or *togerchet*, but it can sometimes be fatal to livestock and children, causing a kind of diarrhea called *karambaza*, which is diagnosed by herbalists in a special divination rite called *takobar*: the herbal medicine woman spins a clay pot around as she calls out the names of particular food or other items possibly wanted by the offended smith. The pot stops at the name of the item wanted by the smith. Smiths insist that, in order to declare *tezma*, in principle a diviner must ask the *takobar* (pot) if it concerns different items, for example, rice, beans, tea, in order to find out what caused it, and who is guilty. Some people use sand that is under the *takobar* as a medicine, steeped in water and administered diluted to the sick person.

Despite local socioeconomic transformations and wider cultural encounters, in rural areas *inaden* still have the right to claim gifts wherever they go in addition to fees for their work. This is the main reason why they are most feared for *tezma* by non-smiths, particularly those of aristocratic background. All smiths, with the exception of those few among them who have become Islamic scholars (*ineslemen* in Tamajaq), are believed to possess *tezma*. Although as noted, this acts automatically, smiths are still held responsible for misfortunes attributed to the effect of this power. Violence against smiths is traditionally rare, many local residents explained, "because they are a protected people, against whom it is not appropriate to express anger without denigrating oneself." Occasionally, however, violence occurs.

In the countryside, as well as to some extent in Agadez, where *inaden* constitute a large portion of this town's total population (of approximately 100,000) and continue to play prominent social as well as artistic roles as jewelers, I was to some extent absorbed into the noble-smith client-patron relationships. Many local residents of diverse social origins tended to treat me as "noble." for several reasons. As noted, in the rural Air region, I usually boarded with relatives of prominent chiefly, marabout, and aristocratic families. Longterm residence with chiefly and noble families was encouraged as more acceptable to local residents, and often, I found, tourists passing through the area tended to stay with inaden. Thus, I was told, if I wished to be taken seriously as a researcher, I should reside with the more officially "prestigious" families, or as locals termed them, " those who are respected." But I often visited, stayed for varying time periods, and traveled with, inaden families and individuals, observing their work at the forge and social interactions in their homes, and closely observed and participated in noble-smith interactions, including rights and obligations at rites of passage and more generally in everyday life. Although I appeared to many local residents to be wealthier than most persons of noble origin are today, nonetheless, *inaden* tended to classify me, as they did most outsiders—whether researchers, tourists, aid volunteers, or NGO workers, as "non-smiths." As also noted, until recently, *inaden* predominated as go-betweens and gatekeepers for outsiders to Tuareg society, continuing their ambassador roles.

Thus *inaden* and children were the first to approach me upon my arrival in the field, and although I frequently relied upon them for certain services—as did aristocratic families, I, like most anthropologists, sought to get to know persons from a variety of social backgrounds, as well. Thus I walked a delicate "line" in these relationships; for many non-smiths continually warned me about what they considered to be smiths' "trickiness." These warnings were in noble viewpoint justified when, on one occasion early in my research, I engaged a smith to arrange an interview with an elderly healer in a small, distant nomadic camp, and also rented a camel from him for us to travel there, paying him a rather high fee for the camel and also, paying him daily for accompanying me. He assured me that prior to our trip, he had visited the healer and arranged for our interview. But upon our arrival, we found that the healer was on extended travel. Only her daughter was at home, who could not speak for her mother except in her mother's presence, since she was still an apprentice (Rasmussen, 2006). Although we waited for several days, she did not return. Annoyed, I finally returned to my "home" and host family, in the semi-nomadic village where I lodged and worked much of the time, exhausted from my "wild goose-chase."

My host family expressed sympathy over this mishap, sadly shaking their heads, but insisted "Ah ha! We told you so...never trust an *ened*!" On the other hand, the contradiction here is striking, since normally smith/artisans act with integrity as go-betweens and are in fact trusted by many chiefs in that endeavor. Here, the problem appeared to be a difference in degree of allegiance to local patrons versus outsiders, such as myself—in particular, outsiders newly arrived in the community and not yet fully trusted, by either *inaden* or their patrons. Perhaps the aristocratic families, contrary to the surface implications of their warning me and comforting me against the "trickiness" of *inaden,* really wished to maintain a monopoly over *inaden* services for themselves, or perhaps they feared a divulging of cultural knowledge by the smith/artisan man. In other words, perhaps this precaution—of guarding their clients' first allegiance and possible, also, testing my own character until they knew me better—was what really motivated them to warn me of the latters' "dangers." Again, there are approximate parallels here to precious resources protected by denigrating them on the surface—whether esoteric knowledge or nuclear power—which can be used for good or evil, and which can be leaked and appropriated by outside parties—long seen as threatening to Tuareg communities, who have suffered invasions and massacres historically (Claudot-Hawad, 1993,1996; Rasmussen, 2001b).

Although my relations with most *inaden* were usually much more cordial, and grew closer and more positive over longterm and subsequent field residences, nonetheless, *inaden*'s first loyalty was to their local patrons. Indeed, much of their go-between role has historically involved buffering and protecting the local community from outside intruders, and negotiating truces between hostile parties. Yet even in these roles—for example a historical battle described by Bernus (2006), the smith/artisan may interpret events independently—in effect, giving voice to alternative views of history and culture. Moreover, recently, many smiths have been more aligned, in the eyes of some non-smiths, with outside interests for example, tourism and global transnational trade connections, in effect, distracted from their old obligations to nobles, in particular, by lucrative work in tourism and other industries. In an environment with a history of raiding and wars, this role was extended into cautionary relationships with researchers (who until accepted socially, were often assumed to be tourists—welcomed for revenue, but nonetheless outsiders, or to be connected to militia or governments—these latter greatly feared). Only after extended and repeated visits was I able to win trust from persons of diverse backgrounds. Here, one level, the value of *inaden* as culture-heroes vividly emerges. Perhaps the smith/artisan who accompanied me to the outlying nomadic camp early in my field residence simply wanted to get to know me better—or perhaps, his aristocratic patrons had wished him to do this, before allowing me greater access to cultural knowledge. Although this case of the "wild goose-chase" did not involve *tezma*, it illuminates *inaden* roles as mediators and social critics.

At any rate, I was frequently warned by others, though not by smiths themselves, about smiths' alleged negative traits such as "tricking" (*temarqas*)—"they play tricks like the fire *djinn* spirits beneath the sand dunes!" as well as their *tezma,* advised to comply with their requests, and initially at least keep my distance from them. The families' warning of outsiders "away" from inaden could, in this light, be compared to guarding the true value of one's property or resource from potential thieves by pretending to denigrate it in their presence.

Yet more is at play here. The case of *tezma* that I caught, described earlier, from a smith man who was reputed to have particularly strong powers, which I had felt as cold and fever-like symptoms while staying near his village, and which vanished suddenly overnight after I belatedly gave him food—his second choice, after eye ointment—when he later came by, illustrated different processes: namely, how expatriates are in some other contexts, replacing nobles in local client-patron relationships. True, this incident suggests the significance of globalization on one level in the directions of *tezma* power, but its implications are more complex; for this also suggests that local definitions of historical and social processes persist, and are superimposed upon these intruding forces in conditions that, although involving transformation, also involve drawing upon longstanding modes of understanding power. Paramount among these is *tezma*'s ability, as in a litmus test, to cast into relief others' character traits, such as generosity or lack of it. Tezma is also a nmenonic device reminding others of the importance of reciprocity and of smiths' and non-smiths' ideally mutual obligations to protect each other, their livelihoods, and their cultural knowledge and autonomy.

In other words, *tezma* is, as Evans-Pritchard (1950) termed it long ago, "refracted" through many contexts of social practice and has many levels of cultural meaning. Moreover, this power has persisted throughout many different kinds of social tensions in Tuareg communities; it has neither ceased nor emerged under more "modern" circumstances, but rather, resurfaces periodically in particular social contexts of interaction which, global influences notwithstanding, remain highly personal and intimate, and re-define *tezma* according to context of accusation and situatedness of accuser and accused.

Hence the relevance, I argue, of social processes I call re-surfacing and orchestrating in the operation of ritual powers and others' definitions and re-definition of them. In effect, I may have been a welcome "lightning rod" for local non-smiths, who, while not exactly hoping for or gloating over my own vulnerability to *tezma*, nonetheless perhaps felt relief that I temporarily "took the heat" off them, so to speak, in the flying of this force from the angry heart of the *ened*. Of course, my host family, in particular, was genuinely concerned about my welfare, and constantly sought to protect me from what they perceived (or portrayed?) as dangers—physical and intangible—from the environment—shown in their offers to make religious amulets for me, to prevent me from becoming lost in the desert, and other details of hospitality. And yet—I pondered whether or not "new nobles" might be deployed, on some subconscious level, as a buffer or shield against what locals still felt at a most personal level, in what remained very intimate relationships, despite modifications, flexibility, and wider forces at work.

I do not deny the relevance of wider global infrastructures and policies here, for example, the re-structuring measures of the World Bank and the International Monetary Fund in Africa, which have imposed austerity and pressured local economies toward privatisation.[2] While ostensibly "cost-cutting," these measures have also brought about effects of local unemployment, delay of salaries, devaluation of local currency (the West African CFA) by 50%, shortages of expensive, difficult to import medicines, and forced men into more distant and prolonged migrant labor.

In addition, the intermittent armed conflicts in the northern regions of Mali and Niger have uprooted many Tuareg, who have left some regions as political exiles, migrant laborers, and itinerant traders in another wave in the mid-1990's, and most recently, since 2004, in flights from recurring droughts, a locust invasion, and another outbreak, since 2007, of armed conflict in northern Niger over uranium resources, and most recently, since 2011, an influx of Tuareg returning from Libya in the wake of the civil war and overthrow of Ghadaffi in that country.[3] Smith/artisans, in particular, are compelled intermittently to leave the countryside and even some regional towns such as Agadez on each outbreak of armed violence, since the North was on several occasions temporarily closed to tourists, who now constitute important customers for many smith/artisans.. Many smiths traveled south to Niamey and beyond Niger to Mali, Burkina Faso, France, Belgium, and Italy, to find customers for their artisan work. In peaceful times, this migration for customers farther afield continues for some smiths, though they tend to leave their relatives at home, and prefer to always return to their home when possible, often alternating between home and travel spaces.

Yet these national and global forces, however important, do not entirely account for—either in cause-effect or in meaning—all dimensions of *tezma* at the community level. Local level property relationships and religious orientations are also powerful. On another level, the very personal and local-level relationships—both between smiths and non-smiths and among smiths themselves—remain prominent here as a leitmotif, significant in shaping immediate enactments, reactions, and interpretations of powers. For *inaden,* like other Tuareg, still usually yearn to return to their local community of origin. Those who do return must re-encounter the same "old faces" of the local-level relationships at home, though home is not the same place it once was.These local social actors continue to "read" much conflict in local cultural, micro-political terms. In another incident during my research residence, for example, a family of nobles and prominent marabouts received frequent requests for millet, tea, and sugar from their smith client family, but they tended to hoard these goods, keeping them in a hidden place and trading them with friends and relatives. The mother and her married daughters resided next door to each other. One daughter was married to an oasis gardener. This couple had one baby daughter, healthy until the age of six months, when she suddenly contracted dysentery. Her mother, aunts, and I tried several herbal remedies and some pharmaceutical medicine from Agadez and the United States as well. But the baby eventually died, despite these efforts.

In discussing this tragedy with friends afterwards, they told me that the family suspected their baby's death had been caused by the *tezma* of a female smith whose request for a gift of food from the household had been denied a few days before the baby fell ill. The smith frequently participated in communal work parties (tent construction and repair, mat manufacturing) and also sang praise-songs and served food at this aristocratic family's rites of passage (namedays and weddings). I had seen her recently come to the household, kneel in their tent door-frame, holding out her winnowing basket, and ask for millet, but household members had indicated there was none left. For nobles' fluctuating fortunes today in the wake of droughts, loss of herds, unemployment, and nationalist/separatist armed conflicts make it difficult for them to continue supporting smiths in their traditional client-patron relationships, and they sometimes find smith's continuing requests for presents and compensation annoying. But it is considered rude to refuse directly in noble cultural values of *tangalt*, so usually a noble will indicate there is no more millet or cash or other resource when confronted by a smith's requests for them.

Alongside the continuities in *tezma* accusations are new changes, which are highly significant, also. Sexual pollution figures more explicitly into some more recent noble/smith tensions—particularly in oases. These accusations generally bring greater physical violence. In these contexts, pollution emerges as a kind of metonymy for other concerns, and *tezma* power becomes a synecdoche for the larger turmoil in Tuareg society—seen as uncontrollable and unpredicatable, and thus all the more frightening. In this traditionally endogamous society, smith men who are suspected of romantic liaisons with noble women are resented by noble men as "stealing" these women. Several friends insisted that, "Only in the towns do couples dare to disobey these restrictions, and there only in secret; otherwise, this would be a theft." Thus, the trope of theft refers here to the "draining off" of female fertility, male prestige, and aristocratic cultural (if not currently plentiful material) property.

Although a few nobles and smiths are becoming business partners, many are instead rivals in an economic system formerly characterized by nomadic pastoralism, oasis gardening, and caravanning, and now increasingly moving toward agro-pastoralism, NGO-based business and artisan workshops,, intrusion by transnational mining corporations, and labor migration. Rewards are scarce, erratic, and unevenly distributed. Some nobles resent some smiths' and other formerly subordinate peoples' in the old social hierarchy (for example, descendants of slaves) success in the tourist and other new industries (Rasmussen 2001b,2003). This tension has often taken two forms: of gossip about smiths who disregard the old sumptuary laws limiting "upscale" dress and accessories to aristocratic persons, and more serious accusations of sexual transgressions, such as adultery between married persons.

Consider, for example, a female smith, a resident of a small oasis, who was nicknamed "Tamajeghat" by local nobles (a common generic nickname, a play on the term *tamajegh,* denoting a female noble, given to those who imitate persons of noble descent) because she dressed more finely that usual for a *tenet,* wearing for example, shimmering indigo-dyed and elaborately embroidered robes, rather than the stereotypical rags smith/artisans are supposed to wear, particularly in rural areas. Although her practice was met with some disapproval from local persons of noble origin, nonetheless, their attitudes were predominantly gently jocular; they used this nickname with affection, rather than hostility. That *tenet* was not as economically successful as she appeared in her dress and lifestyle; rather, these reflected her aspirations to higher status and prestige, and moreover, as a woman, rather than a man, she presented less of a threat to impoverished men of noble descent than did *inaden* men. Thus the social tensions in these cases are not always marked by outright hostility, as long as non-smiths do not feel too threatened by the successful smith and as long as joking relations remain effective in diffusing tensions.

More serious are cases of alleged breaking of sexual taboos. In the late 1990's and early 2000's, several cases of alleged adultery between *inaden* men and noble women in the countryside were punished by severely beating the men. One of the smith men accused of an illicit extra-marital affair with a woman of noble origin, unlike some other accused men, narrowly escaped a beating by going into hiding and traveling, and eventually paid a fine, enjoyed unusual prosperity from his tailoring business and oasis garden. He was the object of longstanding resentful gossip in his village, well before his alleged illicit affair.

In another case, a smith man who had long resided with his family in a smith neighborhood in one small oasis was accused of starting a ring of prostitution there. Local residents reported that such organized prostitution had never existed in the countryside before, only in the towns. They were particularly outraged that this man had allegedly engaged a young woman of noble origins in this activity for his profit. Local residents beat him, and ejected him from the community. The man went into exile, and became a mason in a distant region. His relatives remained there on the oasis, however, and this scandal caused a rift between his supporters and detractors.

Thus there are indications of an increase in certain kinds of tensions between non-smiths and smiths recently. There have always been some tensions, albeit of a different sort. These emerging tensions are over new concerns, and they are not just any old tension concerning smiths' compensation or gifts: rather, these are social tensions of a specific type: namely, fears from persons of aristocratic origin that their women will be tempted to conduct sexual liaisons with, or even marry, *inaden*. Yet as shown, *tezma* accusations in general and other more commonly experienced social tensions such as disputes over client-patron reciprocal obligations between nobles and smiths are not new, but longstanding. These predate global IMF and World Bank privatization and restructuring programs, labor migration, regional armed violence, intrusions of mining companies, corporations such as Hermes in Agadez, which around the late 1990's began to employ some *inaden* in their workshop away from the older family artisan workshops, and tourism during peaceful times. Other more longstanding motives for *tezma* accusations continue. In Agadez, many local residents felt mixed sentiments of jealousy of smiths' regular salaries at the Hermes workshop, on the one hand, and sympathy for the *inaden* employed there, on the other, citing their long hours and more regimented work.

Thus it is instructive to tack back and forth between historical and recent *tezma* accusations, rather than treat them as mutually-exclusive in meanings or as sequential "replacements" of each other. In an earlier incident that occurred during the 1970's, while I was traveling back to the rural area from Agadez by agricultural cooperative truck, I saw a smith hail this truck, but the vehicle was full at the time, and passed him by. Several hours afterward, the truck became stuck in the deep mud of the rainy season. Those on board insisted that the smith's *tezma* had caused this mishap. What is interesting about this earlier accusation is that, despite the misfortune of the travel delay believed caused by the angry heart of the smith, there was no physical violence toward him. In fact, most passengers on board the truck joked and laughed about it.

Yet when one examines those few earlier ethnographic references to this force, there is no linear temporal trend suggesting any consistent pattern of increasing or decreasing physical violence toward *inaden* accused of *tezma* alone. The direction of consequences varies, but not on a scale in one linear direction or another. Nicolaisen (1961), for example, described an even earlier incident of *tezma* in the mid-20th century. A Tuareg from Air was returning from Damergou with a caravan of camels carrying millet. One evening, when they stopped to camp, a smith came to ask for a gift of millet. The Tuareg noble answered that the smith could wait until the next morning. It became dark, and the camels were led to the pastures for the night. The smith left. Immediately after his departure, one of the camels belonging to the Tuareg fell and died. The Tuareg was convinced that the camel had been killed by the *tezma* of the smith. He got up, pursued the smith, and killed him with an ax. The Tuareg was condemned to seven years of forced labor. (Nicolaisen,1961:136). This brief vignette, though atypical in its extreme violence, recalls the reason for my "catching" the old smith's *tezma*: delay in compliance with his request. Nobles and other non-smiths must not keep smiths waiting; whereas smiths can keep others waiting. Friends frequently urged me to hurry to comply with a smith's requests, not to keep him or her waiting. The broader significance of this is that smiths are action-oriented, dynamic agents of transformation.

Only in my data on the recent cases that involve the breaking of sexual taboos did I encounter increased physical violence as a consistent pattern. Although thus far rare, deplored by most local residents, and of course not justifiable, these actions have a logical explanation: since noble patrons need *inaden*, and since *inaden* remain valuable as non-aligned mediators to them only if they do not intermarry with them i.e, they remain outside noble descent group alliances and rivalries, becoming potential or actual husbands of women of noble origin would threaten smiths' endogamy and consequently diminish the value of smiths—a disadvantage for both social categories, but more feared by nobles since by extension, these violations also cause smith men to compete with, rather than complement and support, noble men in marital matters. In times of economic difficulty for many, these violations of sexual taboos only heighten personal insecurity over prestige and eligibility necessary for marriage.

Thus *tezma* accusations alone do not always suffice to provoke the physical violence today; rather, the trigger is sexual transgression, with its ensuing pollution based upon the unsettling disjunction or contradiction between the old ambiguous social status of the smith/artisan and his/her new emerging socioeconomic status, in which, at a kind of social "crossroads," noble and smith/artisan pass each other going in opposite directions. It is as though they are traveling on two trains passing one another. Most often, though not always, it is the noble who is becoming poor, having lost herds; and often, it is the smith/artisan who is becoming prosperous, at least relatively, and from the viewpoint of the non-smith. In this process, the old system of official endogamy and social prestige—once based on real property ownership (in noble monopoly over large livestock, the saber sword, caravan trade, and client and servile labor and goods, expressed in sumptuary laws of conspicuous consumption, e.g., exclusive dress and accessories) is perceived as threatened. Yet in actual practice, contrary to noble fears, most *inaden* continue to in-marry, often to their close cousins; thus the fear of sexual liaisons between these social categories is largely symbolic of newly-impoverished persons' fear of loss of status, prestige, and property (cultural or symbolic capital) more generally, particularly men who can no longer easily raise bridewealth to marry into prestigious families. *Inaden* have traditionally reminded their patrons of their prestige; now they remind them of their threatened loss of prestige. In this fear, the *ened* appears particularly threatening, since in his relative prosperity (real or exaggerated—for not all *inaden* are well to do, and not all non-smiths are poor), those suffering downward socioeconomic mobility lose face. Although in fact, many *inaden* suffer just as much as others from droughts, wars, and famines, nonetheless, they tend to become scapegoats for these reasons.

Thus cases of sexual transgressions—rumored or actual—in effect remind the impoverished chiefly and aristocratic men of their precarious position as eligible partners in marriage, at least those who have difficulty raising bridewealth, and thus tend to take on exaggerated proportions in local typifications of alleged *inaden* "traits." Some persons tend, for example, to exaggerate the wealth of *inaden*—though many do benefit from the tourist trade, not all become wealthy from it. In other words, there is some stereotyping. Revealingly, many persons of noble background in their discourses to me tended to emphasize sexual transgressions associated with *tezma* pollution, but not all *tezma* accusations are made against male smiths, and some accusations, moreover, do not implicate sexual transgressions at all.

For example, in another case I collected, a *tenet* (sing., smith woman) I knew was recently accused of *tezma* by one of her noble patron woman's daughters. She had requested, and been refused, sugar at this household, and the daughter fell ill afterward. The smith woman, quite upset, tearfully denied this, but her client-patron relationship with this family was broken. The breakdown was somewhat disadvantageous for this woman, for several reasons. Rural *tchinaden* women have fewer alternative sources of income or customers than do rural smith men and urban smith women. Although this woman was a popular praise-singer, she was somewhat more impoverished than some other smiths. Furthermore, rather than marrying a close cousin according to the usual smith custom, this woman had married a former slave man, who had arrived in that village from the outside. Many years before, his noble owner had used him for bridewealth in his marriage, but the man had escaped from that region. In his new location, a primary school director had given him a job as school handyman. The couple were now divorced.

Marriage to a former slave is less stigmatized than in the past, and divorce does not bring any stigma to women. But this smith woman had also broken a sexual taboo: she had two illegitimate children, strongly disapproved of in Tuareg society despite the tolerance of some pre-marital affairs (though not, as noted, between smiths and nobles). Thus this woman's *tezma* in this case did not emanate merely from her smith social status or alleged coveting of the sugar alone, but rather seems to have been intensified as part of her more general marginality in the community as the mother of illegitimate children, and at a time of heightened upheavals, when some persons searched for scapegoats, and sought to protect against challenges to identity, expressed, again, through the idiom of sexuality and pollution.

In another case, during the cold, dry sandstorm season, when the small daughter of a noble woman in a rural chiefly family fell ill with stomach pains after she ate meat leftover from a wedding the previous day, the mother blamed a smith woman for causing this girl's *karambaza,* claiming she had coveted the meat eaten by her daughter. Stomach problems are less frequent in the cold dry season than in the hot, rainy seasons, thus adding to suspicion of an alternate cause. Smiths are supposed to receive a portion of the meat served at noble weddings after their praise-singing. But this particular wedding, celebrating the bride's second marriage in a chiefly but poor family, was more "low-key," and smiths had not been invited to perform their more usual, elaborate evening praise-songs.

The mother treated her sick daughter be combining several remedies. First, in a small ritual against *karambaza,* she gathered up grains from the foot-print of the smith in the sand in her compound, and threw them into the fire to burn. Next, she took her daughter to the new clinic nearby.[4] There was no further discussion of, or reaction against, that smith's transgression, only gossip that "the *tenet* had coveted the portion of meat eaten by the child."

How powerful are these micro-politics across the region? In and around Kidal, a diverse, but predominantly Tuareg town of approximately 20,000 in the Adragh-n-Ifoghas Mountains in northern Mali, the contemporary social and ritual roles of smith/artisans there (called *inhaden* in the local Tadart dialect of Tamajaq, spoken by the Ifoghas Tuareg there) appear more attenuated than in the Air town of Agadez, and much more attenuated than the close social relations in rural Air. Most *inhaden* in Kidal either work in tourist artisan craft cooperatives, or do repairs. There are much fewer *inhaden* in Kidal than in Agadez. There are only three *inhaden* families there, and one family serves the *amenukal* traditional leader of the Ifoghas and resides near his palace in his neighborhood, called Quartier Aliou. Others manufacture and sell silver and leatherwork at one of Kidal's three markets, in the beautifully decorated artisan workshop building located inside the New Market. Around 2006, there were plans to expand this workshop soon, with NGO support. During peaceful times, Kidal *inhaden*, like those in Agadez and Niamey, mostly work in the tourist industry. But in January 2012, there was a resurgence of the Tuareg armed rebellion in northern Mali, and violence between dissidents and the Malian army propelled 15,000 Kidal residents away in refugee flight. The recurrent political violence in northern Mali—in 1963,1990-96, and 2012—has resulted in massive refugeeing out by local residents of diverse social origins, resulting in greater breakdown in pre-colonial social stratum relationships there than in northern Niger.

Likewise, in the surrounding northern Malian countryside, again, in contrast to the rural Air Mountains and town of Agadez in northern Niger, some social roles of smith/artisans have been attenuated. There, former slaves called Bella, rather than *inhaden,* perform wedding praise-songs. Smiths and griots (oral historians) sing less frequently at Tuareg rites of passage in the Adragh-n-Ifoghas region than do those in the Air region.

A man of aristocratic social origins in Kidal even denied the existence of *tezma* force today. He insisted firmly, "In the past, a smith could follow a noble, and set up camp right next to his well...but now, we do not allow smiths to interfere in our affairs." Interestingly, he regarded traditional longstanding mediation by smiths, usually a positive feature, negatively as "interference." However, his elderly aunt recalled its existence until very recently, but she did not elaborate or explain why she though it had declined.

In northern Mali, particularly the sedentarized towns and villages, smiths' activities appear to have projected much farther outward beyond noble descent groups, whose cohesiveness has been subjective to greater stress than those in northern Niger. Residents intermittently flee the region during sporadic armed conflict outbreaks between national militia and dissident rebel fighters, which alternate with peace talks. Whereas by contrast, in the northern Niger countryside, many smiths remain at least partially embedded within the local community, even in some urban neighborhoods. Yet northern Niger also experiences intermittent political violence. What, then, accounts for this difference? Agadez is older than Kidal—the former several hundred years old, the latter established early in the 20th century by the French colonial military forces. The Ifoghas amenukal and his family were until that time based, not in Kidal, which was only a water-point for nomads with no permanent settled population, but in the rural pastures around Tin Essako to the east. This chiefly family was brought to Kidal by the colonial and independent state governments. Agadez, by contrast, has for several centuries been a key center for Saharan trading, Islamic scholarship, and its multi-ethnic population, though also somewhat detached from their traditionally inherited client-parton relationships and in residence longer than those in Kidal, includes many more specialized artisan groups, such as smith/artisans, sandal-makers, griots, and traditional wrestlers for the *amenukal* of the Air groups, popularly called the Sultan of Air (Salifou, 1973). Kidal's smith/artisan population , as noted, is much smaller, as is the population of other specialists there; by 2006, for example, only one elderly griot remained in Kidal.

Perhaps smiths' positive integrative go-between and buffering social roles depend, for their effectiveness and positive definition, upon greater solidarity and cohesion of their localized patron noble descent groups. Most aristocratic descent groups in northern Mali have in recent years become more dispersed, more often in refugee flight, although some northern Niger groups have also experienced some upheavals. In rural northern Mali, moreover, smith/artisans tend to be itinerant, passing through villages as general handypersons. The ritual force of *tezma*, in more depersonalized relationships, tends to become re-defined as the negative flipside of otherwise positive, protective, and mutually satisfying social intimacy. Where there is a greatly attenuated social mediating role, as is the case in and around Kidal, there is also an attenuated ritual role, with a corresponding fading of *tezma* *i*n local memory—although, as shown, some ambivalence remains in the attitudes of some persons who face greater uncertainty in their current relations with smith/artisans there. In other words, *tezma* is the other side of the "coin" of smith/artisans' important central (not marginalized) role as culture hero. In effect, the power of *inaden* as ambassador and go-between also involves, like that of translator, some indeterminacy, but not marginality or peripherality. The more distant, impersonal, and commercial the relationships between smiths and non-smiths become, and the more specialized their roles become as artisans/jewelers (for example, silversmiths), the less likely *tezma* is to surface as an explicit causal explanation for misfortune. Nonetheless, this force lurks just beneath the surface in accusations of misuse of other powers, as in the smith-on-smith *ark echaghel* sorcery case.

Thus *tezma* is neither entirely newly emergent as a modern or global force, nor entirely a thing of the past. But, as McNaughton observes concerning the Mande force called *nyama* (McNaughton, 1989), neither is it static or immutable. But I would add further that this force is not subject to neat models of belief/knowledge systems designated as "witchcraft" and "evil eye" in anthropology. It is neither strictly a figment of the local imagination, neither belief, knowledge, nor is it an empirically verifiable "social fact." This force is salient and meaningful for many local residents, however. The directions *tezma*-related accusations take do not always conform exactly to patterns detected in many studies of witchcraft or evil eye emphasizing recent tensions deriving from globalization processes (Ciekawy and Geschiere, 1998; Comaroff and Comaroff, 1993; Englund, 1996). True, the Tuareg data reveal some approximate parallels to the economic tensions traced in some other studies to modernity and globalization: namely, social dislocation in dispersion of populations, loss of livestock and other property, and unemployment. These processes have affected persons of diverse social backgrounds in Niger and Mali, but which especially affect the more nomadic Tuareg of aristocratic origins, the traditional patrons of smith/artisans. Yet there are diverse sources of tension in Tuareg communities, not all from modernity and globalization: some sources of tension are new and alien, generated from the outside, but others are longstanding and intimate, internally generated within the local community.

In sum, the foregoing views of *tezma* power from outside observers— Tuareg non-smiths and myself, the researcher—have yielded some insights into this power's relationships to social tensions, scapegoating, and other exclusionary projects (Bunzl, 2004). But what about *tezma* viewed from within the *inaden* social stratum? How do *inaden* themselves view this power? I now turn to smiths' own perspectives, complementing the foregoing case studies and vignettes with more detailed discourse, comments, and oral narratives from these specialists, presented during our interviews and guided conversations.

INADEN ON THE SUBJECT OF *TEZMA*

"*Tezma*," explained a young smith who also gardened on a small oasis, "is something everyone does, even nobles sometimes. Some people, even if they do not ask for anything, they do it. All they have to do is see what they need. Sometimes, some people seek, and if they do not find (what they are looking for), they activate *tezma*. For example, one year, my cousin was in Hausa country, his wife reserved a ram for him, and the day that he returned, one slaughtered the ram, he ate its meat, and this meat contained *tezma*, so he fell ill. They left to see a marabout, (Islamic scholar), and he identified the *tezma*. After that, he totally refused meat, until afterward he found the marabout to make him medicine and he began to eat meat (once again)." Yet no one, including this man, could recall any case of *tezma* generated by a non-smith or his/her coveting, nor did I ever observe such a case. Thus it appears that most often, *inaden* "seek, but do not find," as this man termed it—that is, mostly *inaden* allegedly covet, in the eyes of both smiths and non-smiths. Perhaps this typification has become internalized within *inaden* viewpoints, as well, although as soon shown, these viewpoints vary, and are more nuanced among *inaden*.

Two elderly smiths I questioned acknowledged that *tezma* exists, but indicated that there is a verse in the Qur'an that cures it, which marabouts can read. These elderly smith men added a sociological self-fulfilling prophecy analysis to this, as well: "With some people," they asserted, "*tezma* is so strong a belief, that if a smith comes even for a short time, (even) if he leaves (without doing anything), they are going to say that he sent (for force of) *tezma*!"

Many smiths also revealed an important connection between *tezma* and smiths' lack of reserve; both are necessary for smiths so that they may accept compensation (remuneration) from nobles for their work, and therefore smiths and nobles must be kept separate; it is this power that underlines their differences in reserved conduct, and these differences that enable smiths to protect their profession. Smiths need this protection of *tezma*, many explained, in order to practice their work and receive compensation. In principle, many *inaden* asserted that nobles' ideal reserve and respect, if properly observed, should protect them from *tezma* attacks. Smiths' lack of reserve, conversely, protects their profession, and is the means by which smiths serve noble patron families. In other words, the ideal here is a complementary relationship between these social categories, and smith/artisans' alleged lack of reserve, backed up by tezma when necessary, should safeguard this relationship.

Thus many *inaden* explained their lack of reserve, respect, or shame in positive terms, as a socially-necessary attribute; by contrast, non-smiths tended to denigrate and scorn this trait. But some younger smith/artisans in the towns, particularly those who were successful economically, appeared to internalize the more negative views of these stereotypes of smiths. They expressed irritation at some practices still conducted in the countryside which express smiths' lack of reserve. For example, several considered it undignified to "go jumping about" as do smiths in their dances in the Air Mountain countryside, thereby redefining lack of reserve as lack of dignity (*imojagh*—a term etymologically related to "noble" and "Tuareg" more generally), and by extension, implicitly challenging older criteria of social distinction between nobles and smith/artisans.

Some smiths also gave a negative reason why smiths lack reserve. This is allegedly because they deceived the Prophet: "There was the prophet who set a meeting or message with God (*anamezil*=message to God) with a smith in order to come, but he missed the meeting. When they met, the people noticed that the smiths were missing." Significantly, in the smiths' own more negative explanation of the origin of their lack of reserve, "official," Qur'anic Islam receives prominent attention. These religious tensions, as well as changes in property ownership and material and spiritual power relations, are crucially important in understanding tensions between smiths and some non-smiths.

Reserve, *takarakit,* is an important Tuareg cultural value, particularly among those of aristocratic origin and in the chiefly and maraboutique (*ineslemen*, Islamic scholar) clans. Although many local residents translate this Tamajaq term into French as *la honte,* and some sources translate this term into English as "shame," *takarakit* is complex: this concept can convey shame, respect, modesty, reserve, and/or embarrassment, depending upon the context of encounter, intention, and social relationship. Persons of noble background should ideally, at least, display the strongest sense of *takarakit.* Their subordinates—namely, smith/artisans and descendants of slaves—are supposed to lack it altogether or have the weakest sense of it. Reserve is closely related to another class-based value, dignity, *imojagh,* a term as already noted, related etymologically to terms for Berber (Amazigh), Tuareg, and noble across various regional dialects of Tamajaq. A "true noble" is not supposed to speak openly or directly about something, particularly a wish, desire, preference, or personal plans for the future, or to ask for something directly of someone else, to express anger openly or complain loudly, or disrespect elders, chiefs, Islamic scholars or parents-in-law. A "true noble" should not eat in public or dress immodestly (Nicolaisen and Nicolaisen,1997; Casajus, 2000). This applies to both sexes within this social category, many still try to observe this ideal value.

The men's turban/face-veil and women's headscarf/shawl (most Tuareg women are not permanently veiled about the face; only men veil their face) express this important reserve/respect in social distance toward respected persons, and/or the high status and prestige of the wearer—complex, indexical associations analyzed in detail elsewhere (Claudot-Hawad, 1993; Murphy, 1964). Smith/artisans, for example, are usually less careful about these details of modest dress. Smith men, for example, often allow their face-veil to droop below the chin—taboo for aristocratic Tuareg men. Also, persons of noble descent are not supposed to pronounce names of deceased relatives on their paternal side, names of some matrilineal founding cultural heroines, of living elders, or of husbands (Rasmussen, 1997). As one *ened* put it, "Since *inaden* (stereotypically) lack reserve, we can recite noble genealogies, pronounce normally taboo names, and sing praise songs and engage in intermediary roles in delicate situations, such as bridewealth in chiefly marriages, taxation, and political negotiations."

In more informal sociability, *inaden* have reputations for exceptional verbal wit, a skill widely valued throughout Tuareg society. Smith/artisans' homes and forges are centers of visiting, gossip, horseplay, and joking. They tend to be less shy about using risqué terms in Tamajaq, and include many sexual euphemisms in their praise songs, as in the following oral verses I recorded, with permission, sung by a group of *inaden* at a rural noble wedding:

> (title): Oh, We are for God
> rhythm: *chiluban* (produced by striking drums with braided palm-fiber drumsticks by that name)
> Oh, we are for God Our Hamid (pseudonym for noble patron) likes us
> He gave me enough to buy a shirt
> Oh, we are for God. Rhaicha (pseudonym) daughter of Mamou (pseudonym, local female in patron family of smith/artisans in that rural village)
> She gave us something to eat
> Fana (pseudonym, older sister of bride) gave us an animal in order to eat meat (euphemism for sexual intercourse)
> Oh, we are for God. Tomorrow one can even to to the city of Kano (i.e. one has enough means)
> because one has found much money
> Oh, we are for God. May God leave (us) for a long time
> with the nobles.

Smiths still have much at stake in maintaining the traditionally balanced client-patron relationships in the countryside, despite some emerging outside opportunities. In rural communities, many *inaden* still rely upon the ceremonial roles as a source of income, since they tend not to specialize as much in silversmithing as some others. Since their noble patrons may now choose among different *inaden,* there arise complex problems of negotiating new roles for their clients. As shown, some non-smiths are now side-stepping the *inaden* altogether for certain tasks such as grilling meat at rites of passage, which may appear trivial to the non-smith, but to the smiths this is important because such an action denies them their fair share of meat portions at these ceremonies. Although inaden in their discourses, like persons of noble background, emphasize smiths' traditionally poor economic condition as an ideal, smiths also emphasize their ideally reciprocal social and economic relations with nobles in an environment of uncertainty and scarcity, and express an ideal of not so much a hierarchical, but more a complementary relationship.

As one very elderly chief of *inaden* in an Air village explained to me on a visit, "Throughout the history of (our) people, the smiths have been beneath the nobles. They arrived with nothing. The (former) slaves, *iklan*, they represented the shadow of the nobles because they worked for the nobles. The nobles who had slaves did not do work themselves. In the past, there were wars and famines. When everyone arrived, they remained in Air. Each one smith/artisan family chose the region where their nobles wanted to live. They did all the work for them (nobles) that they (nobles) needed—spoons, axes, all work they wanted. Today, some smiths (also) do garden work. Before, we smiths did not know any other work outside the forge. Today we want to earn more in order to eat; that is what pushed us (historically, also). Before, even me, I only knew how to pull water from the well, not irrigation with a steer. But today each one knows his work."

I pursued this topic. I asked, "Did you see the events of Kaoussan (Tuareg leader of the 1917 Senoussi Revolt against the French)?" He replied, "At that time, I was very young. Three years old. During the years of Kaoussan, if one was a smith, one did not do anything; we smiths do not fight in wars. Even now, (other, non-smith) men who are honest, they do not fight with a smith (either)." I asked why. He explained, "The noble does not fight with someone beneath him. The smith is poor. Also, the smith he must be honest with nobles. Even smiths, their ancestors were poor." Thus the socio-economic and moral-spiritual dimensions of smith/noble relations are not separate, but intertwined. There should not be domination by one over the other, and relations should be cooperative.

INADEN AND RELIGION

Throughout the foregoing rich exegeses, there is evidence of the complex roles *inaden* play in ritual, mythico-history, and cosmology. Recall, for example, that not solely economic, but also ritual roles are key to smiths' special skills. In many aetiological origin tales of *inaden* they related to me, religious imagery is prominent. Religion is also prominent in much local exegesis of smiths' contemporary social roles. There are ambiguous relationships between smith/artisans, their *tezma* powers, and their spirit connections, on the one hand, and Islam, the Islamic God (Allah), and Islamic scholar/marabouts' *al baraka* power, on the other.

There are frequent connections made between smiths' traditional ideal of poverty and religion. Some stories, for example, refer to God having given smiths in the remote past a golden thread, which made them wealthy, but would remain effective only under condition they would never reveal this secret of their wealth; when a smith disobeyed God's condition, God took away the golden thread, and smiths became poor. As a local chief of smith/artisans in one small rural semi-nomadic village of nobles, smiths, marabouts, and descendants of slaves indicated during a visit, "even if smith is rich, he must be obedient; he must not be disobedient (*ahelek*). Also, whatever his wealth, he begs...The marriages of smiths and nobles are not the same...Smiths are poor, their bridewealth (*tagalt*) is the toolkit/workshop, if one knows this work...(but) nobles, they must have camels (for bridewealth)."

Some oral tales that explain the traditional poverty of *inaden* emphasize their close relationship to, not the Islamic God, Allah, but to the spirits, as in the following brief oral tale I recorded, with permission, from an old smith man:

> There was a smith who arrived at a wedding
> They were having a wedding camel race
> He also he gave his help (by participating in the songs)
> When the race was over, he began to drink
> *eghale*, (a beverage made from millet, dates, goat cheese, and water frequently served at rites of passage), and he at his turn said "Bissmillah" (pronouncement of a blessing or benediction)
> The spirits disappeared, and they took everything (everything disappeared, there remained only the smith and his camel there
> For he did not know that it was a spirit ceremony, (i.e., a spirit wedding rather than a human wedding)
> There remained only the footprints of a single man (the smith) in the sand.

Interestingly, here the smith is portrayed as participating in an "official" Islamic rite of passage: a wedding, featuring special ritual food, prayer, and pronouncements of blessings for the marrying couple and families. Yet at the same time, he discovers that this wedding is not that of humans, but rather, of spirits—outside the purview of Islamic and human sociality and morality. In local cosmology/philosophy, not only *inaden*, but also some other persons are considered close to the spirit world, but in ways distinctive from *inaden*. Children, also, are said to sometimes come upon spirit weddings in remote places outside villages and camps in dried riverbeds. Inaden and very small children both can see spirits more easily than other humans. Each in their own manner stands close to the spirit world, particularly that of the non-Qur'anic Kel Essuf spirits of the wild or solitude. *Inaden*, however, are distinctive spiritually from young children in another respect: the former are represented more iconically in local cosmology as small fire djinn spirits who live permanently beneath the sand, work there with tiny anvil and forges, and sometimes play tricks on unwary human travelers who step over them . This power conveys the potential uses of "weapons of the weak" by *inaden* in cases of being "stepped on" in social life, i.e., scorned by some nobles who renege on their obligations to them or by other non-smiths who somehow bypass the safeguards in smith non-smith relationships. Whereas by contrast, children are vulnerable to the pull of spirits back toward the non-human world, expressing concerns over the high infant mortality rate, as well as more philosophical musings on children's proto-social status, alongside elders, as pre-and post-ancestral at once (Rasmussen,

1997), in some respects approximating the positioning of children among the Beng of the Cote-d'Ivoire (Gottlieb, 2004).

Another oral tale given me by a smith/artisan further elaborates on this smith/spirit relationship, and makes a direct connection between smiths' ideal of poverty and spirits' protection of smiths:

> There was a year, when an old smith named Idi was walking in the middle of the night, the spirits (*eljenan*) came out, in front of him, trying to snatch his baggage from him, but he said to them, "What are you going to do with (the belongings of) an old smith who is worthless and who is your brother?" And the spirit left him alone, so smiths are protected from spirits because they are close to them, like brothers.

In the view of some non-smith Tuareg who have inherited the Islamic scholar profession in *ineslemen* (maraboutique) clans, smiths (who have not inherited this profession in clans) are reputedly "less religious." These marabouts who inherited their profession in clans commented disapprovingly, following a trip when they closely observed *inaden* fellow-travelers, "Inaden skip some steps in ablutions, they do not wash after sex, except possibly, a few smiths who have (trained to) become marabouts," implying that any adherence to these standards of conduct required real effort on the part of smiths. Another person of aristocratic background in a maraboutique and chiefly clan disapprovingly complained to me that a smith had joked during prayers that he and a companion were conducting, an act this noble interpreted as "intentionally trying to distract us." Yet some smiths in northern Niger do become Islamic scholars rhrough Qur'anic study, since this profession among Tuareg may be either inherited in clans or acquired through excellence in Qur'anic study (Rasmussen, 2006). At the core of these attitudes are concepts of deception, or at least modification, of the central tenets of the Tuareg cultural interpretation of the Islamic moral system. An old smith man explained to me that, " it is said that smiths once deceived God; that is why, in (widely-held) local beliefs, a smith (now) deceives (*taghdire*)."

Another elderly smith, by contrast, provided more positive religious imagery, disputing the foregoing negative religious imagery. He alluded to the patron prophet of smiths, Dauda (David), a motif in many *inaden* mythico-histories. He explained: "It is because the Prophet Dauda (David), the first smith, their prophet, dropped his hammer, holding it behind him in respect when he heard the call to prayer, that some smiths are thus marabouts (Islamic scholars), and (also because of this) that God gave the trade of the smiths *al baraka* (Islamic benediction or blessing). At first, Dauda did the work of iron and wood, and then God made it easier for him to break stones; is because of that, that the smiths invented soapstone (*asol)* work. With the aborak (tree) wood, Dauda constructed a ladle, a spoon, the saddle that one clutches. With this (stone), Dauda constructed the *iwikin* (men's stone armbands, both decorative jewelry and protective amulets), and along side of the camel he made *aroki* (the carrier for transporting baggage)." Here, Dauda's position as a patron prophet of *inaden* is important in his teaching of skills to make the material products of smiths' trade. In making stone armbands, however, *inaden* again become merged with pre- and para-Islamic ritual and cosmology: some Tuareg men earlier wore these armbands as part of a rite of passage, but very few now do so, particularly those in groups where there are numerous Islamic scholars/marabouts, who disapprove of these armbands as "un-Islamic," harking back to a time of more laxness in the organized (Qur'anic) religion and greater adherence to pre-Islamic Tuareg rituals. These latter rituals are still subtly interwoven into some healing practices and rites of passage, but are often "officially" denigrated by Islamic scholars (Rasmussen, 1995,2006). The stone armbands on men's arms now tend to be rarely seen; I only noticed a few armbands being worn by Tuareg men recently, usually those who belonged to groups where marabouts were less influential.

Smith/artisans' disputed and complex relationship to Islam, already hinted, is expressed in other verbal art. Some oral tales suggest an elevation of Islamic practitioners over smiths, perhaps conveying smiths' efforts to align themselves with organized "official" Islam. Consider the following oral tale I collected and recorded from a smith in a village near Mt. Bagzan about a smith named Agaga:

> One day, Agaga climbed a large fallen tree. He was seated, and the tree did not move. He attached Qur'anic books to the trunk of the tree. He spoke to the cadaver of the tree, he said, 'Tree, you must take me to Tchizewirate.' [There is belief that a prominent marabout once flew to Tchizewirate on a tree trunk.] He shut his eyes, and the tree did not move. He said, 'I believe that until the present time, we have not the same value of the marabout.' But now he has become mentally unsound and poor (*akhalak*).

According to another oral tale, briefly paraphrased for me by an older smith who was also a marabout, there was a smith of Agalagha who was transformed into a stone by a marabout for alleged arrogance. In both these tales, there is emphasis upon competition and rivalry with other Islamic scholars who are non-smiths, but also affirmation of the latters' religious powers. The position of this teller of the second tale is significant: as a smith who became an Islamic scholar, he validated his own devotion to organized religion (i.e., Tuareg cultural interpretations of Qur'anic Islam), thereby allaying any doubts on this by telling this tale that subtly reprimands a smith who challenged marabouts' supremacy.

Nonetheless, smiths and marabouts, though often opposed in local symbolism, traditionally share some similar ritual and sociopolitical roles: both ideally refrain from fighting, raiding, and until recently, from departing on salt and date caravans to Bilma, Niger and Kano, Nigeria, and they are supposed to own only a few livestock. Both traditionally require the protection of aristocratic warriors, but are also both needed by nobles: the former, as go-betweens, jewelers, handy-persons, and musicians, and the latter as Islamic scholars, scribes, healers, and legal adjudicators. Traditionally, noble patron families were supposed to bring back sacks of millet from caravans to their smith client families and even now, many rural nobles still give millet, tea, sugar, and cash on demand to their smith client families. Marabouts nowadays acquire animals through religious alms donations, hospitality arrangements, and healing ritual treatments requiring animal sacrifice, but ideally, they should re-distribute most of the meat as alms (Rasmussen,2001a,2004).

Several Tuareg of aristocratic background asserted that "a smith can be a marabout, but not an *imam* who leads the call to prayer." Smiths, however, contradicted this, asserting that they can also become an *imam* at prayer, and one smith man indicated his grandfather had been one. "It is sufficient to obtain authorization with a blessing (*al baraka*) from prominent marabouts to do this," he explained.

These contradictions express ambivalence regarding smiths' relationship to, and roles in, organized "official" religion (i.e., Qur'anic Islam in local cultural interpretation), particularly ritual. In my view, such contradiction and ambivalence strongly suggest that, upon Tuaeg conversion to Islam, there needed to be a symbolic reconciliation between Islam's call for equality of all believers and Tuareg social hierarchies. Important was a need to at least symbolically curtail the older powers of smiths in the local indigenous African religion pre-dating Islam. Yet smiths' spiritual roles were so compelling that they could not be suppressed entirely—indeed, in a creativity of power, these spiritual roles became nested within the new order, but carefully controlled.

Historically, Tuareg and other Berber (Amazigh) peoples initially resisted Islam in their mountain and desert fortresses, only gradually taking it up between the eighth and eleventh centuries C.E. (Norris, 1975,1990). In several other African societies, likewise, with belief complexes surrounding smith/artisans and their ritual powers that are very similar to those of the Tuareg, smiths' longstanding important ritual, cosmological, and social roles pre-dating organized scriptural/textual religions such as Islam and Christianity, smiths' alleged "mystic" powers are viewed as problematic because they present cultural contradictions. These contradictions must be resolved by continually re-defining smiths' powers, over and over again, and attempting to clarify and/or realign them to greater cultural satisfaction of the "traditional" elite or officially dominant classes. These religious strands of so-called "indigenous" (traditional) African and "official" (organized) religions are not strictly opposed; for they also interweave in other contexts, and are not always contradictory in every context. Where tensions are present, they arise from cross-cutting religious and socioeconomic configurations of power.

In the past, Tuareg smiths were protected by non-Quranic spirits of the wild (Kel Essuf), principally the "hot" fire *djinn*, against being killed in raids; thus smiths belong to the people of the *tawsit* (descent group) who took their ancestors in a raid in the past; the ancestors of the smiths (though from outside the noble descent system, and of outside origin) took as their affiliation (descent group) the names of *tawsit* of nobles to whom they belonged. As soon shown, imagery of illegitimacy and taboo-breaking surround some smith aeiological origin mythico-histories. Illegitimate children among the Tuareg are often called children of the wild or spirits (*bararen n essuf*, or Yessouf—the latter, notably, ambiguously close to the Qur'anic name Yussuf denoting Joseph (Rasmussen, 1995,1997, 2006). Some illegitimate children are raised in the wild by maternal grandmothers, can be named for a wild animal such as Eggur (Jackal), or take the mother's name; matrilineal elements are retained to varying degrees by different Tuareg groups, but Islam introduced Qur'anic and Arabic patrilineal institutions which became superimposed, with nation-state law, upon those earlier matrilineal institutions.

Another example further illustrating this ambivalence over smiths' power is from everyday sociability: the custom that only smiths may eat directly from the cooking pot; whereas nobles must eat from the dish or plate after food has been transferred from the pot there. More generally, the purpose of social stratum endogamy marriage ideals and their associated taboos for each social category, in many elderly smiths' viewpoint, is so that there can be client-patron attachments between them; whereas by contrast, according to many nobles, its purpose is to protect from smiths's pollution, since they are impure or "dirty" from work of the forge.

Hence the importance of smiths' and non-smiths' viewpoints, their self and mutual perceptions, and assessments of power, in current identity and historical memory. Indeed, even smiths' own accounts are not monolithic or consensual, but reveal some internal disagreements and variations. The unpredictable and debated nature of smiths' power reflects efforts—at times conscious, at times unconscious—to cope with larger problems surrounding organized and "traditional" or indigenous religious influences in Tuareg society. These belief systems sometimes interweave and overlap, and sometimes conflict and compete. *Inaden* in their ritual roles, social relationships, and oral narrative*s* remind non-smiths of longstanding contradictions, but also flexibility and negotiability in these systems.

NOTES

1. *Ark echaghel*, by contrast, is believed to be intentionally activated, directed at a specific target the instigator wishes to harm, even to kill. There are several methods used, some of which involve the collaboration of former slaves and interestingly, occasionally marabouts, whose *al baraka* blessing power is in these cases subverted or "corrupted" toward destructive goals. See Nicolaisen (1961) and Rasmussen (2004).
2. See Comaroff and Comaroff (1993), Moore and Sanders (2001), and Stewart and Strathern (2004) for analyses of connections between these policies and conflicts over wealth expressed in the idiom of witchcraft and sorcery, and also Grinker and Steiner (1997) for discussions of these policies in Africa more generally.

3.   There have been several Tuareg armed nationalist/separatist conflicts against
      the central governments of Niger and Mali, and their causes over longterm have
      been complex. In my view, the tensions have more regional than ethnic bases.
      From French colonial eras until recently, the northern, predominantly Tamajaq-
      speaking regions of these countries and their residents have been marginalized
      by uneven development programs initiated by first, colonial powers and later,
      state agencies. Many Tuareg were initially underrepresented in higher
      education, new jobs, and functionary positions, fearing early schools as centers
      of cultural hegemony, and have tended to reside far from decision-making
      centers. Many early aid programs pressured nomads to sedentarize, and
      disrupted ecological balances between herds, wells, and pastures. The 1963
      rebellion based in Kidal, Mali, initially broke out in tensions over food relief
      distribution, and there were massacres by some military commanders there. The
      1990-96 rebellion erupted in the wake of massacres of civilians in Tchin
      Tabaraden, Niger and Lere, Mali, following simmering tensions over
      unemployment of youths returning from exile and labor migration, and leaders'
      demands included greater autonomy for northern regions, as well as
      representation of Tuareg in government and jobs. Later, in 2007 in Arlit, Niger,
      fighting resurged in conflict over uranium contracts awarded to transnational
      companies, in areas used for pasture that residents allege have become
      contaminated by the mining. Most recently, in 2012, another armed conflict
      broke out between rebel dissidents in northern Mali and the Malian army after
      the former returned from Libya following the overthrow of Ghadaffi. Although
      there have been efforts to negotiate peace, these countries have very low
      budgets and some promises of peace pacts have been difficult to implement in
      peripheral zones. See Loughran and Seligman (2006), Claudot-Hawad (1996),
      Kohl (2007) Rasmussen (2001a).

4.   This clinic opened around 2000, but is often low in medical supplies. Many
      rural residents remain skeptical and timid of bio-medical personnel, particularly
      those from outside the region, and tend to go there only as a last resort after
      trying local healing specialists (Rasmussen, 2001a,2006).

CHAPTER TWO

INADEN ORIGINS, HISTORIES, AND PROFESSIONAL PRACTICES

MYTHICO-HISTORIES

Numerous, sometimes conflicting traditions relate the origins of *inaden*. According to Benhazera (1908), for example, a woman named Tamanenet was the ancestor of all smith/artisans. Smith/artisans' separate origin traditions, their tendency to practice social stratum endogamy more so than other Tuareg today, and their "secret" *inaden* jargon, nowadays only occasionally used, called Tenet, express the distinctiveness of this group. Tenet, which includes terms formed by word-plays on standard Tamajaq, rather than a different grammatical structure altogether, is today spoken only in specialized situations.

Etiological mythico-histories of *inaden* origins are regionally somewhat varied, but all tend to fall into two categories: within each *inaden* group (clan), some variants have in common Biblical and Qur'anic origin themes, on the one hand, and other variants have matrilineal ancestress themes, on the other hand. As in aristocratic descent groups, both motifs—those with "official" Qur'anic religious imagery and those with matrilineal pre-Islamic imagery pre-dating "official" religion—are present. But the *inaden* mythicio-historical ancestral founders are in both cases distinct from those of the aristocratic groups, the latter already analyzed elsewhere (Rasmussen ,1997,2006). For example, in the Adar region near Tahoua, Niger, and in the region of In Gall, Niger, most traditions trace artisans' beginnings to two prophets in the Islamic and Biblical traditions, David and Noah.

In general, all Tuareg origin mythico-histories tend to share a common theme: many variants trace origins to a founding female ancestress. But the *inaden* origin stories that I collected differ from those of the non-smiths, in several ways. First, the matrilineal female ancestress is usually different from that of the noble matrilineal ancestress, even the ancestress of the noble descent group to whom the smiths are attached. Secondly, as already hinted, many *inaden* variants also emphasize the outside religious origins of smith/artisans, or they emphasize a once common religious origin, but later divergence from it by the *inaden* for some reason, usually an action by an ancestral smith who stood out from the ancestral nobles and/or committed a transgression.

Despite their common themes (both with each other and with some noble origin mythico-histories), *inaden* oral mythico-histories that I collected are not internally monolithic or consensual. In their details, these origin accounts display some variation, even within this social stratum, and within the same region and local community. Not surprisingly, perhaps, one explanation, widely recognized by scholars (Mudimbe, 1992; Hale, 1999), is that these variants express the widely-practiced "impression management" and manipulation of history and genealogy found throughout many oral traditions more generally, for example, those of West African griots/bards. But to account for some finer nuances of difference, in my view, one must distinguish between those origin myths by the *inaden* themselves and those origin myths related by non-smiths about them; for the latter are often reported speech (Bakhtin, 1965[1986]), that is, collected from non-smiths by some early French and other European travelers, colonial administrators, soldiers, missionaries, and other outsiders with ties to the French colonial administration of then-French West Africa.

In my research on these oral mythicio-histories, I found that many *inaden* themselves trace their descent to matrilineal ancestresses, prominent in Tuareg cosmology, myth, and ritual healing pre-dating Islam (Rasmussen, 2006) though as noted, these ancestresses of smiths are different from the noble descent groups' female ancestresses. The *inaden* mythico-histories related by smiths themselves also mention, in the same or different accounts, additional Qur'anic and Old Testament themes, some of which were also presented concerning the origins of smiths' status, power, and relation to religion. There are similar noble Qur'anic themes in noble origin accounts given nobles, but these differ in their details; for example, they include such figures as the first marabout (Islamic scholar) who converted people in the area or sank the first well. Whereas smith Qur'anic themes are quite different: these latter tend to relate more ambivalent relationships to both Tuareg cultural and Islamic religious elements. For example, in the Air Mountains near Mount Bagzan and also in the nearby town of Agadez in Niger, several elderly smiths of the Kel Ewey Tuareg recited for me the following variant of their origins:

> Our ancestors did the same career as Dauda (David).
> At the moment of creation of people, all people were the same. People were with David and together and the same
> Dauda (David) hid behind a tree and God told him, "May you always stay with trees."
> And after that David did the work of wood
> And after the people who were near, (living) as neighbors with Dauda (David), took up the same career as he did. They had the name of smith.
> That is the word that our parents gave us
> And after that, the smiths with their work,
> the nobles began to have need of that.
> (So) They lived together with nobles (always).
> The smiths they began to live next to nobles
> Now the smiths they seek to be beside nobles
> They receive the name of the descent group of their nobles
> For example, the smiths of the Kel Tchimilan, they live in the same place as their nobles
> The smiths of the Kel Nabarro live in the same place as they
> Those of the Kel Igurmadan also live in the same place

It is for that that they received the noble descent group name; the name of the *tawsit* of smiths is found just in the region of the nobles (i.e. they receive the name of the noble *tawsit* to whom they are neighbors)
Also whenever nobles need work, they tell their neighboring smiths (it is geography, even in origins, the traditional relationship base)
And afterward, when the smiths work one pays them
If it is a wedding or nameday, or a work the smith does, on pays him
To be a smith is nothing profound; it is sufficient to not have reserve
Even if you beg too much, that is being a smith
You walk with an old pair of pants, toward home, which is the forge
Basically, everyone (all humans—nobles, smiths, and everyone else) has the same father and mother: Adam and Hawa (Adam and Eve)
It is different work careers, (that make the difference),
Smiths work in wood and iron and begging.

In this oral account, similar but not identical to several others offered me by several other local *inaden* near Mt. Bagzan, there is emphasis upon not solely smiths' separation from, but also their close relationships to non-smiths. Although *inaden* have separate origins from their noble patrons, their social connections and mutual dependence are given the most emphasis. Also, their work is distinct and specialized, but their identity with others as all children of Adam and Eve, stands out.

Yet many elderly *inaden* also emphasized smith's traditional association with poverty and the practice of begging, and their lack of reserve (*takarakit*). Consider, for example, the following oral mythico-history, recited to me by an elderly smith I shall call Yussuf:

A year ago, I left for a village at the foot of the Bagzan,
When I arrived there, someone told me, 'There are the ruins of the ancestors, where they lived a very long time ago. They lived beside our noble ancestors. Because of that, you must come help us do some work we need.'
Also, all my relatives (parents=*marawanin*) who are old, they had herds, but as they were smiths, they respected their nobles (i.e., had fewer livestock.)
They did all their work for them, that they wanted, and the nobles paid them."
"Also, even if the smith is rich, he must be obedient
All the smiths, if they find a place where their nobles are, they must obey them
All that they obtain, they bring to their children and they eat together (Smiths do not eat what they receive from nobles on the spot with nobles, but they share it at home among smith relatives)
Whatever is his wealth, whatever his wealth, he (a smith) begs
You (researcher) want to know if smiths have their own descent group? one has not had this information, but (sometimes) we specify only the other (attached noble patrons' own descent group, to which some of us believe we belong, but others believe we are not, but have our own descent group
Each (aristocratic) descent group has its own (attached) smiths, even the livestock brand indicates the same (descent group) as the nobles, but the brand on their smiths's livestock is sometimes a modified, "twisted,"(inverted or reversed) version of brand on the nobles' livestock.

As for us (here), our relatives are Kel Igurmadan (a local descent group) because they come from upper Bagzan Igurmadan. They are neighbors of the Igurmadan who are your (researcher's noble hosts') fathers. [Note how this smith viewed me as absorbed as a fictive daughter into my host family's genealogy.] They were the noble patrons of my parents (relatives). (i.e., patron-client relationships were inherited through the generations).

Yet Yusuf himself also offered hints of contradictions, even within his own narrative:

About Dauda, sometimes others they say that the smiths deceived God. That is why the smith deceives (*taghdire*)
This, according to everyone, it is like that
Our occupation is that specified for smiths, because the smith who does not know any career is neither noble nor smith, and this smith cannot find *al Baraka*
The smiths in Hausa country are called Massassikitan (in Tamajaq, designates a distant artisan to the south, in Hausa, called *makeri*), they make black wooden bowls for us. The prophet Dauda told us and them that we both, like all smiths, have the same smith work to do, the same career to do
All the prophets, each one was important
To be a smith, that is a career (occupation)
Begging is the source of smiths' income, with their ax over their shoulder, always.
If I wear clothing that is clean and I walk around here in it, no one is going to say that I am a smith (opposite in the countryside from in Agadez, where smiths dress up more)
According to our parents, the profound significance of being a smith is having to know the profession or career (*tazale*)
My history, how I came to this village, it was marriage that brought me here
There are a very few nobles in a large oasis near us who know the work of the forge Now even they make sabers!

I asked, "Do smiths like that?" and he replied, "No, but they are not going to say anything. Some nobles are less reserved or ashamed to do this work. Also, if no smiths are living nearby, it may be necessary. I have not seen a noble recently prevented from doing the work of smiths. That is a question of knowledge, if he knows it, he can do everything he wants, if he is not ashamed to do so. (i.e., if he lacks the traditional noble ideal of reserve.) In the past, however, nobles did not ever do the work of smiths. Now, it is not like life before, it used to be shameful for nobles."

Some other oral origin tales, including those reported by outsiders, also emphasize smiths' origins in Qur'anic and other "official" (organized) religious scriptural traditions. Yet the positions of the outsiders who recorded these themes is significant: Pere (Father) de Foucauld, for example, was a missionary among the Kel Ahaggar Tuareg in Algeria around the turn of the 20th century, during the French military subjugation of the Sahara. According to Father (Pere) de Foucauld in his dictionary (1951-52, 3:1300), "some of them (*inaden*) were of Israelite origin, having come from Morocco in a distant age, from ocean shores, after the Berber tribes that conquered Adagh." Other early European travelers' and ethnographers' accounts, also, mention "Israelite" (Hebrew) origin, for example, some early French ethnographers and archaeologists, such as Henri Lhote (1955:323), who believed that many of them are descendants of Jews of Tamentit who were exiled from Touat in 1495 during the Inquisition, and who subsequently intermarried with African slaves.

A Tuareg intellectual of smith/artisan origins, who no longer practiced his smith work of the forge, in conversations with me in the United States also supported this view. However, some other *inaden* with whom I spoke in Niger and Mali did not agree, asserting that trade across the Mediterranean, rather than geographic origins in the Middle East or Judaism, accounted for these associations.

I do not seek to "resolve" this mystery of the "true" origins of Tuareg smith/artisans. My purpose, rather, is to analyze the connections between these mythico-histories, concepts of ritual power, and social practices relating to *inaden* here, and in later chapters, in other smith/artisans in African societies with similar belief complexes. The important point is that, whether "true" or not, many of these origin mythico-histories concerning *inaden* involve reflections on identity, relatedness, and otherness. In the era of French military operations in the Sahara and Sudan and subsequent colonialism, the missionary Pere de Foucauld was attempting to draw the Tuareg into the European Judeo-Christian tradition in order to more easily convert them (as Muslims) to Christianity. He worked in a political environment in which the Tuareg branch of the Libyan Senoussi Islamic religious order was conducting armed resistance against the French forces. Pere De Foucauld was later killed in the Ahaggar (Hoggar) Mountains. Henri Lhote, also, for much of his career, worked in the colonial era.

The important point is that these earlier authors had a political interest in detaching Islamic (and specifically, the Tuareg branch of Senoussi resistance) influences from Tuareg society in their portrayals, and perhaps for this reason, they tended to exaggerate the divisions within Tuareg groups. The ambiguous and conflicting origin mythico-histories of the *inaden* with their contradictions offered them an opportunity to do this, in order to divide and conquer. In other words, it would have been against colonial interests to emphasize complementary, overlapping, or interrelated religious and other cultural influences uniting the Tuareg.

Yet undeniably, in some contexts there are indeed collisions between hegemonic official religion and pre-Islamic Tuareg religious influences, as shown in the mythico-histories and ritual and social practices and relationships between smiths and non-smiths. *Inaden* in effect have always straddled both worlds, situated as they are on the fault-lines of power. For recall that some *inaden,* in additional accounts I collected, also asserted their separate origins, sometimes even within the narratives of the same smith, in a sense similar to those internally polyphonic voices Smith found among former Algerian *pied-*

noirs residing in France (Smith, 2004). These local variants I collected do not have the same agenda, however, as did those outsiders writing about the Tuareg *inaden* in the early twentieth century during French subjugation of the Sahara. What, then, can we make of these oral origin mythico-histories that I collected from *inaden* who themselves emphasize their distinct origins?

Additional insights are provided by narratives of origins that portray ancestral smiths' simultaneously outside origins and mediating roles, sometimes in contexts of apparently anti-social actions, as well as those that emphasize smiths' connections to the spirit world. These motifs are conveyed in several oral mythico-histories I collected and recorded from an *ened* from the border region between Niger and Mali. Below, he related smiths' roles in the origins of the Ifoghas, a descent group in the Kel Adagh confederation in the Adragh-n-Ifoghas region of northern Mali:

> A woman of the Tafaghist (feminine for Ifoghas, a descent group of Tuareg within the Kel Adagh confederation, who reside in Mali and on the Mali-Niger border) had a child
> Her child was illegitimate, the child was born outside marriage (=*barar n essuf*, literally "a child of the wild" i.e., of the Kel Essuf spirits of the wild)
> When she had (the child) she left her family
> She went, went, went, until she arrived in Agalal (a village in the Iferouan region, around the Niger-Mali-Algeria border), when she arrived in Tadak, she was accepted by the Kel Tadak (group of Tuareg in the south of Air)
> She stayed there, stayed, until the smith of Agalal married her,
> the Tafaghist woman. The smith married the Tafaghist woman
> Her real (own) relatives rejected her. When he married her, he had one daughter
> The Ifoghas went to look for their daughter (the rejected woman who had left)
> That day, the smith woman married, she had a daughter (i.e. this woman had two children, one illegitimate one, and one legitimate one with her smith husband)
> The one who was (named) Amazaq, organized the marriage, the smith of Tadak, Tadak, a region of people from the region (between Mali and Niger)
> He told them that the smith belonged to him: "You have abandoned the woman, and I married her to my smith man. If you want your woman, you can take her (with you). So if you want, you can take her, but the (legitimate smith man's) daughter will not go."
> So the second daughter stayed with the smith man
> So they took back their rejected woman. They left with the woman they had rejected.
> The little girl (the child of the smith man and the woman, who stayed) grew up, she became a woman, got married, she gave birth to the Ifoghas descent group (*tawsit*).

Origin of the Ifoghas of Kel Takiza Icherifan (a group having Islamic healing blessing powers):

The smiths of Tasedregh in Air
Kel Takriza, the icherifan (Qur'anic heaing clans claiming descent from the Prophet Mohammed), Kel Takriza, Tadak Tasedregh, Tasedregh (clans) are the origin of the smiths named Sidraghan (whocame from Tasedrigh, another Saharan region). Then they were married, they became Ifoghas, but were from Sidreghan originally
It is thus for the Ifoghas (i.e., there are two groups of people in this account: Ifoghas and Issidrighen).

Origin of Smiths of Kel Tezzelat:

The smiths of Tezzelat, Tezzelat, here are their origins:
A noble woman was tricked by a smith, she did not know he was a smith
He married her, (and) then (afterward) she discovered her husband in the process of making spoons, and he told her, "It is put aside; finished," (i.e. the wife was surprised, and he said that he would stop smith work)
(Nonetheless, even so) She chased the smith, her husband, so they became the smiths of Tezzelat
You understand—there existed smiths, gardeners, slaves, free (*imajeghen* noble) people, all at the same time. These are mixed groups; each group has its smiths
A woman named Handede is their grandparent, it was she who founded their family, and it was she who created the Issidrighen."
There exist also those of the Tezzelat, there are also those who were slaves.

In the foregoing three mythico-histories, there are processes of displacement, exile, and distancing, but also mediation and close interconnectedness. Whether exiled themselves, or sheltering others who are exiled, *inaden* protect. They mediate between the human social and moral community and the spirit world of the "wild," or *essuf,* the latter concept central in local worldview and philosophy (Rasmussen, 1995, 2008), and associated with anti-social, but also creative behavior outside the community of home and tent. Like humans, there is fictive kinship adoption of a child who was born outside marriage. Illegitimacy is a great shame among Tuareg, despite free social interaction and courtship between the sexes.

Thus *inaden*, like some other African smith/artisans described in subsequent chapters—especially the Cameroonian Kapsiki *rerhe* (Van Beek, 1992) and the Malian Mande *nyamakala* (McNaughton, 1988), therefore articulate internally polyphonic messages: on the one hand, they remind the community of older indigenous local ritual and cosmology/philosophy, and on the other, of more recent Abrahamic religious overlays (in the Tuareg case, of later Berber and Tuareg conversions to Islam). As shown in the attitudes toward *tezma* power, these different strands interweave, but also conflict, in the contemporary communities where they resonate. These specialists often mediate between institutionalized, organized and "indigenous," popularized forms of religion. In fields of overlapping practices and concepts of power, oppositions of ritual power and social identity are negotiated—at times harmoniously, at times acrimoniously. .Smith/artisans stand at the intersection of discourses and concepts and actions that alternately honor and scapegoat these "culture-heroes."

Like the Kel Essuf hot fire spirits in the Tuareg pre-Islamic pantheon, there is also an unpredictable and fleeting quality to *inaden*, in their alleged playing tricks (*temarques*) on unwary humans. Recall that hot fire spirits work on tiny forges underneath the sand dunes, and sometimes pull tricks on unwary travelers; likewise, as shown, *inaden* are widely feared to trick their noble patrons and other non-smiths by various means, including shape-shifting.

Socially, this alleged shape-shifting takes a form that mirrors some nobles' fears (real or imagined) of smiths' sexual transgressions, encountered in tensions of alleged "adultery" and other actions described earlier. Even milder courtship transgressions provoke disapproval and gossip by non-smiths. For example, one *ened* man in a village in the Air was accused of "masquerading" as a noble man, in order to court women in a distant village. As observed, underlying these rumors and gossip are fears of smith men's potential appeal to aristocratic women, which have some basis in the socio-economic upheavals in Tuareg society in which many (though not all) persons of noble origins have lost herds and face unemployment, and many (though not all) smiths are becoming prosperous in the tourist trade.

Yet also striking in the foregoing three oral mythico-histories of smith origins, particularly in the Kel Tezzelat tale, is a subtle disapproval of, and warning against "chasing" *inaden* away: nobles need them—not solely for material cultural products, but for "grounding" their own prestigious social identity, now precarious and economically threatened. *Inaden* must remain intricately embedded within the community over long-term in order to remind everyone of this identity, which they in turn have depended on until recently. Tensions arise when persons of noble background become aware of, or are remineded that inaden have alternative sources of income nowadays. Hence the importance of mythico-histories told by smiths themselves emphasize the continuing value of smiths' work for everyone.

Consider another origin mythico-history that reminds others of the need to appreciate smiths' usefulness, and more: the need to recognize not solely their difference, but also their connection, to Tuareg society and Abrahamic religious traditions. This *ened* raconteur also further elaborated on the important connection of Dauda to *inaden* in the following oral tale, which he titled:

Dauda (Patron Founder and Prophet of the Smiths)

Dauda (David) the prophet of the smiths

A smith betrayed him, he (the smith) also betrayed the Muslims
At that moment (when) the smith went behind the tree, he seized it, held it; he hid behind the tree because he was afraid of battle, appearing to commit treason for not fighting a battle
They followed the prophet Dauda (David)
The prophet Dauda at the moment there was a battle between the prophet and the Christians *(ikufar)*
At that moment the smiths said that they betrayed our prophet (Dauda)
May peace be upon him
So they ran towards a tree
At that moment, he (Dauda) said to them, "All your subsistence will come from (be provided by) these trees."
The prophet Dauda said, "Also, it is him (David) who works iron. David gave us, smiths, the power to work iron."
This word, you know the word, the prophet David you know that the smiths when the war began, the battle began, they battled against the Christians
You understand, the smiths were afraid, they hid, they held (clutched) onto the trees ; for smiths do not customarily fight in wars
The prophet Dauda said to them, "May God make you earn your living from trees (i.e. wood-working)."
You know that everyone descended from Adam and Eve; she Eve, he Adam.
So now the prophet Dauda returned to the side of the smiths (i.e., re-approached them, forgave them but made them specialists)
The smiths remained smiths, nobles remained nobles, clients (*ighawelen*—long-freed slaves who gave trribute) remained clients, slaves (*iklan*—newly-captured slaves) remained slaves.
Only now in our days they resemble each other, now they are the same, these divisions no longer exist.
Now all these things have disappeared
Now everyone resembles each other.

Striking in this account of *inaden* relations to Islam, Dauda, and other Tuareg is the assertion that *inaden*, in not fighting a war against the Christians, but instead "hiding" behind trees, (an act this smith/artisan narrator demonstrated to me by miming, in crouching behind a wooden mortar that was handy) express their traditional non-fighting status (in contrast to the noble and tributary warriors). Also in contrast to the latter, *inaden* hid behind trees in fear of the battle, and these trees became iconic for one of their specialized tasks: woodworking (making spoons and ladles and garden pulleys for nobles, for example). Here, mixed reactions to *inaden* non-combatant status (as go-betweens, ambassadors, and mediators) is expressed in the accusation of treason and some disapproval from Islam. Yet there is a paradox here. For Islam also insists that all Tuareg were equal, in contradiction to their social hierarchy. Thus the prophet Dauda (David)—found in Qur'anic, as well as Old Testament Biblical traditions— assigns the *inaden* to working with trees (wood) in perpetuity. This mythico-history evolves from initial rejection and punishment and separateness to ultimate occupational skill and specialty, ending on a hopeful note of social reconciliation, thereby mirroring that ideal of complementary social harmony, but also ambivalence, over the smith/artisans' problematic relationship to Islam. The tale reflectst on this paradox, and attempts to resolve it.

Nevertheless, several smiths explained, "We do not marry nobles. We do not court noble women. In the tradition of our parents, the smith marries a smith woman, and the noble marries a noble woman. The slave marries a slave woman, it is like that...a (custom) we have from our parents. The origin (*arassal*) of our parents, each person must marry a woman of his own (social) origins. Their *tawsiten* (descent groups or clans) all have their (brand) sign, on the neck of their livestock."

The next tale is a variant on a common matrilineal aetiological mythico-history of many *inaden* in the Air region, and concerns a female founding ancestress, Khadede (or Handede) and her husband, named Khadan. This tale was collected from an old blind smith man in a small nomadic camp near the semi-nomadic village where I resided during much of my research:

Khadede or Khadede (ancestress of local smiths, her husband, Khadan)

The first village they lived in was called Effafe, to the west of the Tamgak mountains and beside the mountains. Their food was the fruits of the wild trees, for example, the doum palm, the *aza*, the fruit of *tashghare* (thorned tree) and *krem-krems*, (like burrs), they pounded them and transformed them into a cereal called *agarof*. They had their herds of goats and camels, but not many. One day, Khadede left to lead their goats and Khadan also left to look for his camels. They met near a *guleta* called *tarinkit* (a tree that grows always wrapped with another tree, like a cord, like in some houses in towns). They spent the night there, as though they were at home (i.e., the nuptial tent). [There is a local taboo against sleeping in the oeuds, associating this with illicit love; many tourists to the region are assigned this place to camp in; whereas even the nomads ideally "camp" in clustered small communities defined as not the wild but the home] It was because they did not have reserve (*takarakit*). That was also the reason (cause) they had for having a child (i.e., that lapse of reserve—spending the night together in the oeud outside villages and camps, caused them to have a child; she got pregnant).

Now, we also say that when one makes love outside the home, (i.e., in the wild, essuf, outside the nuptial tent), that child will be very open (i.e., lack reserve). They had fifteen children in their family, nine girls and six boys, among the children. There was only one who did not know the work of the forge, he only did begging, he was called *Ezanban* , from this was invented (derived) the *tezma*,(smiths' alleged malevolent power).

Ezanban married the woman called *Bourssa*, this name, from which they invented the name *albourousa* (the *inaden* mumming ritual shaming noble patrons for transgressions against them). Their neighbors did a ceremony without inviting them. As both of them begged, they became poor, they did not want to work , all smiths inherited (their) begging. The village of the woman of the beggars was named Boton, the name comes from *batou* or *behu* (denoting "lie"). One day, Khadede asked her husband to move in order to go a little closer to the south. The next morning Khadan brought their camels closer, they moved away in order to leave the origin village in order to come to another village, where they camped, they found a smith couple, whose leader was named Yofa Yinadan, Yofa Yinadan is an ancestor of a current smith leader/chief in your (researcher's) host family's village.

They were there, marrying among themselves, when they became a large family, they dispersed everywhere in the Air, because on each side of the Air massif one heard news of a village where there were only smiths. Certain noble persons came to that village in order to invite the smiths to their homes because they needed some work, each smith was invited by someone they then stayed with always, and became his smith.

Years ago, nobles did not know how to skin or tan the animal, and as the they were all nomadic livestock herders, every time they had animals that died, (or) when they slaughtered the animal, they needed smiths and smith women also, who tanned the hides. The hides were made for noble youths, they wore pants of leather at that time. There were not many clothes, but the tents of nomads, also, were made with the hides of large animals. That is how the smiths came to live among the nobles.

Again, in this matrilineal etiological narrative of *inaden* origins as in the more Qur'anic and Biblical-themed narratives, there is imagery of nearness and distance, transgression and re-integration, outsider and insider positions. Self and other are not, in *inaden* formulations, detachable parts. Other prominent images here—also recurrent throughout many *inaden* motifs—are illegitimacy, illicit love, lack of reserve, and association with the wild. There are also allusions here to *tezma*, that ritual power of *inaden* , as well as allusions to their *albouroussa* mumming rites conducted in the countryside in order to shame nobles who neglect their patron duties toward smiths. The tale also reiterates the pervasive cultural typification of *inaden* as beggers, and by implication, their idealized poverty and lack of significant income in livestock herds (though as observed, some *inaden* do own herds); hence their primary income derives from working for nobles. Just as the previous tale explained the origins of working wood and metals, this tale explains the beginnings of working animal hides in leatherwork. [In Tuareg society, smith women cut, dye, and embroider leather; women of other social origins now also do some leatherwork, but generally do not perform these specialized phases of leatherworking.] There is a juxtaposition and tension here, as in many narratives by *inaden* about themselves, of smith/artisans' simultaneously peripheral and central position, and their important role in Tuareg society, on which *imajeghen* noble patrons depend.

Inaden in their own origin accounts therefore often state that they stand outside the local Tuareg descent groups, and most, as already noted, continue to practice endogamy, despite upheavals in Tuareg society, including modifications of their client-patron relations with nobles in the countryside, and their near (though not complete) breakdown in the towns. Not all the foregoing accounts assert exactly the same details of their origins; for example, the story of Dauda recurred, but not all tellers agreed on this or its significance in terms of the religious affiliation of contemporary or ancestral *inaden*. But in general in *inaden* accounts, there are re-assertions of belonging and complementary social roles, not solely transgressions or banishments. As we shall see, there are elements of both belonging and disaffiliation in social relationships between smith/artisans and non-smiths, particularly aristocratic patrons.

These *inaden* accounts, as noted, generally emphasize pre-Islamic matrilineal origins, as do the aristocratic Tuareg clans, though the latters' respective founder/ancestresses are different (Rasmussen, 2006). The *inaden* accounts also emphasize, again like those of nobles, Islamic/Qur'anic motifs and Judeo-Christian motifs, thereby reflecting the fluid and dynamic, rather than fixed or static, religious affiliations formerly present in the Sahara, the Horn, and the Sudan, before the greater divergence of the organized religions in those regions later.

These apparently "contradictory" themes reflect these blending and merging processes and local preoccupations with them. These motifs can become, in some contexts of social practice, agonistic, re-directed toward constructing Otherness, in exclusionary projects—constructed both in some local non-smiths' and in some outsiders' early reports on smith/artisans and their origins. In my subsequent comparative chapters, I show how different religious motifs are implicated in sociopolitical and economic processes that do not always produce a romantic syncretism or pluralism; religious intolerance and hegemony can also assert themselves in conflicting interpretations of African smith/artisans' roles in society.

CONTEMPORARY AESETHETIC AND SOCIOECONOMIC ROLES OF *INADEN*

Tuareg smith/artisans' past origins related in mythico-histories provide an illuminating, but only partial, view of their complex ritual power. Also instructive are their aesthetic and socioeconomic roles.

Within the *inaden* smith/artisan social category are different specialists: *inaden wan-tizol* (artisans of metal), who make weapons and jewelry (lost wax technique) using basically the same implements throughout Tuareg regions; *inaden wan-talaq* (artisans of clay), who work in wood and whose name comes from their homeland, the Talak plain, west of the Air Mountains in Niger; and *inaden wan-Tamenannad*, who also work in wood and are reputed to make best camel saddles; in addition, there are stone-workers of gypsum in the Air region, locally mined there by the smith/artisan specialist stoneworker families on caravans. *Ikanawen* (singular *ekanao*), are potters associated with southern Tuareg, Tellemidez and Ayt Awari; *Inesfaden* (sing. *anesfada*) are stewards or even messengers for chieftains. In the Air Mountains of northern Niger, I found that some of these categories of specialists often overlap, and local residents of diverse social origins usually use the general gloss *inaden* (sing. *ened*, masc., *tenet*, fem.) to refer to smith/artisans in general.

Art patronage remains a vibrant activity in Tuareg society for all but the most poverty-stricken families. Until recently comprised of nomadic livestock herders, caravanners, and (formerly subordinate) servile and client gardeners on oases, today rural Tuareg of diverse social backgrounds usually combine, to varying degrees, livestock herding, oasis gardening, caravan and other itinerant and market trading, tourism, artisany, and labor migration. Many still need goods and services, preferably made by hereditary inaden recognized as most skilled in these arts, for these occupations: namely, household, farming and herding tools, jewelry for the marrying bride, and oral history and song performances at rites of passage. Urban residents—Tamajaq-speakers and other ethnic and linguistic groups—order jewelry, and in some smaller towns such as Agadez, call on smiths to officiate at rites of passage and other public events. Although there is much less exact correspondence between prestigious social origins, descent, and occupation, the *inaden* generally remain most closely associated with their traditional, albeit changing, artisan role, and this role (with thus far very few exceptions) is still associated with their inherited social stratum identity. Smiths remain easy to identity, since they remain predominantly endogamous, even in towns.

Inaden are indispensable in making and repairing weapons, household, herding and gardening tools, and jewelry. In some regions, in particular the countryside around Mt. Bagzan in the Air Mountains where I conducted most of my field research, many *inaden* also act as oral historians, musicians, poets, and go-betweens in marriage arrangements or other delicate social and political matters. Yet all these persons are generally called, and call themselves, by the gloss or cover-term *inaden* (sing. *enad*) in Tamajaq, regardless of specialty, followed by the name of whatever regional confederation (e.g. Kel Faday, Kel Ewey, Ifoghas, Kel Ahaggar, etc.) of the aristocratic descent groups they are attached to. A few *inaden* I knew identified themselves with the local descent group of their noble patron families, but many others did not, emphasizing, as shown in the foregoing accounts, their separate descent group. Also, many urban Tuareg smiths tend to call themselves *les forgerons* (French for "blacksmith") or increasingly, among the younger smiths, *les bijoutiers* (French for "jeweler"), reflecting the increasing specialization of many in silversmithing and goldsmithing in the towns, where in addition to continuing to manufacture these products for Tuareg urban families (and more rarely, nowadays, former rural *imajeghen* noble patron families), the urban smiths also make them for African functioinaries and European and American tourists and expatriates.

Here, it is instructive to briefly devote some attention to those elements in their visual arts that are relevant to issues of power. Also, these practices and products cannot be viewed as separate, for several reasons. First, the Tuareg smith/artisans, like many others in Africa and beyond (for example, in parts of the Middle East, Afghanistan, and India) are converters of materials from nature into culture. This has become largely a truism in studies of African smiths (Herbert, 1993; McNaughton, 1988). I do not contest this important observation. But I do question the assumption that this is the definitive, sole explanation for their ambiguous status and others' ambivalent attitudes toward them. Also, one could make the same observation about many other specialists around the world: for example, farmers and herders, factory workers, and midwives, to name a few. Indeed, all humankind converts the natural into the cultural. Also, art and technology have also been merged in many other fields of specialization, as for example, in special effects of films, herbal medicine, and other diverse professional skills (Rasmussen, 2006).

What I am concerned with here is the problem of how, if converting nature into culture is so important to concepts of smith/artisans' alleged *tezma* power, this practice becomes continually re-defined, alternately associated with sometimes positive and sometimes negative power, and what ideological and socioeconomic factors shape the outcomes: in other words, what kinds of political ramifications these processes have for those who are vulnerable at the same time they are powerful. Here, the concept of anomaly (Douglas, 1966,1977,1992) is not adequate, either; for in contrast to such figures as twins, albinos, and other allegedly "betwixt and between" figures, smith/artisans' complex, dynamic transformations cannot be reduced to rigid structural attributes; and they are not, despite surface appearances, reducible to "minorities in the middle," or even always "strangers" (Berland and Rao, 2004; Simmel, 1950), for they are not entirely marginal (itself a very relative and subjective concept), but also central to Tuareg society.

Much *inaden* work merges art, science, myth, and history. Their work is intimately bound up with, rather than standing outside, a moral and social landscape. Recall that Tuareg male artisans work in metal, stone, clay, and wood; their wives are specialists in leather (Bernus, 1993,2006; Rasmussen, 2003). They carry their materials with them, which are generally not cumbersome, but two of their tools are heavier and less manageable. The anvil is a cast iron piece, often set in a block of wood. The bellows (*anahod*), from *ahod,* the hot and dry season wind, believed to bring illnesses but also to herald the coming rains and their cooling *efare* wind, thereby suggesting the fertility and ultimately regenerative role of the action of the smith's forge, is a leather pouch with wooden handles that pushes air into a piece of hardwood fit with a metal pipe ending in a clay nozzle. The anthropomorphic, yet also superhuman powers of smiths in Africa more generally are vividly shown in imagery surrounding their tools and works (Herbert, 1993). Bernus (2006:77) in a brief but rich description of *inaden* visual arts reports that a riddle portrays this bellows as alive, "breathing like any living being."

In my view, such anthropomorphism has a significance for ritual power that Bernus does not pursue: this symbolism serves to remind smiths and non-smiths that, even apparently inanimate objects in the universe have connections to humans, and there is in effect, a "story" underlying all material objects that links them to social and spiritual relationships. The material object cannot be divorced, as it were, from the human being. This theme cannot be easily reconciled with official Islamic injunctions against anthropomorphism and its implied idolatry. But the *inaden* seem to be saying, in these words, that objects, words, and other expressions of creativity should not divide people, but rather, unite them in ideally complementary and reciprocal social relationships. A large village in northern Mali, between Gao and Kidal, where I also conducted research, is named from a regional dialect term for bellows, in reference to its geographic and topographic form, and also, local residents explained to me, an allusion to its historical and social, as well as geographic position as a crossroads between peoples and regions.

Materials for all parts of the bellows are enumerated, even the soft *adaras* wood that surrounds the bellows and the hard *aboragh* wood and the metal *(tama*, iron) and earth (*talaq*, clay). In short, with his bellows, the metalworker is a master of elements, and of fire, in particular. In the town of Agadez, where I conducted the urban phase of my *inaden* research, this was vividly illustrated to me once, when I inquired whether the sandal-makers (called *mai takalmi*) there were considered *inaden,* since these famous beautiful sandals are also in leather (cowhide), and a smith woman friend there explained, "No, they are not; for the sandal-makers, though they use leather and make leather products, do not work with fire; only we *inaden* work with fire. *Inaden* must work with fire."

This statement is interesting for its implications. In addition to underlining the importance of fire as an integral element in *inaden* power and relatedness, it also suggests that—contrary to some current Tuareg ethnographic preference for the term "artisan" in both English and French to the terms "smith" and "*forgeron*" respectively (Casajus, 1987,2000; Loughran and Seligman, 2006), the more adequate (albeit still imperfect) translation of *ened* into English is, in fact, "smith," rather than "artisan," since these artists and ritual specialists themselves distinguish finer categories in classifying "artisans" than the European language terms do.

In other words, although some compromise in translation is necessary, and all English and French terms for these Tuareg and other African specialists are approximate rather than equivalent, I consider the term "artisan" alone inadequate to convey the nuanced complexities of *inaden* roles. Although the wives of the Tuareg *inaden,* called *tchinaden,* (fem.plural), work in leather, they are still considered as distinct from the Agadezian leather sandal-makers, since *inaden* work with fire and marry in very closely, even in the multi-ethnic town—often to first cousins. This suggests that another key criterion of classification for *inaden* besides working with fire is endogamy; for the two groups of artisans in Agadez do not intermarry, and do not consider each other as belonging to the same group or coming from the same origins. Indeed, the *mai takalmi* artisans are of Agadezian origin, a group related to the Songhai, early inhabitants of Agadez, who until around the early twentieth century, spoke their own language, a Songhai dialect called Uraren, which disappeared following massacres of its speakers by the French colonial military (Rodd, 1926). Nowadays *mai takalmi* speak Hausa, and consider themselves more "Agadezian" than either Songhai or Hausa, though they sometimes intermarry with these latter groups, but only rarely with Tuareg and never, as noted, with the *inaden.* Other tools, such as hammer and sledge, shears, file, burin, punch, scraper, and crucible, are carried in a leather tool-bag.

Woodworking requires fewer tools: an axe, adze, and iron awl for pyrography. The wives of the *inaden* of metal and wood cut the leather, using a very wide, flat knife and scissors, as well as metal cans for dipping brushes into glue. They dye and stitch, and also do cut-out and embroidery designs, and in some regions such as the Adragh-n-Iforghas Mountains and its town of Kidal in Mali, insert tiny mirrors, on leather satchels, bags, camel-harnesses, cushion covers, and other hide products with a razor-blade. Leather is also used to make tent canopies, various kinds of sacks, waterbags, some amulet covers, women's hair decorations, camel and donkey decorations, buckets, and cords that raise water from deep wells.

Until relatively recently, iron *(tama)* produced south of the Sahara came from blast furnaces of rural peoples, for example, Hausa *makiri* smiths, who were experts at smelting ore from ferruginous concretions. But today, iron is mostly salvaged from automobile carcasses. Copper ore has been found near Azelik, Niger, and copper was made there in the very distant past. Its production resumed in the Middle Ages, but stopped at the end of the fifteenth century (Bernus, 2006). Today, copper is salvaged from various sources, including public faucets. Silver, the metal most often used in Tuareg jewelry making , was until approximately the early 1980's sold at the market in the form of Maria Teresa dollar coins from Austria, which consisted of approximately 75 percent silver rand 25 percent copper, and were called in Niger *souletan.* Recently, these have been replaced with sterling silver.

Iron is used to make weapons (swords, javelin launchers, knives) and decorated implements (e.g. padlocks). Copper and silver, and more rarely gold, are used to cast or fashion jewelry and to decorate chiseled plates that adorn amulet cases, weapons, and padlocks. Wood is made into furniture (tent pegs and beds), as well as domestic items (cups, milking bowls, ladles, spoons), and pastoral implements (pulleys, saddles, packsaddles).

The most elaborate objects *inaden* produce make use of multiple materials. The saber sword *(takuba),* for example, requires working iron or steel, as well as copper for the hilt and leather for the scabbard. The camel saddle with a cross-shaped pommel *(tamzak)* calls for very precise woodworking for twin pieces that fit together and are joined by leather; the raised portion or "rest" at rider's back, is decorated with colored leather embellished with metal or copper plates.

In Saharan towns such as Agadez, Niger and Kidal, Mali, as well as in the countryside, *inaden* still tend to reside in their own quarters or neighborhoods. For example, in Agadez, one finds most smith/artisans in Sabon Gari, Chinadaban, and Indoudou. In Kidal, smiths (in the local Tadart Tamajaq dialect, called *Inhaden*) tend to reside mostly in either the neighborhood of the *amenukal* of the Ifoghas confederation, or near other specialists such as herbal medicine women. But these residential arrangements are not mandated, and are flexible. Unlike the rural Hindu caste system, wells and other facilities are not separate. In the Saharan towns, *inaden* households tend to be more intertwined among non-*inaden* households in even those neighborhoods where they cluster or predominate. In other words, smiths are more prevalent in some urban neighborhoods than others, but are not rigidly obliged to live spatially segregated. Whereas in rural areas, there tends to be greater segregation: there, smiths tend to reside in more distinctive areas, exclusively alongside each other: their households are either in separate neighborhoods altogether, well distanced spatially from those of aristocratic, maraboutique, and chiefly families, or in exclusively *inaden* villages located near, but not inside as part of, other villages and camps in the area. These spaces are occasionally made physically even more distant by subtle barriers, for example, by allowing bushes to grow between the different neighborhoods, in times of heightened social tensions.

For example, in one major semi-nomadic oasis near Mt. Bagzan in the Air Mountains of Niger, there are two major extended *inaden* families. A few *inaden* households came to that village recently, in the 1970's, for reasons of marriage and work, who were originally from two small smith villages nearby. But most *inaden* families in that larger village are longstanding residents who arrived there early in the 20th century with their aristocratic patron families from Mt. Bagzan, and also returned with them from Damagaram or Hausa country in the South following the Tuareg flight from the French massacres in the Air region suppressing the Tuareg Senoussi revolt in 1917. The chief of the *inaden* works as a go-between for the chief of the local noble descent group there, the Kel Igurmaden, and still conducts important rituals for the latter's family, such as handling the chief's drum or *ettebel* and assisting in tax collection. The *tchinaden* women in this smith chief's family, likewise, serve the women in the aristocratic chiefly families, even to this day, in such tasks as hair-dressing, shaving the week-old baby's hair at the nameday, singing praise-songs, and preparing and serving food at nobles' namedays. But many noble families outside the chiefly family tend to seek smiths living closer by for these tasks, for convenience, rather than strictly the traditional (inherited) smiths.

Thus there is a gradual change toward more flexibility even in the countryside, though not yet a complete breakdown of smith-noble client-patron relationships there. A further impetus for this flexibility has been the sporadic (1990-96, and currently, since around 2007) armed Tuareg rebellion and government militia fighting, in whose violent cross-fire the local residents have been sporadically caught. In November 1997, and again around 2002, many local residents of diverse origins were forced to flee from this violence and migrated about five kilometers away, up into the foothills of Mt. Bagzan. Thus upon my return to that region, I found that many residents were displaced— some persons temporarily so, who later returned to their village, and others permanently, who started oasis gardens in their new area. Later, only one smith family remained as refugees in the Mt. Bagzan village where many had previously fled the 1997 violence; all other smith families later returned to their home villages within about five months of that event. Consequently, residents in the new area had only one smith family for goods and services, not really sufficient, and had to walk or ride several miles to their older home area for

work by smiths who had returned there. Several women of noble origins in the
new site began hairstyling, though they still called on their traditional smiths
from afar to come serve at their rites of passage (namedays and weddings).

A few villages on and around the base of Mt. Bagzan in the Air remain
exclusively *inaden* villages to this day, despite some out-marriage with other
inaden and increasing male labor migration and itinerant trading of art objects
abroad. In one such village, which I shall call Anou—the scene of what many
local residents suggested was my own *tezma* "attack" described in the opening
pages of this book—there is one large extended family of smiths, in about
twenty-five compounds, though some of the young men are often now absent
part of the year working in Libya. Although traditionally they serve nobles in a
nearby oasis and herding community, they do not identify with the latters'
descent group(s); instead, many there indicated they belong to a smith clan or
descent group called Issidraghane, who in their origin mythico-history, as
shown, trace their ancestry to the same founder. This is an origin distinct from,
not solely the neighboring non-smith/artisans, but also different from the other
smith/artisans of that region, though all *inaden* say "we are all cousins," and
freely intermarry with each other. Issadraghane, a village or region between
Mali and Niger, which was the place of origin of many smiths around these
small villages, and recall, was mentioned in a mythico-history. Important in their
origins was that female founding ancestress named Handede or Khadede, also
mentioned earlier in the wider regional mythico-history. There, as within each
smith village and also among some urban smiths, a preference for close cousin
marriages persists: those between father's brother's children.

Many male smiths in that small all-smith village once worked only wood,
but since the 1980's, many have been also working *asol* soapstone, which they
transport on small caravans from nearby mines, for the tourist industry, and also
tend livestock and oasis gardens, the latter formerly an occupation associated
with the stigma of past servitude in Tuareg society, but now taken up by many
persons of diverse social background. Many of these *inaden* men make garden
tools, which demand intensive labor. It takes an entire day to make a garden
pulley for a well, for example. In contrast to the situation in the larger semi-
nomadic communities where I worked, where there were inaden working in all
specialties—of metalworking, leatherworking, stoneworking, and woodworking,
only a few persons in that small smith village work metal at the forge, since their
nearby patron nobles can no longer easily afford jewelry. Nonetheless, most of
these smiths still sell their products to local rural Air residents in nearby villages
and camps. Women there repaired my leather billfold with tools made from
local wood and discarded iron (for their awl), which had been made by smith
men in that village. The *tchinaden* women own these leatherworking tools once
they are made, and keep them on divorce. It takes approximately six to ten days
for the women *tchinaden* to make a goathide *anwar* water-bucket and other
containers, but the *tenet* does not slaughter the animal only for this purpose;
instead she uses hides from an animal already slaughtered for a ritual or holiday,
such as a Muslim prayerday or a rite of passage. These *inaden* also continue to

perform songs and serve food at nobles' rites of passage, but not strictly for their inherited patron family; rather, also for other non-smiths, on demand, who reside nearby in their region.

These rural and urban contrasts and transformations in residential patterns and work roles reflect, to some degree, the increasingly fluid relations between the social strata and the relatively greater breakdown of the old client-patron relationship in Tuareg society more generally, especially in the towns. The roles of some *inaden* in Agadez continue, however, albeit in much modified form. Most no longer have hereditary client-patron ties with their old aristocratic families to whom they were once attached in the countryside. They serve diverse families—Tuareg of both aristocratic and other origins, as well as non-Tuareg— in towns such as Agadez and Kidal, but in more commercially-based relationships, which feature choice of *inaden* based on personal rapport and preference, and featuring predominantly monetary transactions, rather than the older payment in foodstuffs (though some millet and parts of the animal's meat are also included, even today, for rites of passage duties). *Tezma* allegations, not surprisingly, tend to be rarer here, and when they do surface, tend to be taken more as jokes than serious fears. The *albourousa* mumming rite in which smiths embarrass patrons for reneging on their obligations toward them have disappeared there, and furthermore, young people in Agadez I questioned had never heard of that rite. But urban smith/artisans retain their special status and continue to in-marry closely.

Another example of gradual modification of roles and relationships is at Agadez weddings: whereas in the Air countryside, Tuareg wedding songs called *baowole* are sung by old smiths as they bring the bride toward the nuptial tent in a very slow procession (a short distance from her mother's tent), by contrast, in the town of Agadez, this performance is much more casual, abbreviated, and restricted: at weddings there, I observed only a few elderly *tchinaden* smith women sing them, and very softly—almost timidly, under their breath—and spontaneously, as they simultaneously ate the food later in the wedding celebration. They reacted with some shame to my recording of these songs as we ate, although they gave me permission to do so. Smiling a bit self-consciously, they explained to me that "only we very old smith women know these songs." These songs, often ribald in their sexual imagery, were perhaps more shameful in the urban context with its official Islamic influences, or perhaps, remained only a remote memory on part of the elderly smith women—or both factors may be at play here.

Yet these rural-urban and other contrasts should not be taken as absolute binary oppositions or as a "disappearance: or "death" of all cultural knowledge or practices pertaining to *inaden*. There are varying degrees of rural and urban, and settled and itinerant Tuareg smiths; they do not form two neatly opposed, polar, or discrete categories in this regard. Many *inaden*, as well as other Tuareg, tend to spend part of the time in the towns, and part of the time in the countryside, out at pastures or oasis gardens, seasonally, and have kinspersons in both places. But the point is that, in general, most *inaden* nowadays serve both impersonal customers (including some non-Tuareg) as well as, or instead of, their noble family to whom they are attached through inheritance.

Inaden are also guardians of cultural and intellectual knowledge and property. Throughout Tuareg regions, there is a striking consistency among all material visual art and technology objects made by artisans. Some of these so strongly evoke Tuareg society that they have become its logo or icon: for example, the ornate turquoise and red camel saddle with a cross-shaped pommel; the sword. Miniature versions of the saddle, as well as the cross, are often seen in tourist art, on travel agency desks, and airline companies. In jewelry, the Agadez Cross pendant (locally called *talkhakim*) is widely considered emblematic of Tuareg culture. This takes various forms, and is worn by women of all social origins. In west of Niger, in region of Ayerou and Bankilare, Bella (or Buzu) women, former slaves, all wear silver jewelry, or rarely copper, and beads, in many different styles, as long necklaces or fastened in their hair. The top of the Agadez cross pendant, a crescent, connotes according to some observers the sky; the bottom, with its open-worked circle, connotes the earth (Loughran and Seligman, 2006). Symbols can be interpreted according to the way these items are worn. On certain pieces of jewelry, all that is represented on the sky portion connotes masculinity (grandfather, father, uncle, son, husband, or their objects); what appears on the earth portion connotes femininity (mother, daughter, wife, and utensils pertaining to women). (Bernus, 2006).

There remains much speculation concerning the origin of the Agadez cross, beyond the scope of the present analysis. Recently, in the capital city, I saw an Agadez Cross pendant motif on the Niger telephone directory cover, on a paper-dispenser in a restroom, and in the name of a hotel. These recent uses of this pendant are interesting; for during the sporadic conflicts between Tuareg dissidents and some central governments, the Agadez Cross was once frowned upon by some in the capital city. During my Peace Corps teaching at a girls' lycee there in the 1970's, parents heatedly debated whether or not to allow their daughters to wear the Agadez Cross, at that time a symbol of the intermittent Tuareg armed resistance to the central state. Nowadays, however, despite intermittent resurgences of armed conflict, this design appears everywhere in Niger, and is accepted as a common motif on tourist art, not solely in the predominantly Tuareg regions, but also in museums and workshops in the capital city, Niamey, in the South.

The camel saddle is interesting in its iconography and relevant here in its implications for the issue of power. According to Bernus (1993,2006), each part of the saddle bears a name that, like the bellows, often is anthropomorphic: the capped metallic point beneath the pommel is called "the lower beard," in relation to "the upper beard," that is represented by a leather strip that juts out below the saddle's cross motif that the rider clutches. The two lateral branches of the cross are called ears, and upright part, from bottom to top, called the bottom and neck. The dark leather that covers the saddle's pommel's three crossing branches is called "veiled," in reference to Tuareg men's turban/faceveil. The vertical protrusion of cross and the protrusion that tops the mantle are both named for the Gazelle *dama—ener* in Tamajaq—with the first is called the front gazelle, and the second the back gazelle (Bernus, 1993:220). This is placed between the man and the camel, and thus this saddle serves, in Bernus's view, as a bond between two bodies (Bernus, 2006). In my view, these cross motifs also strongly resonate with crossroads symbols elsewhere in Africa (Stoller, 1994), suggesting junctures, intersections, mediating forces, assembling dispersed humans and elements, and fateful decisions.

Therefore, although the saddle is an inert object, and *inaden* are, as noted, identified with the spirit world, it is linked to the world of the living--of animal and human beings through anatomical terms, alluding to the gazelle and to humans, that are used. Such metaphorical vocabulary is often anthropomorphic. Even the name of the decorated saddle, *tamzak* (the deaf woman), refers to humans and to the ears of the cross. Deafness is a defect. Yet there is more alluded to here than merely ridicule. The point is that these tropes highlight the importance of verbal art (tales, poems, songs) throughout Tuareg society, and underline smith/artisans' crucial role in performing it orally. Although others, also, do this, smiths traditionally perform distinctive genres, such as praise-songs, play distinctive musical instruments such as small hand-drums called acanza used to announce nobles' rites of passage, and in the past, recited poems praising battle-heroes in their chiefly and other patron families.

As I see it, the problem here concerns motivational and contextual meanings of a sign, in effect, recalling semiotic floating signifiers. This and other material products of *inaden* convey the dynamic, fluid, and sometimes contradictory roles of the smith/artisan. The parts of the sword, like parts of the saddle, also have names referring to the human body: the pommel is she of the white head; the grip is bone marrow; the hilt, the shoulder, the blunt edge is the back, the sharp edge, the mouth or that which eats, and the point, the tongue. The mouth and tongue are potent symbols for eating (and by symbolic analogy, sexual intercourse and by extension, marriage), as well as the verbal art so highly valued in Tuareg society.

The point is that smiths' visual art cannot be compartmentalized as solely "technical", solely "aesthetic," or even solely "visual/material" culture. Material, social, human, and spiritual powers are all interwoven into a seamless whole in the work of *inaden*. These visual objects, though not the major focus in the present book, are nonetheless important in revealing another key point: despite living in precarious and harsh Saharan and Sahelian conditions, care in aesthetics is never sacrificed, and these objects are never solely functional. These works serve as nmemonic devices to remind others of the important, multiplex roles of these specialists. These works also complement, and refer iconically to, the important verbal/oral roles of the *inaden*: in arranging marriages and negotiating bridewealth, in reciting nobles' genealogies and singing praise-songs at noble rites of passage, and in also listening, as confidantes and go-betweens.

Also, *inaden* in their creativity (visual and verbal) bridge worlds of animate and inanimate beings—a theme to which I return in greater depth in subsequent sections. These qualities (or more precisely, practices) make the Tuareg *inaden* and other similar specialists elsewhere both admired and unsettling—whether poor clients of the aristocrat, or well-to-do artisans of the tourist and functionary, they can evoke ambivalence and envy. In addition, this power reminds Tuareg of their locally rich cultural knowledge, whereas Islam encourages more universalistic affiliation. Finally, *inaden* make non-smiths' prestigious material wealth possible to express. Thus power is dangerous and protective simultaneously.

Among Tuareg weapons, only the sword (*takuba*) is still carried by predominantly rural and older men. Today, a few smiths make guns for hunting. Rebel fighters in the sporadic Tuareg armed rebellion against the central governments of Niger and Mali prefer imported Kalashnikov rifles. The shield has disappeared; the javelin launcher has become very rare, as has the dagger. There are different local Tamajaq language classifications of sword types, however. Marks and inscriptions on some blades make it possible to determine origin for some of them (Briggs, 1965; Gabus, 1968). From the end of the fifteenth until the seventeenth century C.E., blades made in Solingen, Vienna, Padua, and Toledo crossed the Sahara (Bernus, 2006). But originals are rare, owned only by chiefs. Others have been copied south of the Sahara.

Many decorative small knives are made into letter-openers for tourists now. Visitors to my American home in 1999 arrived with back-packs crammed full of these knives, intended not at all as weapons, but as art commodities to sell here as decorative letter-openers. Upon their later return visits later in 2000 and 2001 following the travel restrictions of Homeland Security in the wake of the World Trade Center bombings, they could not bring such items in their carry-on luggage. Thus the continually transformative art of *inaden*, and re-definitions of their art and their power and skill, even in global contexts far from their home community, respond to the surrounding social and political dynamics. From knives to letter-openers and back to knives again—this process iconically, and also ironically, conveys (with new political meanings) much of the unpredictability of changes in perceptions of their ritual and social mediating powers. Of course, the airport security did not articulate this in the idiom of *tezma* fear, but rather fear of possible "terrorism," though not by *inaden* specifically. Despite some harassment and persecution of innocent persons traveling with "Muslim or Arabic-sounding names" reported in airport travels following 9/11, the *inaden* in this transnational travel context were not feared because of their culturally-specific *tezma* power, but rather because of powers that were feared as potentially activated by any traveler. In other words, inaden identities in that context became submerged into wider identities—of negative stereotypes of terrorists.

In sum, much symbolism surrounding Tuareg jewelry and other visual art forms can have multiple and shifting meanings, including references to religious, gendered, and nomadic life. These blended aesthetic and symbolic influences are articulated and meditated on through changing social and economic channels of power.

NOTES

1. Nobles' themes, for example, do not mention Dauda. Men and Islamic scholars in *imajeghen* families tend to emphasize descent from a prominent marabout who brought Islam to their region, such as Sidi Okba in North Africa, (Norris, 1975) Atkaki around Mt. Bagzan, and/or a prominent noble warrior such as Boulkhou, Firhun, or Kaoussan. By contrast, women in those families tend to emphasize matrilineal founding ancestresses (Rasmussen, 2006).
2. The Ifoghas, in the Kel Adagh confederation in the Adragh-n-Ifoghas Mountains of northern Mali, have traditionally been military rivals of the Kel Ewey in the Air Mountains of northern Niger. These groups are separated by desert and today, by the (artificial) nation-state borders of Mali and Niger. They have not extensively intermarried, and their dialects of Tamajaq are significantly different. I noticed that few residents of each had been to each other's regions, though the recent Tuareg rebellions have tended to promote greater contact and alliances between eastern and western dissidents, and leaders of this movement appeal to Tuareg to unite on the basis of their shared language and interests.
3. Until recently, most *imajeghen* nobles disdained gardening, and in some regions, its stigma remains strong, associated with servitude. In the Air region of Niger, oasis gardens have been somewhat more successful, since the water table is not so low, and sedentarized, semi-nomadic agro-pastoral villages have been present since at least the early 20th century if not earlier (Bernus, 1981), and also because Kel Ewey there have tended to enjoy close cultural ties with not solely North Africa, but also farming peoples of the South, such as the Hausa, through caravan trading and also in flights from droughts and wars in the Air. In these and some other more sedentarized areas, land tenure issues are more prominent than in more nomadic camps, although *imajaghen* in all regions in the past monopolized property, whether herds or gardens, and gave military protection to subordinates who worked for them.

CHAPTER THREE

POWERS, TENSIONS, AND MEDIATIONS

OUR SMITHS AND OUR NOBLES

Thus the *ened* has multiple roles, and stands at the confluence of distinct but converging worlds. *Inadan nena*, denoting "our smiths," is in rural areas the most frequently heard expression still used by noble patrons to refer to smiths in longstanding, albeit modified, client-patron relationships in the countryside and sometimes, and also is still heard used to refer to smiths in some families in Agadez. Smith/artisans, for their part, reciprocally refer to their aristocratic patron families, even in times of more attenuated and uncertain client-patron relationships, as *imajeghen nena*, or "our nobles." Many persons of aristocratic origin confirm that, in the past, nobles had to ask an old smith chief from their own small *tawsit* (descent group) for permission before using the services of *inaden* from another nearby *tawsit* not attached to them, for purposes of residential convenience, but they no longer have to ask this permission today. Now, nobles can use smiths' services from another *tawsit* if they live nearby, are renowned for certain works, get along better with them, and/or are more convenient. Thus geographic residence is as important as descent group and inherited client-patron relationship nowadays for noble-smith relationships; whereas, traditionally, they must be in same *tawsit* (e.g. Kel Chimilan), or more precisely, *inaden* had to be those attached to the nobles' *tawsit* through matrilineal inheritance (each noble woman brought a smith family to her marriage, as she brought former slaves in the past). But many local residents also considered personal rapport still important.

Smiths and non-smiths often use these terms for each other with the possessive pronouns affectionately, in both reference and address. Nonetheless, as shown, they acknowledge some tensions and mutually ambivalent feelings in their relationships. Many Tuareg of aristocratic background say that the smith is "disparaged" or "denigrated" (expressed as *denigre* and *meprise* in French) But these terms should not be taken at face value, as do some ethnographers who tend to assume that the denigration and disparaging implies "character flaws" on *inaden*: Bernus for example, reports that the *ened* is considered to be a coward, a liar, and untrustworthy (Bernus, 2006). These characterizations, although sometimes taken from direct speech of local residents, still tend to be culture-bound; for they emphasize moralistic and psychological imagery unmediated by social context. These characterizations of smiths tend to be official viewpoints of chiefs and aristocrats. In the early twentieth century, for example, *amenukal* Moussa Agg Amastan stated: "You, artisan, ...(you) slave who keeps camels, of no dazzling feats are you capable... at war you killed not even a fettered donkey" (Pere de Foucauld, 1925, I:409). Leaders' and missionaries' statements are illuminating, but as noted, are biased and need to be situated in wider power relationships.

In my view, some of these early biased accounts may convey the views of those in conflict with the smith/artisans. Consequently, some make the *inaden* sound almost shiftless. Nicolas, for example, assumed that denigration has the same connotations as in his own cultural values: "The metalworker always knows how to make him(her)self indispensable, even though he(she) is always a born traitor...has no needs or ambitions, ...no one is as ill-esteemed as the metalworker" (Nicolas, 1950:191).

As interpreter and intermediary, the artisan is ambiguous; this implies a quasi-official role, not easily controllable, which could be transformed into that of emissary and spokesperson, journalist, even "spy." One level of significance I offer is that smith/artisans often take advantage of this "disgraceful" reputation by behaving according to others' stereotype of them, as unconstrained by rules of propriety—in particular, by aristocratic values of reserve, dignity, and restraint—that others follow. For example, the *ened* enjoys a freedom of speech and gesture that allows him/her expression and critical commentary, in their own view somewhat like journalists—a comparison frequently made to me by smith/artisans themselves. Following the complaint of an American Peace Corps volunteer that he went from her home to the home of other volunteers for multiple hospitalities, thus in her own viewpoint, showing disloyalty to their friendship, an Agadez smith/artisan commented teasingly: "I am like a journalist, a fly...I am buzzing everywhere, my nobles cannot be rid of me!" In effect, what she viewed as disloyalty he viewed as his normal peripatetic, integrative, circulating role. When a smith/artisan in Agadez invited all Peace Corps volunteers and other expatriate aid workers to his child's nameday celebration, an American there grumbled under her breath, "I see that all the *anisara* (foreigners, i.e., Americans) are here!"

Indeed, in the town of Agadez, in the 1970's and 1980's, in the wake of droughts making noble patrons unable to support their smith/artisan clients, expatriate aid workers were in many ways taking the place of nobles for some *inaden*—albeit on a subconscious level. To the *inaden*, these aid workers were all similar, despite differences in personalities; they all constituted a form of new patronage, so going from one aid worker's home to another was not in their own viewpoint, disloyal, but instead, a continuing of the *inaden* role of intermediary. In many smith/artisans' viewpoints, this was a service, and within the older client-patron system, exclusive friendships were not important; rather, this mediating quality made smith/artisans indispensable to everyone. Recall that some themes in the mythico-histories included acts of chasing away smiths, but also their sheltering of others who were also exiled from their communities, as for example, in the tale about the origins of the Ifoghas Tuareg group.

The smith/artisan's social status is therefore ambiguous, and is not reducible to stereotypical "character flaws" in a psychological, culture-bound sense. This status needs to interpreted in more nuanced terms, as simultaneously "abject," to use Butler's term (Butler, 1993) and heroic, (my term), central to cultural reproduction. Ritual processes hint at this: for example, patterns at animal sacrifices at religious festivals such as Aid al-Kabir, popularly called Tabaski, marking the end of the Ramadan fasting month; at rites of passage such as weddings, and in more informal everyday sociability (visits of distinguished guests). At rites of passage and Islamic holidays, usually a sheep or goat is slaughtered, though rarely a steer, for a large wedding, or, in Ahaggar or Ajjer, Algeria, a camel. After the animal's throat is slit, its carcass is suspended from a tree-branch to be carved. The distribution of different parts of the animal varies depending on the occasion and according to region; certain people at a religious festival, visit, or wedding are given the best pieces, and sometimes the internal organs and stomach (Nicolaisen and Nicolaisen, 1997; Rasmussen, 1997). One piece, however, is always reserved for the artisan: part of the chime known as *tanazermeyt.* The animal's back is divided into three parts. Among the southern Tuareg, part of the chime reserved for the artisan is often called *seknes inaden,* denoting "make the artisans argue," for it often provokes quarrels of several artisans present who all want this same piece of meat.

Some local residents also used imagery of pollution in discussing another alleged stereotypical trait of inaden with me: namely, their alleged "dirtiness" *(win jargonen* in Tamajaq), often explaining it in terms of these specialists' work at the forge, with fire, and also, occasionally, in terms of their origins from outside Tuareg society. Although smiths often visited nobles frequently and shared much news and gossip with them, *inaden* usually sat on separate mats, and did not share food or tea with the others. But this characterization should not be taken at face value, and should be balanced by the viewpoints and voices of the smith/artisans themselves, with a balanced attention to both language and practice.

Smiths' perspectives on these issues are found in the following discussions of several interrelated topics: the cultural value of reserve, role reversals at rites of passage, and details of the smiths' mumming ritual called *alburusa.* Two elderly rural smith brothers elaborated on these practices while explaining to me why they lack aristocratic ideals of reserve or shame *(takarakit)*: "Nowadays, nobody has reserve, neither noble or smith. But at rites of passage, we still observe this (value of) reserve: when smiths marry, nobles behave without reserve, and when nobles marry, smiths behave without reserve (i.e., they reverse roles at each other's ceremonies)." I asked, "Why do smiths reverse roles with nobles in each others' ceremonies?" They replied, "That shows that they (nobles and smiths) have strong social ties, solidarity *(amssimghare* or *simghare).* But nobles must not exceed more than one day being (behaving like) smiths (i.e., behaving without reserve or modesty, joking, etc.). If they do, we do our *albourousa.* The roles of smiths in nobles' ceremonies, they serve the guests with tea, food, they cook, they install the mats. At smiths' ceremonies, nobles do this."

Alboubousa (or *ilbourousan* plural), that dreaded smith ritual protest, resembles a mumming ritual, and is enacted for a fine when nobles transgress certain rules in noble-smith relationships: for example, when nobles wear clothing inside-out, when nobles play the role of smiths outside the permitted ritual reversals, or when nobles bypass their smith in organizing events that normally require the latter to officiate or mediate. For example, *inaden* must sing praise songs at nobles' rites of passage; they must serve as go-betweens to negotiate bridewealth for the marriages of nobles. The purpose of this *albourusa* ritual is to protect *inaden* professional interests when these are threatened by disobeying these conventions. In such cases, all smith/artisans conduct *ilburusan* against all nobles in their area as a protest against even one noble infraction (for example, if one individual refuses to pay compensation or remuneration for smiths' goods, and/or neglects to use smiths' services at rite of passage).

During interviews and conversations about *albourousa*, I recalled the reference to this in the oral mythico-history about Khadede, and remembered a recent incident of this mumming ritual. I asked, "Have you recently seen any (additional) *albourousa?*" One of the brothers replied jokingly to me, " The one that I have most recently seen was that small *albouroussa* conducted for you because your blouse was inside out(*agriwal*)." [I had unintentionally worn a local blouse inside-out several months earlier.] He went on to explain in detail the more elaborate *ilboursan* (plural) protest rituals for more serious infractions:

> If nobles marry, and they transport the (bride's) baggage themselves, (and by-pass us smiths) one does *albouroussa*. It is we smiths who do it. And if a noble receives a visit from his daughter-in-law and slaughters the animal (for that occasion) himself, without calling in a smith to do this, that is another action provokes the *albourousa*, it is the big one in this case. Because he slaughtered the animal himself, and you , his (attached) smith, are (supposed to do this) for you are his smith. If the smith is not informed about this, especially, then it is a loss for him, of his part of the meat (*izouza*) Even here in this village, I 'pushed' (initiated) the *albourousa*, at Moukha's (pseudonym). We had one at Takhia's (pseudonym) also, because she left to (formally) greet her sister-in-law without looking for a smith to serve at this ritual. For Aliou (pseudonym), he gave his baggage to someone other than a smith, he brought them when he got married and moved to Mount Bagzan, he brought that baggage to the Bagzan. So I assembled the smiths, we did the *albourousa*, we made the entire village pay (a fine)! Normally, the nobles must disdain the smith's work. If nobles do the work of the forge, we'll do nothing to them, and we won't prevent them from working nowadays (i.e., only in the past, were we strict about that). Now, one still does not intermarry with them.

When he raised this topic of marriage, I asked, "Why do smiths marry among themselves only?" He explained, "because many nobles do not like smiths, most are ashamed to marry smiths. As for the smiths of the West, the nobles and smiths, there are some who intermarry, but not among the Kel Ewey Tuareg here (in semi-nomadic communities around Mt. Bagzan in the Air). We have a few exceptions: someone who married a (former) slave, our cousin, you know him. There was a noble teacher who married a smith. There is a smith in Agadez who has two noble wives. But among the Kel Ewey (a dominant large descent group within the Kel Air confederation), one does not do that. Among the Kel Ferwan (another large descent group of Tuareg) one does that. But everyone, nobles, smiths, they are brothers basically. All people come from Hawa and Adam (Eve and Adam)."

The *inaden* also listed some restrictions they must follow in their own work. For example, on Saturday all smith women who are married do not do hairstyling. No one knew where this custom derived from, but a *tenet* (female smith) briefly explained to me that she thought it was because "our grandfather (ancestor) declared that day a holiday."

I asked for details on *izouza* meat parts: "What is *izouza?*" The elderly *inaden* explained, " The part of *izouza* is the following: in a bull, the neck, the head, the paws, some pieces of the stomach, some pieces of the intestines. In a small animal, it is the same thing, with also the skin At a special bull wedding (where bridewealth includes a large bull, steer, or cow), the breast belongs to the bride. Between the paws it is for smiths." Here, again, the interstitial position of *inaden* is symbolized by this meat part distribution. The elderly smiths continued to explain further, adding to each others' comments: "*Izouza* is important, this is how they do it." I also asked, "What is the meaning of the expression 'to grease the throat?'" They explained: "That is just a manner of flattering our nobles." I then asked, deciding to tease provocatively as *inaden* often do in their conversations: "Historically, were smiths and slaves the same? "We are more important than slaves. Slaves were bought. A slave (in the past) or a person of servile descent (today) cannot inherit a smith. However, there were some smiths in Tahoua (a large oasis in northern Niger) who (in the past) had slaves." [Slavery was abolished at mid-century.]

These comments on the connections between the *albourousa* mumming ritual, *izouza* meat distributions to smith/artisans, reserve and lack of it, and social identity and difference reveal the complex "nesting" of *inaden* in Tuareg society, notwithstanding their ambiguous and allegedly outside origins. In *albourousa,* occasionally still held in the countryside, smiths can ruin a noble patron's reputation, or at least, embarrass the noble by walking as a group around the area and shouting out loud what that noble did or did not do to violate the rule. This process was vividly illustrated when a man of aristocratic origins neglected to use his family's attached smiths or any other smiths' services for an

important ceremony called "Greeting the Tent" (*tineseslem*) that he held for his second wife's relatives and in-laws in 1991. So smiths went around the wider area and broadcast this infraction, despite the man's pleas to stop. He was compelled to pay the smiths attached to his family a fine in cereal grains. The organizer/participant in this *albourousa* went on to describe its details vividly:

> One year, we did an *albourousa* to Ahmed (pseudonym), since he had held a
> *tineseslem* or "Greeting the Tent" ceremony for his second wife and relatives

without seeking smiths to help. [This ceremony is held soon after a move of the married couple to the husband's home, usually following initial uxorilocal residence until bridewealth payments are completed and the parents-in-law approve of the groom.]

Yehiya (pseudonym for a smith in his village) came to tell us we are initiating an *albourusa* at Ahmed's

We arrived at his home (in a neighboring village, about a half mile down an unpaved road from the narrator's), we told him, "We are going to do the *albourusa* to you."

He responded (pleadingly), "You must not. I am going to give you 15,000 CFA."

We smiths said, "No, what we'll find in all those villages will be more."

We then left for all the (surrounding) villages in the area

we received much millet over there from nobles, we had a donkey that transported our water. One made three days' trip while getting our supplies together. Our donkey ate the barley given to us (as part of the fine).

If people saw smiths doing the *albourousa,* they hid their supplies.

We arrived at another noble's home (in narrator's village)

We ate all her wheat!

Oumba (pseudonym) gave us 1,000 CFA (about US$2.50) and told us jokingly: "You must go to Tabelot, in order for the people there to see the *albourusa.* It has been a long time since they have seen it."

The song (we sang) while traveling had verses that sang," Our father is dead!"

We sing these verses in order to show that we are not happy (about the breech in noble conduct).

Real smiths have no reserve!

I then asked him, "Why do you put on sandals over your ears during *ilbourusen*)?" He explained, "In order to (as some say) make us look like we have hyena ears, and (also) to make us smile like the devil, or the animal with a tail... We also (sometimes) put on beads of goat dung (balls) in order to be interesting (entertaining) to look at."

Albourousa (pl. *ilbourousen*) can also be performed by smiths, enacted for a fine, when nobles attempt to imitate or play the role of smiths, for example, as when they wear clothing inside-out, attempt to do work at the forge (taboo traditionally, though now a very few nobles starting to do smith work), or when nobles attempt to by-pass smiths' services. While I was lodging with a family of noble origins, a female smith attached to my host family once performed a small *albourousa* for me, when I unwittingly wore a blouse inside-out. She did this by loudly ululating and extending her hand out to me in the traditional smith begging gesture pervasive at rites of passage, though she did this very good-naturedly and jocularly, in formulaic style, without hostility, to collect the small fine I "owed" her. For this was an infraction of longstanding sumptuary laws concerning noble and smith differences in dress, accessories, and work.

Why, exactly, was my small, seemingly trivial infraction so important? Only smiths are supposed to enact reversals and inversions, not others. Only smith/artisans are supposed to linger (either standing or sitting) in a door-frame of a tent or house. Children who become mentally disabled are sometimes believed to have been left as babies in that space. That space constitutes, as Stoller and Coombs terms it in discussing Songhai cosmology (Stoller and Coombs, 1994), a crossroads symbol, which, in the Tuareg case, potently conveys smiths' interstitial roles.

Gradually, during informal conversations and more structured interviews and oral histories, I learned more details on the meanings and practices of *albourusa* (pl. *ilbourousen*). All smiths in an area conduct *ilbourousen* against all nobles in an area as a protest against even one small noble infraction (for example, refusing to pay a fine and/or neglecting to use smiths' services serving food and tea at a noble namedays or weddings, or not allowing smiths to announce and invite guests to these rites of passage, but circumventing their services). In the countryside, where face-to-face relationships remain important socially, smiths can ruin the noble's reputation in this ritual

Smiths during their *albourusa* ritual can in principle destroy nobles' property, dump out water, even seize belongings, if this concerns a serious infraction of rules. Their aristocratic patrons/customers cannot call in any police or other authorities in these circumstances. As an old *ened* explained to me,

> The *albourousa* is inherited by smiths
> *Ilbourusen* represent the conduct of someone, a commentary (on it)
> Also they represent the benefit of smiths
> In history, one says that the Arabs did that
> All nobles who have played the role of a smith, one does this to them
> Even if you use a small smith child, one cannot do *alburusa* to you (i.e., you must at least call on one smith child, at minimum, to do a task that is done by smiths, or else you are subject to the *ilbourusen*)
> Albourousa represents our heritage
> The origin of a noble, if his daughter marries,
> normally, he should seek a smith: (for example),
> The baggage of the marriage, if it arrives first, a smith woman must touch that, and she must ululate, and only after that
> should the noble sees that baggage (presents, *tamegi*, from groom to bride, in addition to bridewealth).

The foregoing oral narrative and conversations revealed that, from the viewpoint of *inaden*, the *albourousa* ritual expresses the interest smiths have in protecting their craftsmanship from others who infringe upon these rights. In effect, they are protecting their collective specialization, approximating a guild or union. In the countryside, as well as the town of Agadez among some Tuareg families recently arrived from the countryside, smiths still receive their traditional *izouza* parts of meat at namedays and weddings: the leg, the breast, half of the stomach, the liver, the heart, and the fat found inside the stomach, which are expressly reserved for them as their right.

Yet the hyena alluded to in the mumming rite's symbolism (of sandals attached to smiths' ears) is very distinctive from the animals whose meat is eaten. As in many other African societies, hyenas are ambiguous and subject to ritual restrictions, somewhat like the pangolin (Douglas, 1977). Hyenas are not eaten; in fact, they are considered an anomalous animal. Many Tuareg believe that hyenas are hermaphrodites, and/or can change sex back and forth. Thus the transformative qualities of *inaden* as mediators are conveyed in these symbolic mumming props—sandals worn over the ears—that some identify metaphorically with the hyena. Also, the excrement of animals such as the hyena and the goat are, of course, the antithesis of human food—here the inverted behavior of smiths' aristocratic patrons prompts the latter to mockingly "play with" the edible/inedible categories: this playful critical commentary is expressed by the goat dung beads.

Also mentioned was an additional image: of the devil. Here is another hint of smith/artisans' ambiguous position in local religious worldview: as standing apart from orthodox, Qur'anic Islam, in being associated alternately with spirits and the Devil, on the one hand, but on the other, also being associated with prophets such as Dauda.

Many older smiths insisted, "*Ilbourusen* are smith's heritage. For example, if a noble's daughter marries he should seek a smith; a smith woman must touch the baggage of the marriage when this arrives, and she must ululate, and the smith takes all leftovers home from the wedding." A smith woman whom I frequently accompanied to babies' namedays explained to me that "*Izouza* represents compensation for our (female smiths') work of shaving the infant's hair and (all smiths') marriage-arranging (for nobles). Both *izouza* and *ilbourousen* rights are inherited by smiths. Smiths who conducted these rituals also expressed their important journalistic role in either maintaining or challenging their patrons' reputations in a balance of power.

A young smith from an all-smith village in Air remarked to me, "Two years ago, we have enacted an *alburusa*. The motive for that was an oasis gardener from our neighboring (patron) village, who had a visit from his son-in-law, and he did not seek us smiths for preparations. Rather, he got busy grilling the animal (for the celebration) himself! That was our reason for having the *albourousa*. We made all the people in that village pay. We did not even warn him, (for he should know about this!), we did it suddenly. And he paid us!" Thus these ceremonies traditionally have functioned in maintaining complementary occupational specialization and preserving a balance in wealth accumulation. But today they are less effective since some non-smiths resist them.

Yet smiths and non-smiths vary in the extent to which they experience tensions, and alongside these social tensions are also, ideally, joking and supportive relationships between *inaden* and their patrons. According to a smith in the Kel Ferwan Tuareg descent group who alternated between Agadez and Niamey, "Kel Ewey Tuareg (the descent group who predominate around Mount Bagzan) disdain smiths more; whereas (we) Kel Ferwan smiths and nobles are like brothers." Many smiths there attributed the disdain of smiths by some (though not all) Kel Ewey Tuareg to the latters' Hausa influence—accurately or inaccurately, I do not know. But even many Kel Ewey Tuareg insisted that, "*inaden* are like our cousins, or like women; you must not get angry with them, but joke with them."

These apparent contradictions or variations in degree and type of social ambivalence and tensions were illustrated in the experience of numerous families in rural Air, particularly in rites of passage. At a baby's nameday that I attended, for example, a smith woman shaved the baby's hair. At the end of the nameday, women in the baby's family and smiths, including an old smith man, played a game called *taboulan*, denoting wrestling and horseplay, translated as *la lutte* and also locally compared to *erawan* or play. Participants explained to me that this game was provoked by someone saying "the tea is good". It involved a brief dance, and mock fighting combined: the participants threw food at each other, and then wrestled. Many guests at the nameday explained to me that this is done "just for fun," i.e., as part of the ideal joking relationship between smith/artisans and their aristocratic families to illustrate their famililar and complementary (fictive kin) roles.

Even beyond formal rituals, these multi-dimensional relationships are evident in everyday informal sociability and work. One smith/artisan man I encountered in a rural region provided a vivid illustration of this. One day, he was making a mortar for my host family, who were of aristocratic origin, and in exchange, the male household head gave him a squash from his garden and paid him a small monetary fee, to even the transaction. The wood came from a tree rare in that region, and the work was demanding, requiring several days' hard chopping and sculpting—in effect, "wrestling" with the tree trunk. This smith/artisan, whom I shall call Siliman, related to me in a very familiar and playful manner, teasing me in much the same way as he did his aristocratic patrons/customers, since I was staying with them. He grabbed my hand, held it tight rather than more formally shaking and withdrawing of it as is conventionally done between most persons there, and complimented me on my perfume. Then he tried to sell me a colorful rug from Libya, hinting that my host wanted it. This embarrassed my host, who later confided to me that this tactic had made him uncomfortable. Siliman later also asked me where my husband was. Then he touched my cheek, and asked why my face was moist (I replied that I was wearing an ointment, explaining that it protected from the sun's rays, i.e., sunblock). Then, he touched my back and asked, "Why is this so bony?" [Many rural Tuareg prefer fat women.] Then he left, but peered mischievously at me and my research assistant through a small window as we crouched on a mat inside an adobe house and worked on transcriptions and tapes.

Later, around noon, Siliman brought more of his supplies to the small village of my host family, and set up his own small camp beneath a tree near my host's compound to work on the mortar. Beneath the surface "play" and conventional, almost formulaic camaderie of this relationship, however, were some tensions. My host commented under his breath that this smith was "unusually familiar," and also " too ostentatious for a smith." Siliman was indeed very well-dressed, wearing long flowing robes and a new men's turban/veil *(tagulmust)*, in contrast to most rural *inaden*, who, as observed, in principle are supposed to appear poor, often dressing in rags and refraining from wearing Islamic amulets or jewelry, although they manufacture them. Other *inaden*, for example, asserted to me that they "disdained (wearing) jewelry" themselves. But Siliman wore a large silver amulet case with Qur'anic verses inside it around his neck, and thus, according to the noble man who commissioned his work, seemed "more like an Agadez (urban) smith."

In the countryside, each noble family officially still has a smith family they inherited through marriage, still knows who they are, and also has an alternate or back-up smith if the primary attached smith is unavailable. This relationship remains recognized, even though, as noted, nowadays each individual noble can also choose a personal smith on the basis of skill preference or even personal rapport, for certain tasks, in a voluntaristic friendship. In one village near Mt. Bagzan, residents include approximately half *inaden* and half non-*inaden*, (families of aristocratic and servile origins). The smith households were almost all located near their original aristocratic patron families, and socially interacted with them. There are now about 130 households (in all) there. Some *inaden* accompanied their patrons' entire descent group or clan to the area from on top of Mt. Bagzan around the middle of the last century during wars in that region.

Yet many smiths hesitate to answer questions about the identity of their own *tawsit* or descent group because, they explained, "we consider ourselves all relatives *(imarawen)*, on the basis of our common social stratum and origin; we are kin in the same clan or descent group, and descend from the same ancestress." Some smiths emphasized their association with the *tawsit* or descent group of those nobles to whom they are traditionally attached. But most do not really consider selves to belong to this noble *tawsit*, since they are not related by kinship, marriage, or descent to nobles, whose clan or descent group calculates descent from another founding ancestress.

According to the chief *(amghar*, also denoting elder) of a local group of rural smiths in the Air Mountains, "the main distinction between nobles and smiths is that the prophet *(annebi)* of nobles is Mohammed; whereas the prophet of us smiths is Dauda. Also, after death, we smiths go to a land apart from both Paradise and Hell. Also, we smiths lack *takarakit* or reserve; whereas nobles have this." He later explained that smiths need this freedom, in order to arrange noble marriages and to recite genealogies and others' oral histories. Importantly, here lack of *takarakit* is defined in positive, rather than negative terms of denigration, in which non-smiths—including some outside ethnographers and travelers—have tended to define it.

He continued: "We smiths "belong" to nobles, but not as slaves once did, since we are given compensation (remuneration). Smiths are, rather, available to nobles." Other low-status men who are former slaves or descendants of slaves also sometimes become "*manoeuvres*" or handypersons for nobles, doing repair-work, mechanic works, etc., but not, as yet, manufacturing jewelry or tools, or serving in ritual or social roles of the *inaden*. This is significant; for suggests that the practice of manual technical labor, which some scholars of smith/artisans in Tuareg and other societies consider the main reason for their "denigrated" status (Berland and Rao, 2004; Herbert, 1993; McNaughton, 1988), does not explain everything; for there are striking differences, in local viewpoints of persons of diverse social origins, between smith/artisans and slaves. Tuareg smiths themselves abhor comparisons with former slaves or their descendants, and non-smiths, although making less of a distinction between them, nonetheless often say, "smiths and slaves are next to each other, though different." Rural gardeners and caravanners seem to have the strongest ties with *inaden,* due to work needs (for tools, etc), but as shown, *inaden* serve many additional roles besides making and repairing tools, and one does not as a rule give just any task to a non-smith; thus those persons called *manoeuvres* and *inaden,* although overlapping at times, are not exactly equivalent in their social status.

Most persons of noble origin remain ashamed to do work of the forge. But they are beginning to sell smiths' work. Several men of aristocratic origin I knew went to Nigeria and sell jewelry to Africans, Europeans, and Americans there. One related to me how he sold art objects made by smiths, especially silverwork, regularly to a woman at the American Embassy there. Another spent about half the year in Lagos staying with a male relative, who lived there all the time and worked as office staff at an airline. Others have formed business partnerships with *inaden,* but these relationships can be strained.

Another practice of Tuareg smiths that makes them distinctive in their own and others' viewpoints is that special jargon or argot that they occasionally (nowadays very rarely—at least when others and I were present) speak among themselves, called Tenet (also the fem. sing. form of "smith"), which only they know. Both smiths and non-smiths described this to me as "twisted Tamajaq," featuring much word-play. Significantly, *inaden* did not reverse this association, that is, they did not insist that Tenet was "standard" and non-smiths' Tamajaq was "twisted Tenet." There are parallels here with other symbolic differences between smiths' livestock brand designs and aristocratic patrons' livestock brand designs, and smiths' dancing starting on the left foot, and with smiths' entering the nuptial tent when they led the bride there at the wedding on its left side, as opposed to nobles' right side symbolic emphasis.

A detailed analysis of Tenet is beyond the scope of the present book, but many researchers have reported that this is spoken primarily when artisans want others not to understand, by most Tuareg smiths in Ahaggar, Adrar, Air, and Tamesna (Bernus, 2006; Casajus, 2000; Lhote, 1984:57). One brief incident in my field research, however, is illuminating here. I rarely heard Tenet used conversationally, only specific terms in jest, such as *oujembek* for *ened* (smith in the singular). Many inaden I knew well responded positively to some outsiders—for example, myself as a researcher and prior to that, a Peace Corps volunteer, and other Peace Corps volunteers in Air who befriended them, using the former term in joking address. Other *inaden* I knew less well, however, tended to frown, thereby hinting that this term has a certain "inside" familiar quality that keys the relationship on a level that requires mutuality in long association, and approval of the smith/artisan. On another occasion, when I explained to my hosts that I had a sore throat, using the term *igourzan*, they laughed and explained that I was using the Tenet term, and explained to me that the "correct" Tamajaq term was *izourgan*. Official viewpoints here thus tend to consider Tenet "non-standard."

Casajus (2000) considers Tenet a specialized occupational jargon (or *argot*, French), although it is also spoken before others, non-smiths, as a kind of "secret" language or euphemism. Ida and Johannes Nicolaisen (1997) describe it as a kind of "slang" derived from Tamajaq. In Bernus' view, it appears that syntax, conjugations, and feminine and plural forms of this Tenet are the same as in Tamajaq (Bernus, 1983:249). Although some words clearly derive from Tamajaq terms, many others do not. According to Casajus (1989:125), the presence of the same affixes could imply derivation from older Tamajaq terms that have disappeared.

The point here is that smiths often conduct delicate negotiations as go-betweens for official authorities. As already observed, they are active in bridewealth negotiations, even to this day. In the political domain, some *inaden* act as special emissaries to the traditional *amenukal* leader of the regional Tuareg confederation, and to the local traditional chief, whose name, *ettebel*, also denotes a drum made of a very large receptacle carved from hardwood *ahtes* (*Faidherbia albida*) or *tuwila* (*Sclerocarya birrea*), the latter also used in many herbal medicinal recipes (Rasmussen, 2006), and is covered in white cowhide. Its inner surface was covered with inscriptions from *suras* of the Qur'an. Inside it are amulets, a leather envelope holding Qur'anic verses on paper, and small gold nuggets that would make a sound whenever this drum was moved or beaten. Inside the tent, this *ettebel* drum is suspended from two posts, and is brought out when it is to be used. During my research, this drum among Kel Ewey Tuareg was brought out at the feast at the end of Ramadan fasting, and was played by, not a smith/artisan, but by the son of the chief of the smaller clan within the Kel Ewey descent group of the Kel Air Tuareg confederation, predominant near Mt. Bagzan, called Kel Igurmaden. At other times in various Tuareg groups and regions, two metalworking smiths, one holding it in his right hand, the other in his left, would hit it with two soft beaters called *iteker* (sing. *atakor*), braided leather stuffed with rags at their tip, which are, I noted, the same beaters used by smiths in their praise-singing music, called *chiluban*, during Kel Ewey Tuareg aristocratic rites of passage.

During travel in the past, one of the metalworking *inaden* would transport *ettebel* on his camel. The smith/artisan would go behind it, beating it at regularly spaced intervals to signal his position, never allowing it to touch the ground. When beaten at a faster rhythm, this drum would be used to rally warriors. Thus in the past, metalworker artisans would beat the war drum (*ettebel*) at the *amenokal*'s behest, as recounted for 1867, the year when the Kel Denneg went on a raid in the Air, under the command of Musa ag Bodal.

There is some regional and confederational variation on these patterns: for example, in Kel Ewey communities of the Kel Air in the Air Massif near Mount Bagzan, I saw smith/artisans perform drumming mainly on another drum, constructed from a mortar, called a *tende,* primarily during rites of passage and at spirit possession healing rituals, as they performed praise songs called *tedeban.* But the important point here is that *inaden* tend to be specialized drummers as part of their important role in various ceremonies throughout Tuareg society.

Some smith/artisans prepare tea and arrange a site for guests to stay in on behalf of a chief. Formerly, this specialist, called *anesfada* (pl.*inesfaden)* not only looked after day-to-day affairs, but could also stand in for his analogue, the noble descent group *ettebel* chief and confederational *amenukal,* serving as ambassador before other chiefs or foreign authorities, such as French military officers who sought to subjugate them. Bernus (2006) relates how, at the end of the 19th century, two famous warriors—El Kabus, of the Kel Fadey descent group, and Aghali, of the Kel Nan—wounded Musa agg-Amastan, the future *amenokal,* and killed his young brother Bello as these brothers returned from a raid launched by the Kel Ahaggar. Several years later, Musa led a large troop back to avenge his brother's death. When they arrived in the proximity of their enemy, he sent Abbas, his *anesfada,* to ask Mohammed El Kumati, the Kel Denneg *amenokal,* to hand over El Kabus, who had killed his brother. In response Mohammed sent his *anesfada,* Badidan, with a message to tell Musa he was refusing to hand over El Kabus. The role of the smith/artisan messenger here was to avoid a direct, offensive oral refusal. According to Ghubayd agg-Alawjeli, the Kel Denneg, who up to that time had had no contact with the French, kept out of the cities and settled in the Azawagh, only on December 31, 1901 did Mohammed send the metalworker Badidan in his place, and the latter signed in his hand the letter of allegiance. The letter announced that Henri Gouraud, representing the French president, accepted the allegiance of the Iwellemmeden confederational descent groups, who recognized the authority of Mohammed, on the following conditions: "The Iwellemmeden will not incite battles with anyone without permission of the (French) captain who is in Tahoua" (Ahubayd agg-Alawjeli, 1975:142).

The point here is that this historical event was a major treaty committing these Tuareg factions to dependence on the French army and putting an end to their political autonomy. Badidan, significantly, was a powerful representative of the *amenokal* of the large regional confederation.

I noticed that, in both rural and urban Niger and Mali, some *inaden* still serve important roles as intermediaries and gate-keepers between Tuareg and outsiders—both "official" local authorities and less authoritative outsiders such as tourists. On several occasions in the countryside, I observed smiths organize local residents in a rural village, record their names and household census information, and line them up to receive food distributions and even immunizations from the government and aid agencies. Some local *inaden* assisted a local chief with tax collection. These roles confer additional unofficial power to these specialists, at first backed up by the authority of the French military, and later, by the Niger and Malian governments, as well as international non-governmental and other agencies. Thus the position of some *inaden* as intermediaries between sometimes hostile parties is delicate, and at times there is suspicion resembling attitudes toward translators reported in some other African societies (Achebe, 1958).

Many *inaden* are renowned poets, although other women and men of diverse social origin may also excel in this art. Badidan, who recounted several great battles in 1850, went along on them, but did not fight, composed a poem about them, quoted in Ghubayd agg-Alawjeli (1975:76). Thus in Tuareg society, at times the *inaden* have served roles similar to griots (oral historians and bards) among their neighbors, though some Tuareg today in towns use the services of griots, as well as *inaden*, often in the same event, for example a wedding. But these specialists are recognized as very distinctive in Tuareg society; many residents felt, for example, that griots tended to never keep secrets, hinting that they trusted smiths more than griots to intercede in delicate matters. *Inaden* therefore have complex multiple roles beyond a purely manual or technical activity, giving them a more ambiguous character, with freedom of speech and occasionally, in their service to important figures, the opportunity to interpret events and shape policy, albeit indirectly. But they also have the obligation to be discreet in some contexts as go-beetweens—this latter trait is the one most often mentioned as lacking, allegedly at least, in griots.

Today many smith/artisans have transcended (though not entirely escaped or replaced) their chiefs' and aristocratic patron families' control, in marketing their visual art objects beyond Tuareg society to supplement their income in urban functionaries' and tourists' and more general global demands internationally for their jewelry. Initially, when the Sahara opened up to tourism, many (though not all) persons of aristocratic background tended to shun direct encounters with outsiders, and at first sent unknown travelers to *inaden* households. Upon my first arrival to begin my field research in a rural, then more nomadic Tuareg community, I was lodged in a chiefly family, since I had prior contacts in that community based on my earlier Peace Corps volunteer work in that region. Still, at first, mostly smiths and children approached me on visits, and nobles remained a bit reserved and even shy with me. By contrast, a European tourist who arrived shortly after I did, unknown in that community, was sent to a smith/artisan household. Initially, predominantly (though not exclusively) *inaden* started travel agencies in Agadez. Gradually, local attitudes changed, and later Tuareg of diverse backgrounds also worked in tourist agencies. But overwhelmingly, it is still the *inaden* who make Tuareg jewelry. Inaden therefore protect cultural knowledge, but also innovate in transforming it.

THE ECONOMICS OF RITUAL, THE RITUAL OF ECONOMICS

Like the specialisms of doctors, scientists, priests, and artists, smith/artisans' knowledge and power can be defined as used for ill or good (McNaughton,

1988; Herbert, 1993). But who decides, and how? The directions this knowledge takes, and ways its practices are defined and re-defined in broader social turmoil and upheaval are unpredictable, and can be interpreted and manipulated by anyone, regardless of social origin, in diverse ways. For power is in some respects, "up for grabs." There are alternately reaffirmations, contestations, and modifications of these mediating powers according to context and perspective.

These transformations are reflected upon intently, sometimes with worry. In regard to change, an old smith chief near Mt. Bagzan commented, "Life is not the same as before, because before was easier, people had more . The value of smiths to nobles is that they make everything nobles order, but there are many changes, because there are nobles (today) who are jealous of smiths, even if this is over something petty, they do not like that, even if it is a shirt. Recently, some nobles are becoming enemies of smiths." As noted, there are a few persons of noble descent in a large oasis who now know the work the forge, can even make saber swords. A few non-smith women also do hairdressing, but usually where no *inaden* reside nearby. Most smiths do not like what they view as these appropriations of their work, particularly their work with fire and the forge, key sources of their power, but they indicated fewer smiths protest nowadays. For some nobles are less reserved and if no smiths live nearby, they do their work, even though such work used to be shameful for nobles. Many lament the decline in reserve, which used to provide some measure of predictability in these ideally complementary relationships.

A few smiths observed that, "some nobles have become nasty; they now fight when (we) smiths do *ilburusan*, so smiths do these protest rituals less, even if nobles have done something they view as deserving them." Smiths also said nobles no longer give to smiths when the latter beg. But many rural smiths and nobles also acknowledged that they still cannot live without each other, recognizing continuing mutual dependence.

Many rural persons of noble descent, for their part, appeal to cultural values and social practices which have until recently been powerful in noble/smith roles and relationships in the countryside. *Ahelek* denotes disobedience toward an owner or patron, still disapproved if not assiduously avoided by most persons, and figures prominently in complaint discourses of ritual and social power and in everyday relations between the social strata and age generations. A young aristocratic man from a maraboutique family expressed this concept, still salient but now contested, when he remarked, "In the past, smiths feared to commit excessive acts; but now they seek things much more aggressively, from this disobedience." The man considered this is to be a trend, not only among smiths and nobles, but also among youths and elders, especially pronounced in the large towns. "In the past," he elaborated, "there was the belief that if a smith sat on the same mat as a noble, the smith would become mentally disabled and act without any restraint at all. In the past, there was also the belief that if a noble accompanied a smith to the door of his/her compound, the noble would become as poor as the smith." He gave an example of the ramifications of *ahelek:* "If one gave a smith too much millet, he/she would become dependent, and also would tell everyone else around, and they would expect a gift, also. This becomes a habit, and leads to extremely unrestrained conduct." Formerly, the different social categories and age groups were seen as bound to each other in mutual rights and obligations, and ideally, could rely on each others' protective, rather than destructive, powers, though as already shown, the reality was not always as harmonious, even in the past, as many remember it.

Many Tuareg of diverse social origins are conscious of changes in their social and economic relationships, though most continue ritual and ceremonial practices in order, many explain, "to be polite" or "because we are friends" or "for sentimental reasons." Nobles often sell smiths' items, and sometimes arrange to split profits. There are some emerging smith/noble business partnerships, but these are not without tensions. For example, many Kel Ewey nobles I knew around Mt. Bagzan in Air sold wooden spoons and ladles made by local smiths when they went to Agadez. I overheard one noble ask a smith if he could give him a portion of millet for these goods after he sold them in town, as in traditional client-patron relationships, but the local smith replied, "No, I prefer money."

In the Air region, bridewealth used to be four camels for nobles and one camel for smiths. Currently in Agadez and the countryside, bridewealth has become monetarized and also has increased. For Kel Ferwan Tuareg, for example, it is now 125,000 CFA ($250 U.S.) for smiths and 150,000 CFA ($300 U.S.) for nobles, although nobles tend to be less prosperous. Many men do migrant labor and itinerant trading beyond Agadez and even Niger to save up for bridewealth.

A merchant of mixed social origins who sold produce in the Agadez Iron Market pointed out a well-to-do smith woman married to smith man who worked for Sonichar, a French company, and no longer did work of the forge, and remarked, chuckling: "That *tenet* (smith woman) doesn't need to do hairstyling!" Once, after hearing news of a tragic car accident outside Agadez, a non-smith expressed sadness for the victims, but wistfully referred to a smith slain in a car accident outside Agadez as "one of those wealthy *inaden*." A woman of mixed social origins felt that, "Recently, there is an increase in *tezma* because there is less to give smiths, and so nobles refuse their requests for presents and compensation more often." Some nobles asserted that smiths "are now trying to become like nobles; they see themselves as equal to us." Many realize that smiths depend less on nobles than formerly; they tend to travel a lot more often, and more widely. Some nobles complained resentfully that, "*inaden* nowadays are doing work for others and neglecting their traditional work." Smith workmanship for nobles is supposed to be more solid and more decorative than workmanship for tourists. Smiths, they complained, " have become like kings; now they sit on the same mat!" [As noted, if they did this before, there was the belief the smith would become crazy.] Also, nobles now accompany a visiting smith to the door or gate of their compound; before, as noted, if they did this in the past, the noble would become poor like smiths. Some persons of non-smith origins, in referring to the ever-widening travels by Tuareg, believed that smith/artisans, especially, embarked on international travel, and benefited from it, more than other Tuareg (though this observation cannot be verified). Some holding this view complained that, "since smiths have more diverse sources of income, they no longer keep their word." Others—including also some elderly *inaden*—worried over smith's alleged attempts to intermarry with other social strata.

Yet many Tuareg non-smiths, particularly rural persons, still felt that they couldn't do anything without smiths. Many persons continued to emphasize the mutuality of their relationships: for example, they should still always provide food and work for each other. *Inaden* remain indispensable to many. Also, pre-colonial social identities remain salient, widely known, and often alluded to: for example, despite the exhortations of the new Tuareg nationalist leaders in recent years to forget those old social categories, many still appeal to prestigious noble origins to justify or disapprove certain conduct, to distinguish some acts from other anti-social acts, and the chiefly noble and maraboutique clans still attempt to arrange endogamous, politically-advantageous marriages between close cousins. Yet this system is breaking down, and there is some intermarriage between those of aristocratic and servile descent, as well as between a few *inaden* and the latter . However, most *inaden* remain closely endogamous and thus far, most persons of aristocratic background abhor marrying them because of lingering pollution beliefs.

Yet the smith client remains, as shown, usually a close neighbor, extensive travel notwithstanding. For both parties, this is a "double-edged" situation of both beneficial flexibility and uncertain obligations and outcomes, and plays an undeniable role in those negative "witch-craft-like" and "pollution"-tinged *tezma* accusations . Since client-patron inherited smith roles remain strongest in rituals and hairstyling, but other work, such as manufacturing tools and jewelry, allows for individual choice of a smith/artisan from outside this traditional inherited relationship, and some fluid and negotiated relationships result offering escape hatches for both parties. But rural nobles still depend upon smiths as a group for many goods and services; whereas smiths have a wider range of alternate sources of patronage and income: they can serve nobles outside their traditional client-patron relationships nearby, or they can migrate to towns and abroad, where they work for customers beyond Tuareg society and even Africa. Thus there is some asymmetry and imbalance perceived in this relationship.

Many rural smiths were, like former servile peoples who took over nobles' gardens upon their manumission early in the twentieth century, the first to take up oasis gardening, work that some (though not all) persons of noble origin still resist, or practice reluctantly. In addition to their traditional work of the forge and rites of passage services, many rural *inaden* now also do other work such as herding, tailoring, tourist guiding, and tourist art production. Tailoring is now taken up by many Tuareg, mostly men, and although an art, this is not considered a traditional smith occupation, and is paid for in cash all at once, on the spot, by whoever orders work, to whoever does the tailoring, regardless of social origin. Other traditional smith work, when done for nobles in client-patron relationships in the countryside, is remunerated in some combination of cash, food (usually millet cereal), and tea, and over a long period of time. This arrangement is ideally flexible: for example, a noble can give the smith food from gardens at harvest-time, or can bring the smith a portion of millet from the (diminishing, but still continuing) caravan trade.

Labor migration—undertaken by predominantly men, of all social backgrounds—involves more prolonged absences on travel with less predictable returns, and most of this money is sent to one's nuclear household members, rather than going to *inaden* clients. Rural nobles are now having more difficulty supporting smiths, from these upheavals of droughts, unemployment within the home countries, and intermittent armed conflicts in their northern regions, which have interfered with the caravan trade (also challenged by competing trucks) and diminished livestock.

Almost all herding and oasis gardening work in the Air Mountain region of Niger formerly done by tributaries and slaves, is now replaced by relatives or contract (paid) workers. Noble' traditional privileges in the oasis gardens are now much reduced. Nomadic nobles and former oasis clients and tributaries now, in their own terminology, "trade" (i.e., exchange) goat cheese and dates, rather than practice the old tribute arrangements called *tiwse*, in relationships once called *temazlayt* (denoting "root of the nail") (Nicolaisen and Nicolaisen, 1997).

What emerges here is that, rather than a rigid, neatly-bounded category or social status, *inaden* affiliation—despite endogamy—is increasingly ambiguous and fluid, and can be interpreted and manipulated by themselves and others in diverse ways to suit the situation. As also shown in several mythico-histories, their identification with certain spirits underlines their other-worldliness Thus the persistent imagery associating smith danger with protection, and warnings not to harm them imply an effort to mitigate social tensions. These peacekeeping efforts are sometimes effective, sometimes not.

SUM-UP DISCUSSION OF *TEZMA* AMONG THE TUAREG

The foregoing cases, vignettes, narratives, informal conversations, mythico-histories, tales, and reminiscences suggest that, despite some scapegoating and jealousy of *inaden* on the part of some other Tuareg, there remain some social contracts limiting conflict in *tezma*-related incidents. Most residents, particularly in the countryside, regard each other with affection, and lament the breakdown of social values promoting its cooperation and reciprocity. They blame many (smiths and non-smiths) as violating important values that everyone in those old partnerships once agreed on protecting them both in their patron-client relationships. Not solely one or other social category, but those of both traditional partners, may contribute to this breakdown by reneging on mutual obligations. Moreover, this relationship, as shown, is no longer a simple dyad, but there are third parties beyond it.

Nonetheless, *tezma* these days is often converted into a source of danger for smiths more than nobles (in the occasionally violent retaliation by some non-smiths). Rather than acting to smiths' advantage as it once did, as purely an economic leveling device protecting their profession, this force often acquires an added dimension of sexual pollution, and sometimes reverts back against the smith/artisan.

Moreover, the fact that some highly successful *inaden* are also afflicted with another power, *togerchet* or evil mouth gossip emanating from other *inaden*, suggests a double vulnerability: the weakening of communitas within their own social stratum, as well as the weakening of *inaden* status as a traditionally-protected people within their larger community, as they acquire rewards from outside aristocratic descent groups and become targets of jealousy from both other *inaden* and former patrons, and also, in the nation-state context, they still suffer the consequences of more generalized Tuareg ethnic marginalization politically, even as they act as mediators. For their role in bringing the community together for state-related events such as aid distributions and taxation combines the positive ambassador-like role with the translator's ambiguity. To protect themselves from *tezma* accusations, smiths must either flee the rural community altogether, for example, to the towns of Niger and Mali, or remain deeply embedded within it. Those with "one foot inside and "one foot outside" their small rural community, where the old client-patron relationships are no longer powerful enough to protect them, yet not completely broken down, are particularly vulnerable to *tezma* accusation: this predicament of ambiguous powers, but also tenacious (though selective) social memories, prove difficult to control.

THEORETICAL INTERLUDE: WIDER ISSUES

The foregoing sections revealed Tuareg *inaden* as, above all, skilled mediators of persons, practices, and objects. They manipulate spiritual, human, and natural elements and powers, often balancing opposing forces. A number of social theorists have noted an apparently implicit relationship of simultaneous nearness and remoteness between the mediator and those among whom the mediator intercedes (Simmel, 1950; Douglas, 1966; Berland and Rao, 2004). What kinds of closeness and distance, objectivity and involvement, are present in relationships between smith/artisans, patrons, and outsiders? What are their wider consequences and implications for understanding ritual powers?

I now review briefly some social theories on ritual powers in general that are germane to this study of smith/artisans' powers. Next, I reanalyze ritual powers of other smith/artisans from secondary data on smith/artisans' ritual powers in Amhara communities in Ethiopia, Bidan (Moor) communities in Mauritania, Kapsiki communities in Cameroon, and Mande-speaking communities in Mali. Throughout, I re-visit my Tuareg data and interweave these data with cross-cultural perspectives on ritual powers toward an understanding, hopefully, of alternative interpretations of them. These societies are neither representative of all societies in continental Africa (much less diasporic and global cultural "borderlands"), nor are their belief complexes universal, though they share some common themes with each other and on a more generalized level, reveal some common human concerns.

In my view it is more fruitful to analyze allegedly "mystic" (i.e., superhuman)—sometimes malevolent, sometimes benign, ritual powers not in terms of static structural classifications or essentialized qualities, (Douglas, 1966), but instead in terms of process and practice, following some other post-structural anthropological efforts (West, 2007). Yet there is a paradox here. Some local residents themselves reify and essentialize identities and differences, and impose a kind of local structuralism upon these specialists and their alleged powers that cannot be ignored. But the goal in the present analysis is to connect local classifications to resistance, multiple voices, history, and memory (Malkki, 1995; Scott, 1992; Smith, 2004). Ritual powers that on the surface resemble so-called "witchcraft," "pollution," and "evil eye," (Ciekawy and Greschiere, 1998; Comaroff and Comaroff , 1993; Crick, 1976; Douglas, 1966,1996; Foster, 1972; Moore and Sanders, 2001; Spooner, 1970; Stewart and Strathern, 2003) in their symbolic-religious and social-situational meanings reveal how self and Other are continually reconstructed in ambiguity and turmoil

More broadly, in drawing on these and additional data, I address the problem of interpreting wider exclusionary projects (Bunzl, 2005; Carrier, 1991; Fabian, 1981; Herzfeld, 2004; Mudimbe, 1986; Said, 1978)—both within and across different cultural settings. The concern here is also with the general challenge of how to convey the full richness and complexity of social relations in cultural settings without reproducing stereotypes, when some local residents themselves convey distinctions in these terms, whether in binary oppositions (Wood, 1999) or culturally "intimate" "folk" versus "official" histories (Herzfeld, 2004).

It is important in my view to detach the concept of evil from falsely-accused witch figures, and to redefine this concept as sometimes envy-driven political violence against persons given "abject" status (Butler, 1991,1993) who are also often, simultaneously, themselves powerful in unofficial domains. But in contrast to Douglas's theories of anomaly, these powers and their alleged practitioners are not static, are not "born," but made: they are re-interpreted and transformed in diverse contexts of practice. For as the Tuareg data revealed, smith/artisans' power cannot be reduced to that of accused witches. Although they are sometimes scapegoated, these specialists are not peripheral or marginal, but rather, occupy central places in society despite the unofficial nature of their powers. Here, "evil" does not emanate from a falsely accused "witch," or any particular individual, but rather, from a confluence of processes in that society that cause suffering for many persons of diverse backgrounds.. At times, the accuser, not the accused, stands as marginal here, and the strategies of the accused in part reflect weapons of the weak defending against accusations.

A number of studies have noted African smiths' integration of modes of thought that Euroamerican philosophical systems tend to compartmentalize as "magic," "religion" and "science" (McNaughton, 1988; Herbert, 1993), and have also described some paradoxical and contradictory aspects of their alleged ritual powers and social statuses as needed, yet feared, and as apparently "marginal" and/or peripheral and "peripatetic," yet also mediating figures (Berland and Rao, 2004). Studies have noted that, in many African and some Middle Eastern, Central Asian, Irish, and East Indian communities, there tends to be ambiguous social status attached to smith/artisans and related groups , such as wedding singers, griots, and Irish tinkers. There are ambivalent, but also dependent relations between these specialists, whose alleged superhuman powers are alternately defined positively and negatively, and other persons. Smiths' alleged powers constitute part of wider discourses and practices concerning community, relatedness, and difference. On one level, these processes do in fact approximate contemporary "witchcraft" beliefs (Douglas, 1966,1996; Comaroff and Comaroff , 1993; Stewart and Strathern, 2003) in the fragmentation of old worlds and the consolidation of new worlds.

Yet there is more complexity at play in these powers which, on another level, distinguishes them from peripatetics, witches, and other supposedly marginal peoples. As dynamic culture heroes, these specialists are not peripheral or marginal in the older, static social scientific senses of status and role. Nonetheless many regard them ambivalently in a kind of awe. But this awe is subject to chameleon-like transformations in different socioeconomic and sociopolitical contexts.. Guided here by post-structural anthropological critiques of cultural classification systems and of too literal translation of others' imagined and creative worlds (Asad, 1986; Sperber, 1979; West, 2007), I argue that similar (though not identical) smith-related belief complexes widespread in African and some other regions on the most general level represent attempts to mark off places of memory and consolidate group boundaries where these are, in fact, very porous and negotiable, rather than rigid or non-negotiable. On one level, to non-smiths, smiths' powers, roles, and relations act as touchstones for revival of past identities, but also the coalescence of new ones.

With few exceptions (McNaughton, 1989; Van Beek, 1992), many studies of smiths' and other ritual specialists tend to over-emphasize the viewpoints of non-smiths, non-specialists, and non-peripatetics, --the latter often, in the more stratified societies, noble or aristocratic patrons of non-smiths, or other officially dominant members of society. One reason for this discrepancy is that outside researchers often have difficult access to these specialists' own viewpoints since the latter sometimes discourage outsiders from prying too much into their specialism until one has known them for many years. In effect, smith/artisans and other specialists act as gatekeepers to local wisdom (culture, history, and art and science); hence their own protective ambivalence toward outsiders. Yet the "officially dominant" or less "muted" groups, to use Ardener's (1977) terminology, also tend to regard peripatetics and other specialists with ambivalence.

Thus there is the need for finer epistemological and hermeneutic distinctions in studies of witchcraft, often used as a gloss or cover-term for very different beliefs and practices (Crick, 1977). Yet the data convinces me not to completely abandon the term "witchcraft" as an analytical device. Although there is, I show, no precisely exact correspondence or equivalence between beliefs concerning the powers of smith/artisans as ritual specialists and those attributed to witches, witchcraft is nonetheless relevant in many cases because scapegoating very often targets many ritual and technical specialists, even currently, for example, medieval herbalists and contemporary computer technicians, lawyers, and stock-brokers, whether "peripatetics" or not—and the focus of ambivalence is upon the nature of their powers, usually in predicaments of overlapping but also competing cultural knowledge.

In many parts of Africa, witchcraft is often linked to close relationships in home and the family, rather than to distant relationships with itinerant peripatetics (Ciekawy and Geschiere, 1998:4). Witchcraft is the "dark side of kinship…inherent in the kinship order but is at same time a betrayal of its boundaries" (Ciekawy and Geschiere, 1998:5). In a work comparing and contrasting several different powers among the Tuareg beyond smith's *tezma,* (Rasmussen, 2001b), it is argued that witchcraft-like concepts constitute the "underside" of the Tuareg stratified social order: in the play of these different but related powers, there local residents make a commentary on betrayal of trust in longstanding guardians, mediators , and buffers who normally protect. Recall that smith/artisans and nobles are supposed to be mutually supportive in their traditionally balanced and reciprocal client-patron relations. Likewise, ideally benevolent Tuareg Islamic scholar/marabouts and diviner-healers and their trusting patients and believers, youthful and elder leaders, husbands and wives, are supposed to support each other. Conflicts and tensions that undermine structural safeguards in social relationships often express deep local concern with the selectivity and limitations of opportunities and the differential enjoyment of benefits.

Yet these valuable insights do not completely explain the tenacity of beliefs in "witchcraft-like" powers throughout different regions, in past and present eras, and in times of relative calm, as well as turmoil. Nor do they explain the diversity of the alleged purveyors of different malevolent powers, the accused and accusers who belong to a variety of social categories—co-wives, herbalists, midwives, old women, nephews, uncles, minorities, to name a few in the historical and ethnographic record. Thus smith/artisans' powers have some universal commonalities, but are also culturally distinctive in their meanings..

Many concepts of danger directed toward smith/artisans resembling approximately witchcraft, evil eye, and other purity/pollution "Otherness" beliefs emerge in some religious, socioeconomic, and political contexts, as exclusionary projects that, in effect, construct an "abject" category, to use Butler's (1993) term. But they do not have solely a negative face. Interestingly, abjection can be internally contradictory, rather than unitary in its meanings and consequences. For precisely these processes of social tension also construct and reinforce the mediating roles of the accused, and the accused in turn respond not passively, but actively, as seen for example, in the Tuareg smiths' mumming protest rituals. As such, these processes constitute moral and political discourses, which partly emerge from symbolic and cosmological systems, and partly from political-economy, but do not result from exclusively "modern" or "global" economic or political conditions. Indeed, these beliefs are longstanding, and in their tenacity and/or resurgence, can be used locally to consolidate old powers and preserve privilege, and to protect, as well as to dispute or level status and wealth in collisions with their new forms.

In the next sections, I re-analyze cases from several other societies where smiths' alleged ritual powers are in some ways similar to, but in other ways different from those of the Tuareg *inaden*. Throughout these cases, longstanding moral and philosophical preoccupations shape attempts to cope with multiple and unfinished histories in social memory, as well as emergent social realities.

CHAPTER FOUR

Q'ALB POWER AND AMHARA *BUDA/TAYB* SMITH/ARTISANS

The first case I juxtapose against the Tuareg *tezma* power is that of the alleged *q'alb* power of the *buda* people "of the evil eye", whom many consider to be predominantly smith/artisans (*tayb*), in Ethiopia among the Amhara. Striking here are both similarities and differences between these powers and their respective social settings in terms of property relations, ritual beliefs, and socioeconomic practices. Also striking are the greater social stigma and religious tension surrounding smiths and their alleged power, and the latter's more strongly negative connotations, in the Amhara case.

A number of researchers (Freeman and Plankhurst, 2003; Levine, 1974; Mains, 2007; Reminick, 1974) have described "stigmatized" occupations in urban and rural Ethiopia that involve what is locally perceived as "menial" labor, and these have been associated with traditional craft/artisan workers. There are time gaps, sociopolitical and economic transformations, and changes in anthropology and ethnography between the more recent studies and Reminick's classic article (1974) on people called *buda* or "evil eye" people, overwhelmingly smith/artisans among the Amhara, in which he analyzed their allegedly malevolent power, *q'alb*. Nonetheless, the more recent researchers suggest that many of Reminick's earlier observations apply today in many Amhara regions of Ethiopia. Mains, for example, (2007) found that in urban, as well as rural Ethiopia, issues of occupational status indicate a continuing relevance of the relation between one's social origins and identity and one's production, even in late capitalism, thereby contradicting Baudrillard's (1981) claim that consumption has often taken the place of work in the construction of (social) identity (Mains, 2007:661).

As in the Sahara, West Africa, and in East Africa more generally, the artisan professions in much of Ethiopia—locally defined as carpentry, blacksmithing, weaving, and pottery—tend to be highly stigmatized (Mains, 2007:661). Non-artisans have historically marginalized artisans in space, economics, politics, and social life. Historically, marriage between artisans and non-artisans has been prohibited, and artisans frequently lacked defined rights to land. In most cases, they have worked as tenant farmers on lands of others, and have been required to give products of their work to their patrons, receiving only token amounts of grain in return.

Smith/artisans in Ethiopia do not observe the same religion-based food taboos as Muslims and Orthodox Coptic Christians, for example, they are said to have eaten animals like pig, that do not have a cloven hoof, and certain forbidden wild game, such as monkey or hippopotamus. (Mains, 2007:661). Although Tuareg *inaden*, as observed, eat food similar to that of non-smiths, they do not use the same utensils and tend to eat their food directly from a pot, rather than transferring it, as nobles do, into another dish. Similarly, in Ethiopia, smith/artisans are traditionally not permitted to share the same dishes or utensils with non-artisans. If artisans are guests in homes of non-artisans, they eat from banana leaves or other items that could be disposed of following the meal.

Artisans, whose designation in the Amharic language overlaps with the term *buda* for "evil eye people," frequently are believed to possess a power most authors such as Freeman and Plankhurst (2003) translate as "evil eye,"—only Reminick specifies the local term for this power, "*qalb*" and emphasizes that many smiths called *tayb* are alleged to possess this (Reminick, 1974), which over time, has also contributed to the more general social discrimination these specialists have faced.

Dena Freeman and Alula Plankhurst (2003) argue that concepts of personhood are important in maintaining the marginalized status of artisans in rural Ethiopian areas. Farmers in their study asserted that artisans "are not fully human;" factors cited included their supposed eating habits and lack of cleanliness, and very real lack of access to land and the social relations that are involved with land rights. Even when artisans were able to increase their wealth, this did not translate into status and full social personhood unless they were able to obtain land rights; thus, importantly, money alone has not been sufficient to improve the position of the "lower" occupations in either rural or urban Ethiopia (Mains, 2007:661). This finding contrasts to the Tuareg case; for as observed, many *inaden* have succeeded in upward socioeconomic mobility and enjoy some higher social status, if not prestige in the older aristocratic sense, in their wealth and in their widening gate-keeping and mediating activities vis-a-vis the outside world. This change in social status as a result of greater economic prosperity was implied by many aristocratic Tuareg men's unease over suspected (real or rumored) sexual relations between *inaden* and non-*inaden* women.

Thus I ask here, what accounts for this cross-cultural contrast, other similarities notwithstanding? In the Tuareg case, land ownership has only become important recently, upon sedentarization in the more settled oases, where gardening has transformed former nomads into sedentarized or semi-sedentarized agro-pastoralists (Bernus, 1981; Rasmussen , 2004). In the past, although nobles had rights to a portion of servile and client peoples' garden produce as tribute or tithe, they only owned the date-palms within gardens. The primary importance to Tuareg aristocratic overlords was livestock ownership, and herds were not fixed, but moved around as portable property. Tributary and servile persons had usufruct rights to some animals' offspring. Although in Tuareg communities, there are cases in recent years of disputes over ever scarcer oasis gardening lands (Rasmussen, 2004), thus far, there are spaces to which to migrate, and many oasis gardeners have expanded into areas that were formerly pastureland or desert dried riverbeds.

In all this turmoil, *inaden*, unlike the artisans or alleged *buda* people in Amhara communities, and also unlike the Buzu and Bella former slaves in their

Tuareg society, are not officially barred from owning land. As already noted, in principle, *inaden* are supposed to be poor and own fewer herds, but, as also shown, this is flexible and some *inaden* in fact own herds. Unlike the Amhara aristocrats, many Tuareg aristocrats still tend to disdain farming and prefer livestock herding. Among those Tuareg of aristocratic origin who do not disdain this occupation, for example many Kel Ewey around Mt. Bagzan in Niger, oasis gardening lands are becoming very scarce, and significantly, there are sharp tensions between smith/artisans and some aristocratic, chiefly families there which approach, but do not quite reach, the degree of negativity in the Amhara case. Occasionally, violence has broken out in gardening land disputes in the Air region; hence some parallels in the socioeconomic bases of tensions between more sedentarized Tuareg oasis communities and the Amhara landownership pattern, though I am not arguing here that this is the sole cause of beliefs in smiths' malevolent powers. For as already shown, hegemonic religious factors are also at play. Yet property relationships are also significant. Among more sedentarized Tuareg today on oases, where land for gardening is becoming scarce, tensions between *inaden* and their aristocratic patrons have heightened, with many *inaden*, as noted, nowadays turning to gardening, as well as retaining their artisan skills, and in some cases, selling their art works more widely. Following the French manumission of slaves and the turning of oasis gardens over to them, anyone (of diverse social origins) could start a new garden on empty land. But now, one must purchase land to garden, and plots tend to become smaller and smaller over time.

Thus there are both similarities and differences between the Tuareg case and the Amhara case. An additional point of contrast with the Amhara case besides the nomadic/sedentarized difference is that, among the Tuareg, *inaden* have had other options for occupations that, until recently, were stigmatized by Tuareg nobles, and/or involved properties that were owned and/or whose labor was controlled by them. As soon as the oasis gardens in the Sahara were turned over to slaves manumitted early in the 20th century, occupational alternatives expanded for many Tuareg: for *inaden*, as well as for former slaves and clients of various degrees, new occupational opportunities opened up. Smiths, along with former slaves, were in fact the first to take up once-stigmatized occupations such as tailoring and gardening. Nobles only reluctantly followed, in the wake of a series of droughts which devastated their livestock herds, which are more difficult than gardens to reconstitute.

The Ethiopian case in some respects contrasts socio-economically, but as we shall soon see, in other ways resembles the Tuareg case in some aspects of property relations, and is similar, though not identical to it in religious patterns and ritual roles of smith/artisans (differences between Islam and Coptic Christianity notwithstanding). In Ethiopia, land ownership was until the Ethiopean Marxist Revolution in the 1970's more based in a more entrenched and longterm sedentarized local aristocracy, and the "feudal" system revolved around this (Donham, 1998), rather than a more nomadic Tuareg aristocracy who only occasionally came into the oases and towns to collect tribute/tithe, rents, and taxes (Bernus, 1981; Keenan, 1976; Rasmussen, 1995).

In Ethiopia after the 1974 Revolution, discrimination against artisans and other persons defined as of "lower" status was officially banned by the Marxist Derg regime (Donham, 1998; Mains, 2007). Nonetheless, at the time of Mains's recent research (2003-05), youthful informants claimed that a powerful stigma is still present (Mains, 2007:661), and classified some occupations which resembled artisan-work together under the same "stigmatized" rubric, including even welding, since this work is also with metal.

Thus on one level, it is metal that is key to many beliefs concerning the ambiguity and peripherality of smiths. In Ethiopia, these metal-related occupations are referred to by the same pejorative terms, having to do with dirt/pollution and cultural values surrounding smiths' social and ritual roles, their alleged lack of shame in working metal, and that is locally called "lower work." Why metal? What is its connection to local religious concepts?

Although the Ethiopian Amhara are predominantly Coptic Orthodox Christians, rather than Muslims, the common threads between these societies, I argue, is a submerged discourse of cultural contradictions between older African indigenous religions and conversion-based, "official" organized religion. Metal, I soon show, is a prominent motif in mythico-histories symbolizing local ambivalence toward smith/artisans in their ritual—not solely technical—roles. Mains reports that these occupations, even if lucrative economically, are still shunned by many Amhara for another reason: because of their association with a cultural value called *vilunnta*, "the fear of what others might think or say about one or one's family if one seen performing this type of work" (Mains, 2007:661). But this author does not pursue the broader implications of this, nor does he explore the ritual aspects of this belief complex surrounding the *budas'* alleged *q'alb* power.

Fundamental to understanding some parallels between the ritual powers of Tuareg and Amhara specialists, is a closer comparison of their similar cultural values and the relations between these specialists and non-smiths, their practice of forging iron, and local religious mythico-histories. What is so shameful about working metal? Why is lack of reserve a trait of smiths?

I find that *vilunnta* approximates *takarakit* among the Tuareg. In both cases, reserve, shame, or public face and respectful, dignified conduct distinguish non-smiths—in particular, nobles--from smiths in occupational choice. But in the Tuareg case, recall, *inaden* do not feel that having *takarakit* is always a positive trait, for as shown, it actually constrains nobles; whereas it is precisely this lack of *takarakit* that for *inaden*, is enabling: it defines their distinctiveness as a group, and facilitates their working for nobles in ways that make nobles dependent upon, rather than superior to, them. Yet recall also the strong hints, in my data, of change in this value: recall the urban smith/artisan youth who disdained his rural counterparts dancing and comically "hopping around," particularly their performing a signature dance, called scratching for lice, in their praise-singing. Recall also the comments of some elderly rural smith/artisans to me, that nowadays, no one has reserve, shame, or respect, and that some nobles fight back upon smiths' performing the *albourousa* ritual protest.

Mains's and other researchers' descriptions taken together—especially the work in the more rural areas by Reminick—yield vivid insights into the perspectives of the officially dominant parties to these relationships. This "official" perspective, though limited, sheds much light on the connections between witchcraft-related accusations, exclusionary projects, and power relations. Mains, for example, reports that to higher-status Amhara, "working at lower-rung occupations is felt to be placing oneself at the bottom of relations of authority" (Mains, 2007:661). From this material, only the smith/artisans seem to be subject to insults, negative stereotypes, such as being called a thief, and being uninvited to important social events , such as weddings in urban context (Mains, 2007:662). But it is also instructive to explore resistance or "classifying back" on the part of the alleged "witch." I found that despite some social tensions and asymmetry, the Tuareg client-patron relationship, in both rural and urban communities, is much more reciprocal: ideally, at least, both nobles and *inaden* joke and mutually insult each other, as "fictive cousins." Both parties emphasize this ideal in conversation, interviews, and often act in that manner. The observance of respect or deference, as well as familiar joking, in nominally hierarchical social relations has diverse meanings and consequences, according to immediate social context, as well as over longer term.

In urban Ethiopia, Mains argues that artisan-like occupations are not seen as a choice, and therefore are denigrating. The *demibena* relationship, a client-patron like relationship of mutual dependency and equality, is important "only in the immediate transaction context" (Mains, 2007:662). For this reason, Mains argues, many Ethiopian young men shun even lucrative employment that is stigmatized in the urban sector. Among the Tuareg, as shown, client-patron relationships were much more long-term, and they encompassed multiple other contexts—not solely transactions involving material culture—that is, the buying and selling of their art objects and tools, but rather wider social and ritual life, between nobles and smiths. This is indeed changing in some more impersonal, market-driven customer contexts in the towns of Niger and Mali and abroad, but still, many *inaden* are benefiting from this, rather than suffering, in longterm relationships and monetary gain. Yet they consequently become vulnerable to nobles' and other smiths' envy over the economic success of smiths' new roles. Also, in contrast to the Ethiopian case, a few Tuareg nobles are even taking up work of the forge, though significantly, these persons encounter some disapproval from both smiths and nobles.

These contrasts also have to do with divergent historical patterns of rural/urban differences. Mains's findings, interesting as they are, derive primarily from urban research. Had I only worked among *inaden* in the towns of Niger and Mali, I never would have seen much beyond the economic transactional context, which dominates there; I would have only glimpsed at the profound social and ritual aspects to their roles. Nor would I have seen the intimacy of the client-patron relationship, even as they change, in the countryside. For example, youths in Agadez had never heard of the *albourousa* rite, and adults there believed it no longer ever occurred—but in the countryside, I found otherwise.

In urban Ethiopia, it was in fact with the growth of permanent cities that notions of occupational status began to develop beyond traditional stigmas applied to artisans (Mains, 2007:663). There was expansion of northern settlers into southern Ethiopia and consequent appropriation of land in the late 19th and early 20th centuries (Donham, 1986). In the Jimma region, for example, individuals who received land after the Italian occupation expanded their wealth through farming and trade. The pattern was to have a large piece of land in the countryside and also a home in the city. Money from the sale of coffee funded the building of a house in the city and engagement in trade.

By contrast, Tuareg society has always been predominantly rural, with nomadism and caravanning trading expeditions sometimes entering towns to the South for varying time periods, usually seasonally during the cool, dry caravanning season, and also in times of ecological disaster, such as drought (Baier and Lovejoy, 1977), when nobles traditionally had privileges of shelter and lodgings with client peoples. But these sojourns were usually temporary; most Tuareg, in fact, still yearn for eventual return to the rural Sahara, and even today, many drought refugees, political exiles, labor migrants, students abroad, and expatriates express this preference, and Tamajaq-speaking residents of Saharan towns such as Agadez and Kidal usually have other work, properties, and relatives in the countryside, and are absent part of the year from town in their "home" rural communities. Many Tuareg—particularly those of noble descent—complain that in the towns, they feel more pressured to drop what they view as important customs, such as their Tamajaq language and men's face-veiling.

In fact, among many Tuareg, it is sedentarization and urbanization that are associated with "lower" status within Tuareg society (clients and slaves) and the "otherness" of ethnic outsiders (for example, the Hausa). Even the *amenukal* leader of the Ifoghas confederation, who was relocated to Kidal by the French colonial forces and the Malian post-colonial government, still regards home as the rural desert region around Tin Essako to the east—he and his family travel there whenever possible. In fact, Kidal—a town of approximately 20,000— remains largely semi-nomadic. Cultural preference is not the sole reason for this pattern. Armed conflicts between Tuareg rebel/dissidents and national armies also periodically propel many town residents away, to refugee camps. Thus there is a very different orientation toward land and land-ownership in the Tuareg case.

Another condition relevant to smiths' more denigrated status and allegedly malevolent power in Ethiopia involved the creation of a wealthy land-owning class, especially in the Jimma region, which attracted others to the city. Many moved to the city in search of wage labor for that class. New migrants found mostly menial labor there. The prestige and desirability of government jobs from 1941 onward in the city then developed in Jimma, and remained based on the traditional hierarchical relationship between the nobility and farmers. The government administrator replaced the authority of the *gult*-holding lord, and education took the place of military activity as means for accessing social mobility (Mains, 2007:663).

Thus in socioeconomic transformations in Ethiopia, there arose an occupational hierarchy between those with and those without government work. Government workers had both political and economic power, whereas others generally performed service work and manual labor ; to some extent, a patron-client relationship existed between those two strata(Mains, 2007:663). In much same manner that a rural lord could provide access to land, government administrators and landowners could give their clients urban employment, better housing, and other opportunities. The revolutionary Derg regime (1974-1991) under Mengistu eliminated most opportunities to accumulate wealth through private enterprise, which caused the value of government work to further increase. For parents who came of age earlier under then-Emperor Haile Sellasie, education had been the key; at that time, class sizes were smaller and educational quality was higher, and secondary graduates were guaranteed government jobs (Mains, 2007:663).

Later, from the Derg expansion of education but also its decline in quality, unemployment has increased from declining educational quality and the large educated youth population. Furthermore, government jobs from neo-liberal economic privatization reforms and post-revolution have diminished. Hence the gap now between youths' aspirations and their probable life opportunities.(Mains, 2007:664). But many middle-class young men have social networks to support them, and still disdain stigmatized work such as smithing and welding.

Freeman and Plankhurst (2003) argue that the roots of occupational stigma are found in local movements of people and relations of dominance, rather than in the symbolic qualities of production and transformation associated by other researchers with blacksmithing and other artisan occupations (Herbert, 1993; McNaughton, 1988). Yet I warn against any rigidly positivistic mono-causal or "chicken-or-egg" explanation. Mains found that how one treated workers in lower occupations varied with the quality of one's social relationships with them. Yet even in that urban setting, for most youths, their greater purchasing power did not bring social respect at their community level (Mains, 2007: note 7, page 671).

Similarly, for most economically successful *inaden* I studied, —whether rural or urban,--there were also continuing ambivalent attitudes from non-smiths, regardless of, or perhaps even more so with their more prosperous socioeconomic success. What resulted for many successful inaden in towns of Niger and Mali, in fact, were increased, rather than decreased, suspicions toward them: both from non-smiths over their alleged *tezma*, and from other smiths over their alleged sorcery and negative gossip. *Tezma* remained more associated with smith/artisans by not solely non-smiths, but also by most smiths themselves, though a few mentioned that others are capable of this power, yet only smiths are blamed for it.

The point here is that, in Ethiopia as well as in northern Niger and Mali, economic success enabling one to slip away from official aristocratic patron dominance and from a more face-to-face, intimate, and small-scale community does not guarantee that one escapes from other dangers. Thus there are additional cultural factors making the status of smith/artisans and their ritual powers distinct from other ambiguous or "low"-status occupations, such as slavery, that in economic mobility find less social ambivalence. Indeed, in the towns of northern Niger and Mali, there is some intermarriage between former slaves and persons of other social origins, but much more rarely between smith/artisans and persons of other social origins.

Thus something imbues this specialism with distinctive social attributes beyond strictly economic occupational attributes. This was shown vividly in Ethiopia, in the fact that the stigma of those occupations resembling smiths' occupations (welding, shoe-repairing, etc.), although more flexible in their social connotations, still tended to be modeled on the smith "stigma." In other words, the new stigma of the shoe-repair person or welder was derivative of (though not identical to) the old stigma of the iron-worker, potter, or weaver— but most of all, the iron-worker. For in Africa, as Herbert has pointed out (Herbert, 1993), iron was intimately connected to the older African indigenous religious tradition of smelting, a dangerous activity surrounded by taboos. In my view, these different processes—of material dominance and symbolic capital— need not, indeed cannot be, viewed as mutually exclusive; rather, they intertwine and overlap in their mutual influences. I insist upon the simultaneity of the meaningful and the material, whose confluence and mutual construction are particularly striking in smith/artisans who are also ritual specialists. I also argue that additional factors are at play in shaping the alternately positive and negative definitions of African smiths' powers, which need closer analysis: namely, the relative influence on the long-standing cosmology surrounding smiths' powers, of "official" scriptural/textual/ state-sponsored religions such as Christianity (in Ethiopia, for example) and Islam (in Tuareg communities of northern Niger and Mali, and in Bidan communities of Mauritania, for example) upon the longstanding cosmology surrounding smiths' powers. The presence or absence of religious tolerance or intolerance powerfully shapes some attitudes toward smiths and their ritual powers. Notably, among the Kapsiki in Cameroon, indigenous African religion remains strongest, and among the Mande-speaking people of Mali, an intermediate case here, indigenous religion persists prominently alongside Islam.

There are hints that smiths once occupied a ritual space much more powerful in the older, pre-Islamic and pre-Christian eras, but with the coming of these religions, their roles and relationships—particularly among the Bidan and the Amhara—became more ambiguous, and attitudes toward their powers became more ambivalent and negatively-tinged. Whereas by contrast, as soon shown, among the Kapsiki and the Mande, ambivalence and ambiguity are also present, but smiths' powers nonetheless retain more positive dimensions, they appear less stigmatized and scapegoated, and their older ritual roles have not diminished as much—indeed, they continue to perform important functions in life cycle-related events—particularly circumcision of youths and officiating at funerals. Recall that the Tuareg *inaden* perform as praise-singers and food-servers at noble namedays and weddings but significantly, do not officiate or perform at funerals, suggesting that *inaden*'s roles have become more attenuated, and evoke mnemonically an earlier, previously more extended function that has now been forgotten in the mists of time—or suppressed by other religious authorities.

In examining beliefs in alleged *q'alb* powers of the *buda,* predominantly artisan groups in relation to religion and symbolism in the Ethiopian Amhara context, it is instructive to turn to rural communities. Many Amhara of rural Ethiopia hold to the "evil eye" belief called *q'alb*, which is connected to the status of allegedly "evil eye" *buda* people, mostly smiths. Like Tuareg *inaden*, they are of a different origin, but unlike Tuareg *inaden*, engage in rather minimal interaction with the Amhara people. It is for this reason, and also because *Buda* own no land, that they work as artisans, sculpting pots from clay, forging tools from iron, and weaving cloth from hand-spun cotton and sheep's hair. *Buda*, "the evil eye people," are also known as *tayb*. This term is derived from the noun *tebib,* which denotes "craftsperson," in Reminick's translation (Reminick, 1974:280). Yet significantly, this term is also associated with the verb denoting "to be wise or to be very clever."

Striking here are the connections, not noted by Reminick, between knowledge and power, and the idea that this power can be used for good or ill. This terminology suggests that factors beyond literal occupation and official dominance shape attitudes toward *buda* evil eye smiths and their alleged, more complex power of *q'alb*. These factors, I argue, are related to, not solely the property issues discussed in the foregoing section, but also the exclusionary projects of official, scriptural, state-sponsored organized religion: in Ethiopia, Coptic Christianity and its priests.

In rural Manze Amhara communities, "to be a *buda* is to have the evil eye" (Reminick, 1974:280), but in my view, there are hints of finer distinctions and interconnections among positive and negative powers. The term evil eye is also known as *qalb*, as *ayn og,* and sometimes *kifu ayn.* Q'alb generally designates the power to curse, destroy, and reincarnate—particularly to harness the labor of the dead for one's own ends. The beautiful craftsmanship of the *buda*'s work, paradoxically, is also one sign of his/her status: finely made, well-proportioned water pots with their black finish are unmatched by any rare Amhara "peasant" (i.e., farmer or aristocratic landowner) who would dare to make on one.

Importantly, fashioning tools from iron takes even more skill, and only the Buda tayb smith/artisans practice this art. Again, the role of metalworking stands out in Reminick's, as well as others' descriptions (Berland and Rao, 2004; Herbert, 1993; Mains, 2007), as crucially a sign of "smithness." Although weaving is also associated with *tayb/buda* people, many Manze Amhara peasants have also taken up this skill, not as an inherited trade, but to accumulate needed cash. The non-smiths insist that *buda* or *tayb* people who are artisans by descent know a special form of weaving that Amhara cannot learn. Thus a critical distinction made by Amhara that frees him/her from this stigma of artisanry is that he/she did not inherit this (artisan) trade from his/her father (Reminick, 1974:281). This finding resonates with some more recent findings in urban centers, suggesting that changes in these attitudes toward *tayb* do not always occur in cities.

Most Amhara trace their lineages patrilineally to a close relative or ancestor who had wealth and status, and who was the patron of many who worked the land of their estates. This *rega* or aristocratic landowner's genealogy is known by the community; his relatives and ancestors are known, and for this reason, the *rega* is less likely be suspected of being impure (Reminick, 1974:281). The *buda/tayb* (as noted, not always equivalent, but overlapping in identities) may inherit status through either the mother's or father's line, or both. Thus one cannot avoid the status of *buda.*

Amhara trace the mythico-history of the origin of the *buda* "evil eye" people back to the Creation. Eve had thirty children, and one day God asked Eve to show Him her children. Eve became suspicious and apprehensive, and hid fifteen of them from the sight of God. God knew her act of disobedience, and declared the fifteen children she showed God as his chosen children, and cursed the fifteen she hid, declaring that they would go henceforth into the world as devils and wretched creatures of the earth. Some of the children complained and begged God's mercy. So God, merciful, transformed some of the hidden children into animals so that they might exist with dignity. God left others among the hidden children human, but sent them away with his curse as agents of the devil. These human counterparts of the devil are ancestors of the *Buda* people (Reminick, 1974:286).

Another mythico-history centers on a Christian theme, when Christ was baptized at the age of thirty, related by an old Amhara peasant farmer, which I paraphrase here: the angry devils, envious of God's favoring Christ while they suffered God's curse, tried to kill Christ. But Christ ran, and fled his enemies. He hid in the crevice of a great cliff. While hidden, many children were killed by the devils (spirits) in their search for God's child, but they were unsuccessful in finding Christ. All the animals were asked to betray the whereabouts of Christ, but they refused. But a lizard in the crevice with Christ waved his head from side to side showing Christ's pursuers where he hid. Christ saw this and cursed the lizard. No one could get Christ down out of the crevice in the cliff. Then, the clever *Buda* people made giant tongs of wood and plucked Jesus Christ out of the crevice. The *buda/tayb* blacksmiths also made the nails, and the carpenters made the cross, and while Christ hung on the cross, he cursed those people whose skills made it possible to crucify him. (Reminick, 1974:286).

Although someTuareg motifs portray the *inaden* as closer to the spirit world and less observant of Islam, the latter do not blame smiths, but rather, attempt to show their complementary roles to "official" religion—Islam among Tuareg.

In the Amhara case, however, Reminick did not include a *buda* voice or variant responding to, contesting, or re-interpreting the motif of betraying Christ. Thus it is difficult to ascertain the budas' own perspectives on this theme. Yet the Amhara variant is nonetheless instructive; for it reveals the so-called "evil eye" power as part of the exclusionary project of the hegemony of organized religion, and also offers striking parallels with the persecution of Muslims, Jews, and alleged "witches"—whether midwives or herbalists—and other persons in medieval Europe by the Church under the Inquisition.

In the Tuareg case, as shown, *inaden* mythico-histories I collected also featured some motifs emphasizing their ambiguous religious origins, ambivalent relationships to the Prophet Mohammed, and their ties to Dauda. But in these motifs, the *inaden* are portrayed more positively as peace-makers and ambassadors, as hiding from battle, rather than betraying the Prophet. Recall, also, that some accounts revealed competition and tension between *inaden* and Islamic scholars. Thus the Tuareg motif reveals more multiplex and nuanced relationships between *inaden* and Islam, on the one hand, and *inaden* and nobles, on the other, than those Reminick collected in rural Ethiopia. In both relationships within Tuareg society, smiths emerge as able to negotiate and mediate precisely because of, not in spite of, their marginality. This fact of their positive value was emphasized to me over and over again by both smiths and non-smiths. Whereas in rural Amhara society, the more positive mediating roles of the *buda/tayb* people tend to be de-emphasized at their expense.

Yet the Ethiopian material does include some disagreement about the buda origins. For example, some Amhara contended that the devil is the sole source of *buda* qualities and *q'alb* power, but others claimed the origin of *buda* existence is "different from the source of their power" (Reminick, 1974:286). In other words, there are hints of contestation and manipulation of mythico-history here. Although their existence is associated with the Devil, their power comes from a different source "only questionably related to the devil" (Reminick 1974:286). Consider, for example, this origin given by an Amhara, which I paraphrase here: The source of *buda* power is an ancient man who has immortality. He has no arms and no legs, like a lump of flesh, and just sits at a place called Yerimma, which is a cave of extremely great depth. He is indeed, endowed with supernatural (superhuman) powers. Each year, the *buda* people make their annual visit to this lump of man with their small children, who are just learning to walk and to talk. This ancient man can distinguish between the *rega* aristocrats who may come and the *buda* themselves. He rejects the former, and accepts the latter. The ancient man then teaches the *buda* children all the arts in the *buda* (artisan) trade, and then presents the child with the leaf from the anis plant (also used by spirits to make themselves invisible so as to avoid being eaten by the hyena). And every year, each *buda* must make a human sacrifice to this ancient man. The sacrifice is like a tax, and if the *buda* cannot find a suitable victim by the time the sacrifice is due, he must sacrifice his own child (Reminick, 1974:286).

In this account, there is an inversion of the Biblical theme of Abraham's sacrifice. Thus these *buda* mythico-histories emphasize the outsider status of the *buda* in their origins, and more: their alleged reversal of the rituals of organized Judeo-Christian religions. Again, there are some parallels with the Tuareg imagery of inversion/reversals surrounding *inaden* symbolism, as in smiths' favoring of the left side in rituals and dances, and their livestock brands which are viewed as "twisted" versions of the brands of nobles. But this design in fact resembles a prominent ritual symbol widespread in African religions: of the crossroads (Stoller and Coombs, 1994), a term rendered in Tamajaq by *temlilif.* Inaden themselves emphasize this positive crossroads quality more than the negative "distorted" or "twisted" quality, thereby underlining their mediating role. This view suggests that, as in the *buda* case, there are multiple dimensions of inversions associated with smiths and these may be re-interpreted to either reinforce or refute the hegemony of the "official" religion. In a similar vein, many Tuareg Islamic scholars consider the left side to be "un-Islamic." Children are discouraged from writing with the left hand, for example. But the Tuareg mythico-histories and symbolism, even in their interpretations by nobles, do not go quite as far as the Amhara mythico-histories in "demonizing" smiths. Only a brief motif associates *inaden* with the Devil (called Iblis); they are more often associated with spirits, who vary in their temperaments. This association conveys Tuareg smiths' interstitial position in two respects: first, their ambiguous relationship to Islam; and secondly, their connections with a cosmological spirit order widespread in indigenous African religious, of a world of spirits intermediate between a high deity-like figure (e.g., Chukwu among the Ibo, Kwoth among the Nuer) distant from humans and the human social world (Achebe, 1958; Evans-Pritchard, 1937, 1950; Leinhardt, 1966; Middleton, 1960).

In an Amhara community, anyone whose ancestors are unknown may be suspected of possessing the power of "evil eye" or *q'alb*. Many Amhara *rega* believe that *buda/tayb* may be thinner than usual, because their blood is believed to be thinner than a non-buda Amhara person's blood. A *buda/tayb* may tend to look sidewise at people, may have an eye deformity, or may suffer a discharge of tears or pus from the eyes, metaphorical or iconic images of *q'alb*. Or he/she may have a very light complexion, widely interpreted as having an ashen substance in their mouths, and allegedly unable to spit saliva (Reminick, 1974:280). If a stranger comes to town and is overly friendly, suspicion may be aroused that he/she is too eager to befriend others and hence, possibly over-anxious about concealing their true identity.

Relations between *buda* and *rega* are ideally neither overly peaceful nor overly combative. They mix with each other socially without repercussions, as long as their relations are on a "superficial" basis, for example, they must not marry. The endogamy here is widely practiced by smith/artisan specialists throughout Africa and beyond, although in the Amhara case, the reasons for this practice differ from the reasons offered by Tuareg *inaden* to me: the latter asserted that, along with their lack of reserve, their endogamy enabled them to mediate and also assist their noble patrons in marriage and bridewealth negotiations.

In Ethiopia, there is an ever-present possibility of attack by the *buda's q'alb*. Most rural Amhara are fearful of even mentioning *buda*, especially at night, because if they are overheard by a *buda*, he/she will become angry, and target one's family, causing sickness or death. A person is most vulnerable to being eaten when a Buda sees fear, worry, or anxiety in their potential victim (Reminick, 1974:281). Therefore, it helps to maintain one's composure when in the presence of a *buda*. Someone who is especially good-looking or whose child is considered beautiful, or someone who does something extraordinary, may also become a target of evil eye because of envy believed to be kindled in the *buda*. The *q'alb* attack is not limited to human beings, however: evil eye can attack any living object, for example, livestock as among the Tuareg. It is believed that when one is feeling ill, the body is more vulnerable than ever to an attack by evil eye.

The evil eye attack may occur in one of several different manners. Because of the power of evil eye, *buda* people can change into hyenas and roam the countryside at night. It is convenient to attack a victim in this form in order to conceal his/her human identity. This recalls the idea of Tuareg smiths' association with hyenas, expressed by their props of sandals worn behind the ears in their *albourousa* ritual. Both peoples attach great significance to the hyena. In both these societies, many believe that the hyena can change its sex intermittently.

These beliefs in both societies convey the ambiguous, transformative identity and bridging role of this animal, transposed onto the smith's shape-shifting and socially mediating role which takes on, alternately valuable and disquieting aspects, which among the Tuareg, tend to be more balanced, and among the Amhara, tend toward the negative polarity. Many Amhara also attach great salience to the hyena, partly because they believe in both natural and superhuman (i.e. animal and human shape-shifting) forms of this animal. If the *buda*, in searching for a victim, assumes the form of a hyena, this transformation takes place by his first taking off the hair, and then rolling in ashes of the hearth Once transformed into a hyena, he/she then searches for a victim, and upon finding one, "fixes this unfortunate person with an evil gaze, returns home, rolls in the ashes to return to human form, and waits for the victim to die" (Reminick, 1974:282). The second method of attack involves the evil eye perpetrator finding a victim, twisting the root of a certain plant, and forming a loop with the root "as if one were tying a knot" (Reminick, 1974:282). While this is being done, the victim dies. After the victim is buried, the Buda squats by the graveside and slowly loosens the knot while shouting to corpse to arise. The body is exhumed, and the grave is then closed up again by retightening the knot.This practice recalls *darme* and related "sorcery-like" practices feared in rural Hausa communities in Niger, analyzed by Masquellier (2001), and this author connects this to cases of social conflict indicate the presence of envy. Implied in the Amhara case, therefore, is fear of the dual power of smiths to both open up channels of communication, and alternately, close them or block them. In other words, in my view there is more to the alleged powers of smiths than destruction, though they may be used for those purposes. Different residents tend to emphasize more the positive or more the negative in these powers

The third method of a *buda's q'alb* attack involves aiming an evil eye gaze at the victim, and then waiting for his/her death. After burial, the *buda/tayb* unfolds one piece of flatbread to open the grave and brings out the body. Folding up the other re-closes the grave. Again, what I find noteworthy here is the metaphorical imagery surrounding the alleged *q'alb* powers: many of these tropes allude to the interstitial and inside-outside positioning, or anomalous and liminal practices of smiths: for example, in the open-closed, gustatory, and visual tropes.

People believed to be most liable to be attacked are "those who have a bit more wealth than the average person, who are handsome, and who are proud of their beautiful children" (Reminick, 1974:282). In witchcraft accusations in

European history (MacFarlane in Parkin, 1985), similarly, accused witches were often those who had neither too much nor too little property, but had some wealth.

In Ethiopia, those who become especially liable to be attacked are those who become too familiar with a *Buda* person, which heightens one's chances of succumbing to the gaze of evil eye. Amhara *rega* may come into physical proximity with *Buda* people in daily affairs, but social distance is usually maintained. As in some Tuareg *tezma* cases, anxieties over sexual taboo-breaking and pollution are present. A likely danger to *rega* nobles is the presence of a beautiful *buda* woman or handsome *buda* man. A *rega* who sleeps with a *buda* will grow thinner and thinner because, allegedly, the eye of the buda will suck the blood out of the victim, causing the victim to lose his or her appetite and become weak and helpless.

The ultimate goal of the b*uda/tayb* is to use the victim as a slave (recalling some *voudou*-related "zombie" beliefs in Haiti). After being exhumed, the corpse is taken to the house of the *buda* where it is brought back to life in order to serve the *buda*. But again, as in some voudou-related beliefs, this slave is mute, unable to utter a single sound. The *buda* owns two switches. One switch is used to turn the slave into a pot when visitors come; and when outsiders have left, the perpetrator raps on the pot with the other switch, which transforms the pot into a slave again (Reminick, 1974:283). In this way, outside interference is prevented. When the slave is treated cruelly, he/she will shed silent tears, desperately trying to weep. Reminick notes here that to be silent in the presence of one's superiors and to suffer indignities in silence is "an obligation of children and a trait of dogs". (Reminick, 1974:283). After seven years, the body begins to disintegrate, finally turning into ashes and leaving the enslaver without a helper.

In this concept of servitude through a *buda/tayb*'s evil-eye based power of *q'alb,* there is an inversion of the usual client-patron relationship between the land-owning aristocratic *rega* and the smith/artisan: the *rega* is the one who is threatened with servitude, and the buda is the one who makes the rega work for him/her. In contrast to the Tuareg stories didactically emphasizing how, despite some social tensions, the *imajeghen* Tuareg nobles need the *inaden* smiths, these Amhara themes convey greater fear that the power relations between *rega* and *buda* may be reversed.

Yet like the *inaden*'s alleged *tezma* power, the *buda/tayb*'s *q'alb* power is not completely intentional. *Q'alb* can be a subtle, internal, unconscious desire to perform those activities which make a *buda* so notorious (Reminick, 1974:283). In the *buda*'s daily interactions with the aristocratic *rega* in their still largely stratified yet close-knit rural communities, however, there is really little difference between the two groups. But in rural Amhara communities, this additional power of inadvertent, unintentional, and unconscious desire is widely attributed to these smith/artisan specialists' association with the Devil. This diabolical connection is highly significant; it is believed to confer the specialist an illegitimate advantage over those of higher status (i.e., the rega landowning nobles), who have traditionally held greater legitimate or official authority (Reminick, 1974:283), at least in the pre-Derg Revolution eras. At the time of Reminick's research just prior to the Marxist land reforms, many Amhara *rega* nobles enjoyed a monopoly over land, labor, and products (Donham, 1997). Many accused the *buda/tayb* of attempting to acquire those objects, persons, and services that they coveted from the aristocratic overlords (Reminick, 1974:283).

Even in post-Derg times of socioeconomic transformation, and in the towns of Ethiopia, many persons still regard the artisan professions ambivalently (Freeman and Plankhurst, 2003; Mains, 2007). This attitude is undoubtedly a vestige of the more longstanding client-patron stratified order in the countryside, where many (though of course, not all) persons still believe that the *buda* must be avoided, since they "eat" others in order to better their chances for gaining opportunities and achieving success in daily life among *rega*. The interconnections within the Ethiopian case are clear. These Amhara attitudes somewhat recall the Tuareg case, in those attitudes of some rural and urban non-smiths toward a few more prosperous *inaden* they believed to be "illegitimately" imitating nobles in their dress and habits. They also recall the noble men's reaction to the very prosperous smith who gardened and tailored in his rural community, and also worked for Europeans in the capital city. But *inaden* are not considered anti-Islamic outright; rather, they were more described, and sometimes viewed themselves, as more "lax" in practicing Islam, and as having allegiances more to the ancient indigenous Tuareg religious spirit pantheon, as well as to another Prophet, Dauda, rather than the Prophet Mohammed. Hence the abjectness of their status in this context was not as diametrically opposed to the official, scriptural organized Islam as much as the status of the *tayb/buda* people was opposed to official, scriptural organized Coptic Christianity.

Amhara differ as to whether or not the *buda* people themselves can become a victims of evil eye attacks. Some Amhara insist that, just as *rega* fight among selves for wealth of the lineage, so *buda* people (also) fight and attack each other with evil eye for more equal shares of wealth. But other Amhara deny that, and insist that *buda* had much more to gain from *rega*, and furthermore, surmise that those allegedly possessing this power know how to protect themselves from each other's attacks.

Coptic Orthodox Christian priests teach that one's only protection against a *Buda* lover is to crawl to church on one's hands and knees for seven days. Parents who fear their child is weak and vulnerable to the influence of evil eye on the advice of a clergyman called *dabtara,* address the child in a gender opposite to the child's actual sex. Or parents shave their children's hair, leaving only a tuft of hair over the former fontanel of boys and a ring of hair around the heads of girls, or rapidly spit into the child's face. Compliments are always suspect if not accompanied with the invocation, "Let God protect you from evil eye!" (Reminick, 1974:284). At feasts, all persons must be served equally, lest someone deprived become envious and curse the food, making participants sick. This recalls the Tuareg case of the child's stomach *karambaza* believed caused by the smith woman who had been denied the wedding meat.

Another precaution against *q'alb* by Amhara is to be silent and guarded. When one expresses one's emotions too freely and becomes too outgoing with others, places self in a position of vulnerability to evil eye (Reminick, 1974:284). Tuareg of aristocratic origin, similarly, also promote verbal restraint in an important cultural and aesthetic ideal, called "shadowy speech," metaphor, or *tangalt* (Casajus, 2000). On the other hand, as already noted, there is also an important joking relationship between Tuareg nobles and smiths, which features much relaxed, familiar teasing which is reciprocal; nobles, in fact, reciprocally sing praise-songs at smith weddings. By contrast, among the Amhara aristocracy, laughing and joking freely with others occurs ideally with only close and trusted friends and relatives; at most other times, stolidity and silence are encouraged in order not to attract attention of an envious *buda*, who may resent those enjoying themselves while he/she is not invited to share in the mirth (Reminick, 1974:284). Yet Tuareg noble/smith joking relationships, for all their surface jocularity, also involve caution. One is supposed to avoid too much overt praise or direct statement of one's wishes and plans. One is not supposed to reveal one's true sentiments, for fear of others' envy or covetousness—this applies, however, to anyone, not solely nobles (Nicolaisen, 1961), and the latter drop reserve temporarily toward smiths as confidantes. Other parallels between the two cultural value systems are even more striking: the Amhara custom of concealing the face behind large soft cloak, concealing especially the mouth and nose, is one common way to avoid evil eye; this recalls one important meaning of the Tuareg noble men's face-veil/turban (Casajus, 1987; Claudot-Hawad, 1993; Murphy, 1964; Rasmussen, 1991; Rodd, 1926).

There are several means of diagnoses and cures of this malevolent power from the buda. If a person succumbs to an attack, the family of the deceased may intercede and prevent the *buda* from wresting the corpse from its grave. The family member must guard the grave for forty days and forty nights after the body has been interred, allowing sufficient time for the body to decompose, and thereby deprive the *buda/tayb* of a body to possess. If a family is poor and know a *dabtara* of a local church, they may take the patient to him. The patient drinks holy water and breathes in smoke of a burning root.

Another method is to bring the patient to a medium who has powers to communicate with *zar* spirits. A silver bracelet is placed on the patient's left wrist. The medium then enters trance, seeking possession by a spirit who may reveal an appropriate cure for the illness. In seeking out the attacker, a very hot fire is made in the hearth and a piece of metal, a sickle or knife, blade, is put into the flames and heated until glowing. It is applied to the patient's face, making a small pattern of burns. As the wounds heal, scars will become transferred onto the face of the attacker in the same place and with the same pattern. The family can then seek out the guilty party.

A third method involves an elder in the family. When someone begins biting his/her lip, this is the first sign of an attack by evil eye, although this symptom does not always appear. Relatives first tie the victim's left thumb with string. Then the victim breathes smoke from a dung fire, and thereby gains the power to speak in the spirit and voice of his attacker, and recounts the chain of events that led to the confrontation with his/her attacker and attack. Then the relatives ask the possessed victim what form of compensation should be given to counteract the attack. The victim then demands some filthy matter such as beer dregs, ashes, a dead rat, or excrement. The victim eats this and the voice of the *buda* who has inflicted the *q'alb* cries that he/she has left the victim.

The fourth method involves the suspected evil eye person in a more direct, psychosocial medico-ritual therapeutic technique. When this victim is attacked and begins to bite his/her lip and go into trance possession and jump and shout in tongues, a relative tries to get the victim to name the attacker. If he/she does not, the family ties a rope to the victim and has him/her lead the relatives to the house of the attacker, or if the victim begins crying suddenly, this is a sign that the attacker is in close proximity and that relatives must scout the area and seize the first buda person they come across, who must be brought to the bedside of the victim. Relatives take a lock of hair and a bit of clothing from the Buda, and then the Buda is compelled to spit on the victim and walk over him. A fire is built with the hair and cloth of the buda, and the victim then breathes in its smoke. He/she continues inhaling smoke until he/she cries, in the voice of a spirit, that illness has left the body.

The *buda/tayb* walking over the victim of *q'alb* power very closely resembles the Tuareg smith cure of jumping over the victim of *tezma* three times. In both cases, fire's role and significance are also similar: among the Tuareg, recall, the footprints of the suspected smith "perpetrator" are collected up from the sand, and thrown into a fire. In my view, the power of the forge and work with fire by these smiths are in effect re-appropriated, like a vaccination, toward the ends of repelling the smith's allegedly misused power in this circumstance. Also, the psycho-social impact of these methods directly involving the smiths is probably considerable; the presence of the suspected perpetrator at or near the bedside of the "victim" in effect, makes amends and repairs the damaged relationships. On the other hand, in Ethiopia, if the victim dies, the suspect may be ejected from the community or killed. Although I encountered cases of smiths accused of breaking sexual taboos (as in the accused adulterer) being ejected from the community, I never encountered cases of suspected *tezma* perpetrators being ejected from Tuareg communities, though the ethnographic and social historical records indicate occasional physical violence, including one killing, directed toward them in the past (Nicoliasen, 1961,1997).

BUDA/TAYB ROLES IN THEIR WIDER SOCIAL CONTEXT

The suspected evil-eye people who allegedly assert *q'alb* power are most often also smiths (*tayb*).   In the countryside, these attitudes remain prevalent, particularly in the central highlands of Shoa Province in Ethiopia. Amhara there are settled agriculturalists raising primarily barley, wheat, and a variety of beans.

The primary domain of authority within the larger political structure is the homestead, which varies from a nuclear family to a large hamlet of several related families and their servants, tenants, and former slaves. The institution of patiarchal authority is reinforced by a cultural emphasis on male qualities of aggressiveness oriented around acquisition and defense of land. In the countryside land has been traditionally the fundamental requirement of the old patriarchal system. But land, before and after the Marxist revolution, has always been a scarce resource, and there are often more claims to land than can be supported. (Donham, 1997). Thus closest siblings may unite against a more distant relative to maintain land among themselves or siblings may compete for scarce land among themselves, becoming bitter enemies and dividing the kinship or domestic group.

These social patterns are instructive; for they suggest the significance of nomadic/sedentarized differences in Tuareg attitudes toward *inaden*, and by implication, also suggest that the issue of land may by partly the reason for at least some hostilities toward smith/artisans and their alleged powers. As already noted, more nomadic Kel Ferwan Tuareg expressed some disapproval to me of some other Tuareg for their denigration of *inaden*. A Kel Ferwan aetiological mythico-history portrays the first smiths and nobles as originally two brothers who took up specialized but complementary occupations. Much more distant are relations between the Amhara *rega* nobles and the *tayb* smith/artisans in their communities, who do not share fictive kinship in their mythico-histories, except in the sense that the original children of the Creation split up. In the Tuareg case, their split led to complementary relationships, but in the Amhara case, the split led some to become outcasts. Thus there is a range of "otherness" constructed in attitudes toward these smith/artisans and their powers.

Douglas defined evil eye belief as "a special case of witchcraft belief which becomes expressed at critical social disjunctions between persons who hold structurally generated enmity toward each other" (1970:xxx). In his Amhara data, Reminick (1974:288) argued that Douglas's definition of a witch can be generalized to the Amhara's conception of evil eye people. In my view, this theory also illuminates some, but not all Tuareg non-smiths' conception of Tuareg smiths' power, and only in some contexts.

Moreover, I warn that, from the perspective of smiths themselves, as already shown in the *inaden* voices, these roles are not always so static or one-directional. Rather, the accuser can be the transgressor, constructing an "abject' social space, to use Butler's term, that endangers the accused "witch" or purveyor of "evil eye" powers, even as the accuser considers him or herself to be the "victim." But in social practice, it is often the accused "witch" who becomes the "victim" of scapegoating, very much recalling racism, religious intolerance, and other oppressive exclusionary projects.

The *buda/tayb* with internal and nearly uncontrollable powers are not conceived of as persons internal to the Amhara group, but as outsiders who nevertheless live geographically within Amhara-dominated regions, not as a close relative. Thus, the alleged *buda/tayb* power does not quite fit into any of categories that Douglas proposed (Reminick, 1974:288). However, as I have pointed out, nonetheless, these persons occupy an abject position as "Other," morally exiled from their original sin in the Creation and distanced from their aristocratic Amhara overlords in mythico-historical genealogy more than smiths in the Tuareg case, who despite their outside origins, tend to be more absorbed into Tuareg society as fictive cousins or brothers with whom one jokes. These positions are, I have shown, not static structural givens as Douglas would analyze them, but rather are constructed processes in collective memories and social practices, which emerge from religious and economic collisions.

Yet envy is undeniably a factor in so-called witchcraft and evil eye accusation practices, and merits closer examination. Spooner (1970:314) regarded evil eye belief in the Middle East as an "institutionalized psychological idiom for personification of misfortune,...insofar as misfortune, or fear of it, may relate to fear of outsiders and their envy." Foster (1972:167) in his classic study defined envy as "an act of looking maliciously upon someone; looking askance at; casting evil eye on; feeling displeasure and/or ill-will in relation to superiority or another person." Foster argued that envy, along with the closely associated feeling of jealousy, involves a dyad whose relationship is mediated, or structured, by an intervening property or object. Thus a jealous person is jealous of what he/she possesses and fears he/she might lose, while an envious person does not envy the thing, but rather envies the person who has it. Foster, rather too optimistically in my view, argued also that the function of this definition of envy, like some functionalist definitions of witchcraft, is to "eliminate or mitigate rivalry between persons in different categories of status or between persons in different social classes, thereby lubricating interclass and interpersonal transactions" (Foster, 1972:171). Foster considered the predisposition to envy most apparent in "peasant" societies—where land is an issue, or in what he called "deprivation societies" of scarce resources, where people hold on to images of limited good and where social interaction and transaction is defined and perceived as a zero-sum game, and where one's advantage derives from other's loss. In those societies, it is the relative differences between two parties that triggers omnipresently latent envy into overt expression. Food, children, health, most vital for survival of family, are the most frequent and widespread objects of envy, as are cattle and crops.

Yet I warn that envy can be experienced on both "sides" of accusations of malevolent powers; whereas much of the literature tends to emphasize the viewpoint of the accuser or of the "official" authorities. The value of these insights notwithstanding, there is still the need, in my view, to approach envy neither as a static structural attribute nor immutable, essentialized characteristic of a group, nor as a force in solely a "one-way" dyadic process, nor a strictly individual atomistic, psychological phenomenon. Rather, envy needs to be analyzed as a socially and politically constructed and deconstructed practice in the context of fluid and dynamic relationships, including apparent abjectness. To sum up the Amhara case in Ethiopia: The evil eye people are of non-Amhara identity, and hence can only pose a threat to Amhara by virtue of their being different as "Other". This difference, according to Reminick, (1974:290) is symbolic of what Amhara detest, fear, and dread. *buda* people are strangers to land of Amhara, albeit from the *rega* Amhara viewpoint—a caveat I add here, but which Reminick tended to downplay in his otherwise fascinating analysis. Yet what is significant is that in noble view, since evil eye people originated from a different region, they are landless, and must make a living with their manual technical and artistic skills of smithing, tanning, weaving, and pottery-making. The origin mythico-histories of smiths suspected to have *q'alb* and evil eye power express basic themes found in the local belief system, as well as in certain social situations: envy and conflict between siblings, who are treated differently by a superior patriarchal household authority, the core of Amhara household, are projected onto the larger social context of noble-smith relations. In the mythico-history, envy and conflict are generated by a curse of God for the sins of the mother Eve, in her hiding the children from God. Added to this is the Christian story of God's favoring of his child, Christ, the chosen son of God.

Yet I find it curious that the fictive sibling metaphor in Amhara communities is limited to conflict, but not extended to cooperation or joking relationships. Recall that some Tuareg of noble background assert their fictive kinship relationship with smith/artisans, tensions notwithstanding. Additional tensions come into play in the Amhara case since there are much greater tensions, traditionally, over scarce land. Whereas among the semi-nomadic Tuareg, even on oases, land-ownership has not been so central to noble-smith relationships until very recently, and even now, this is not so deeply entrenched in the local client-patron system, or even in the pre-colonial stratified system. In fact, land tensions were more central to Tuareg noble-slave relationships. Smiths have never been forbidden to own land in Tuareg society; rather, it was slaves in the past who were forbidden to do so, and slaves worked the oases gardens for more nomadic nobles who collected tribute from them.

Also key here is religion. The Amhara story of the envious siblings' hunting down of Christ to attain equality among siblings, Reminick reports, has a strong parallel in real-life situations where a father favors one child with more land, creating sibling conflict over equalization of their rights to their father's land (Reminick, 1974:290). The most serious concerns of Amhara involve sibling and other kin conflicts over unequal usufructory rights to land. Landless *buda/tayb*, dependent on others for a livelihood, symbolize the preoccupation in that society with the threat of becoming landless and without authority or identity, because of the ambitions of a more powerful relative or father's curse of disinheritance. This preoccupation receives metaphorical elaboration in the Creation aeiological mythico-history. In this author's view, there emerges a typification or stereotype of envious status inferiors using illegitimate means to gain an advantage over status superiors who possess a legitimate means of domination. Taken at this level, this belief is in effect, a projection of the *regas'* social relations within the household. But in my view, even more is at play here. For in addition to the patriarchal God in this Amhara motif, there is also the Devil, with whom the *buda/tayb*, not *rega,* are identified. Reminick, despite the valuable insights in his analysis, tends to overemphasize the psychological and de-emphasize the collective religious representations at play. The point is that the demonization of smiths by "official" religious authorities, in the Amhara case by the Ethiopian Coptic Christian priests and in the Tuareg case, to a lesser, more benign extent, by some Islamic scholar/marabouts, powerfully shapes conceptualizations of smiths' powers in societies where Christianity and Islam have come to dominate over indigenous ritual practices. Smiths' traditional ritual roles as smelters and forgers converting nature into culture was important in rituals pre-dating Christianity and Islam. In the three cross-cultural African cases I re-analyze next, there are even stronger indications of these themes.

CHAPTER FIVE

ECHAR POWER AND BIDAN *M'ALLEMIN* SMITH/ARTISANS

The relationships between the community of smiths called *m'allemin* and aristocratic Bidan (Maures or Moors) in Mauritania, neighbors of the Tuareg geographically, who also are Muslim, in their symbolism, beliefs, stratified social relations, and subsistence practices in some respects resemble these relationships in Tuareg society. Bidan or Moors speak a Hassaniya dialect of Arabic. These Bidan or Moor attitudes and practices concerning smiths and their powers are also similar, though not identical, to those of the Amhara in Ethiopia. The common translation of *m'allemin* as "blacksmiths" or *forgerons* (in French), is imprecise, and may even carry negative connotations, associated with "low" personal status. Moreover, like *inaden* among the Tuareg in Niger and Mali, *m'allemin* work not only iron, but also silver, leather and wood. Cervello (Cervello in Berland and Rao, 2004:124) prefers the term "artisans," not *forgerons* or blacksmiths, which conveys their technical, manual, and artistic work.

These artisans' exclusion from the Bidan segmentary lineage system give them a status resembling those in neighboring, and similarly hierarchical Saharan, Sahelian, and Sudanic tributary-like social categories. Bidan nobles in narratives express ambivalence toward manual trades performed for others, activities considered to be "degrading, dirty, and ignoble," but at the same time "socially necessary, and hence, valuable" (Cervello in Berland and Rao, 2004:125).

In oral accounts, fear, mistrust, and disdain are associated with *m'allemin* occupations, and also with their alleged activation of a power Cervello translates as "sorcery," called *echar,* (a term, interestingly, related to the Tamajaq term for sorcery, *ark echaghel*, literally denoting "bad work," but in the Tuareg case, as noted, this latter is a malevolent power practiced by anyone, not solely smiths) (Rasmussen, 2001b). More generally, *m'allemin* are linked to the superhuman world, an important aspect of the Bidan cultural ideology. Additional anecdotes stress foreign origins and a stranger status of *m'allemin,* suggesting, Cervello argues, their statutory distance as "customary strangers" in Georg Simmel's (1950) sense: for they are simultaneously interior and exterior to Bidan society. They are local suppliers of goods and services from outside, and must come from the outside. Another theme that evokes alien origins of *m'allemin* relates how some nobles in Mauritania insist *m'allemin* were originally Islamized Jews or Kwar, two groups who occupy a special place in the ideology of Bidan. Bidan aristocrats are Muslims who assert the primacy of Arab or Arabo-Berber origins for themselves. For a political and religious reason, therefore, the Bidan myths about *m'allemin* emphasize their "foreign" background and stranger status. Yet these parties' social relationships are complex: by engaging in intermediary trade with noble Bidan, *m'allemin* as middlepersons or artisans and traders perform a valuable service, and derive a special sense of mobility and ambivalence "through a synthesis of nearness and remoteness, indifference and involvement" (Simmel, 1950:403).

Since *m'allemin* are perceived as not landowners, they are free of common historical origins and partisan dispositions that bias. Thus these specialists play more prominent, and their relationships with other Bidan feature more mutual dependence than among the Amhara in Ethiopia: like the Tuareg, Bidan employ smith/artisans as confidants and mediators. In the Tuareg and Bidan cases, moreover, smiths' narratives tend to emphasize mutual dependence more than nobles' narratives. According to Cervello, although *Bidan* nobles' views and accounts of smith powers and origins assert that *m'allemin* are despised and dreaded, the nobles in the Mauritanian countryside tend to specify that " it is not smiths themselves who are the objects of contempt, but rather, their non-noble crafts" (Cervello in Berland and Rao, 2004:139). They practice "dirty" manual trades, are always dirty, touch metals, cut wood, and their women touch leather, and dyes—to Bidan nobles, associated with dead or at least inert matter, though to smiths, I argue, these materials were once living and when smiths transform them into cultural materials, once again they come to life. To do all that, in Bidan nobles' viewpoints, these specialists must have ties with the *jnun* spirits, even with Satan the Devil (*Shaytan*). They are also widely believed to be "sorcerers" (*saherin*). That is why many fear them.

Additional local stereotypes of *m'allemin* are more hostile: these include lying, begging, and lacking shame (*sahwa*). Yet many Bidan acknowledge that the latters' professional and personal qualities are needed.

Artisan work as well as gardening in Mauritania, even today, are widely regarded as the sole preserve of servile or conquered groups. But until recently, among both Bidan and Tuareg *imajeghen* nobles, it was "the fact that this work was performed for others, as a service" (Cervello in Berland and Rao, 2004:141) that made smith/artisans quasi-servants. Cultural similarities notwithstanding, the Tuareg case, however, suggests finer nuances: slaves and tributaries, as well as smith/artisans, performed such labor for nobles, but slaves and tributaries are not associated with superhuman power of the same kind, or to the same degree, as *inaden*. Tuareg former slaves and their descendants are sometimes associated with sorcery, *ark echaghel*, but not usually with *tezma* power.

The common thread in all these cultural settings thus far are the following: cultural perceptions of a homology between the professional occupations and temperaments of smith/artisans; some tensions in wealth and property ownership; client-patron relationships, and superimposition, upon conversions in these societies, of organized, scriptural religious ritual and mythico-history upon the earlier ritual roles of smith/artisans. In these stratified and hierarchical, yet fluid and changing societies, class typifications sometimes become ossified into stereotypes, encouraging scapegoating in particular predicaments. Views widely held by many non-smiths, particularly those of aristocratic origins, in these societies emphasize smiths' connections to the superhuman world. The alleged danger and impurity in such connections on one level derive from these socioeconomic and religious contradictions, and on another, reflect creative power's capacity to become threatening and unpredictable, somewhat like nuclear power, particularly in times of uncertainty and upheaval.

M'ALLEMIN AND BIDAN SOCIAL RELATIONSHIPS

As in Tuareg society, the central hierarchical distinctions in Bidan/Moor society separate free peoples from those of servile status, or nowadays, descendants of free persons from those descended from servile peoples. In both societies, cultural ideologies tend to persist in which these statuses remain salient in memory—particularly in rural communities, although importantly, there are also socioeconomic and ideological transformations. Again, as among the rural Tuareg and the Amhara, the Bidan condition of liberty, traditionally associated with the aristocracy, is justified in terms of genealogy, and legitimated with reference to idealized moral and ethical qualities of nobles. Symbolic capital consists of prestigious ancestors since the nineteenth century. The *noblesse oblige* idea, of dominance yet patronage and protection of subordinates, is also powerful, thereby mitigating somewhat the counterforce of rigid hierarchy.

Bidan were formerly nomadic, but are more sedentarized and urban than most Tuaeg today. Aristocratic values include defense of honor, warrior power, generosity, and valor in combat. The freest and most noble are those who are politically dominant over the other groups: these groups may have a warrior, or both warrior and religious (Islamic scholar) status. The least noble free groups are those who have been weakened by wars, famines, or other social or environmental catastrophes, and have been forced to seek protection from aristocratic groups, in exchange for tribute. Yet, as in the Tuareg case, there has always been flexibility and negotiation of statuses; statuses are provisional and never fixed. In contrast to the Tuareg case, however, in recent years, segmentary Bidan no longer recognize tributary status, but emphasize joint warrior and Islamic religious status principles, sometimes together.

M'allemin smith/artisans, classified as free groups, are considered to have a status superior to that of *abid* slaves and *hratin* tributaries, since *m'allemin* are not of servile origins, which remain a stigma (Cervello in Berland and Rao, 2004:128). *M'allemin*, despite their allegedly separate origins, therefore constitute more of a social stratum than an outside ethnic group, in contrast to the situation of *buda/tayb* among the Amhara, who are much more strongly identified with a different ethnic group, albeit speaking the same language. This point underlines the problematics of assumptions of rigid social identity in Africa—for example, in the notorious case of the Belgian and German-imposed "racial" identities upon Tutsi and the Hutu in Rwanda and Burundi—and underlines the political construction of social categories, rather than their intrinsic or immutable characteristics. From this perspective, one must be equally cautious in referring to smith/artisans in any group as unambiguously a different "ethnic" group, despite their outside origins. Indeed, this Simmelian "stranger..far and yet also near" status is the crux of the problem I examine in the present book. For in all these cases, smith/artisans speak the same language as their patrons in the surrounding community, (with the exception of the Tenet "secret argot" only occasionally spoken by the Tuareg *inaden*), though they marry endogamously.

Thus *inaden*, *tayb*, and *m'allamin* smiths all can be considered simultaneously the same and distinct; I prefer to designate them as a social category or stratum; for they are much more than a group of occupational specialists, and in their own and other local residents' viewpoints, there admittedly occurs some essentialization of their identity. As Wood (1999) pointed out in his study of Gabra gender constructs, despite scholarly sensitivity to post-structural critiques of reifications and binaries, the researcher cannot ignore these categories when local residents themselves make them. Rather than merely reproducing them ethnographically, however, anthropologists need to explore more fully the processes underlying the constructions of such categories.

Smith/artisans among the Bidan, like those among the Tuareg, now may change client-patron attachments, but have limited spatial mobility, and are regarded as free but non-noble. *M'allemin* remain associated with Bidan families or religious *qaba'il* families through ties of clientage. In the absence of *iggawin* griots or bards, the *m'allemin* can also assume roles of musicians—a situation also found among some Tuareg, notably the Kel Ewey in the Air Mountains of Niger. Both musicians and artisan/smiths of Bidan society, as in Tuareg and some other Sahelo-Saharan societies (Hale, 1999), have similar roles as mediators, confidantes, and counselors for influential persons.

Thus *m'allemin* activities as smiths and leather workers and social service providers (mediators) are essential to cultural and political life. In these roles, they are very similar to Tuareg *inaden*. Historically, men worked iron, silver, gold, and wood, while women worked leather than engaged in sewing, weaving mats, and dying imported cloth for clothing. Payment has been traditionally in millet and/or milk, livestock, and clothing, though there is increasing monetarization. Traditionally, activities and products have centered around pastoral nomadic life.

M'allemin are therefore surrounded by paradox: they are valuable, but widely described as despised (Cervello in Berland and Rao, 2004:132). Each camp of Bidan included at least one tent of m'allemin. There also was traveling commerce in camps during the harvest. Thus m'allemin produce material goods indispensable to social life, and are artisans of material culture, while also fulfilling roles as intermediaries in domestic affairs (especially in relations between the sexes) and in political affairs, again, similar to what I observed among Tuareg smiths, who are often also confidantes of women, as well as chiefs. M'allemin are not expected to observe the same "code of honor" as nobles.

Cervello interprets the *m'allemin* as culturally Bidan (Arabophones), but of non-aristocratic and "inferior" rank (Cervello in Berland and Rao, 2004:133). There is also a more pejorative term for these smiths: *igdayan* (sing. *agday*) that denotes "rustic, uncouth blacksmith". Interestingly, the term *m'allemin* by contrast derives from the Arabic root signifying "science," "knowledge," or "learning". These smiths are also designated by the term *sunna*, from the root denoting "to make, create or construct," which connotes acquired aptitude through practice. Thus the association of *m'allemin* not solely with inherited status, but also skilled learning, and not solely with danger and destruction, but also creativity. The point here is the existence of both negative and positive roles of smiths, expressed in local language etymologies.

The *m'allemin* in Mauritania do not constitute a distinct descent group or lineage, but are always attached to their patrons' descent group or lineage by relations of protection and clientage. As already observed, the Tuareg smith/artisans vary in their self-identification and affiliation in relation to noble descent groups; some emphasize their affiliation and even merged their own descent groups with those of their traditional nobles, whereas others emphasized their own separate descent group or lineage. Most, as also observed, considered their origins very different from those of nobles, however. As also already observed, the *buda/tayb* constitute a separate descent group, completely outside the *rega* Amhara descent groups. Of course, these differences should be recognized as historically and politically constructed, rather than fixed or objectively "true." But whether "true" or not, the ideological bases of these different degrees of smith alterity and "otherness" in relation to non-smiths are of interest here. On one level, I argue, the lesser degree of smith "otherness" in their own and non-smiths' viewpoints have to do with the relative lack of sedentarization and private land ownership among the semi-nomadic herding Bidan and Tuareg aristocracies. By contrast, there has been greater emphasis upon the alterity or "otherness" of smiths in the context of importance of landowning lineages among the sedentarized farming Amhara *riga* nobles.

Traditionally, *m'allemin* moved as "peripatetic" groups, searching for pastures with their nomadic protector Bidan families. As among the Tuareg, there is sometimes a spatial organization of tents in a (nowadays semi-nomadic) camp according to rank of families. Yet some Bidan smiths are also are sedentary, and like the Tuareg smiths, some have long lived in ancient Saharan towns. Cervello does not report the existence of exclusively *m'allemin* villages in the countryside. In the Tuareg case, however, there is a slight difference from the Bidan case concerning residential settlement patterns: many Tuareg *inaden* arrived in the major Saharan towns such as Agadez, Niger and Kidal, Mali only after their attached nobles either became too destitute to support them, or themselves left the countryside, initially in the wake of major droughts in 1969-74 and 1984. Most *inaden* I studied in my rural and urban research were recent migrants to these towns, over approximately two generations (from around the late 1960's); only a few families there were of more longstanding urban residence. As already noted, until recently, most Tuareg tended to shun towns as longterm residences. Until recently, far fewer Tuareg were fully sedentarized into urban life than Bidan. Some, though not all, client and servile groups of the Tuareg nobles were more sedentarized, and they gave portions of their harvests as tithe or rent to the more nomadic *imajeghen* nobles until approximately the mid-twentieth century.

Thus the Tuareg and the Bidan are in some respects similar, and in other respects, different in their degree of sedentization, urbanization, and land patterns. There are very close parallels in the roles of their smith/artisans, smith-noble relations, and beliefs concerning smiths' powers. These two cases in many ways stand out from the Amhara case, though all three cases thus far also share a few similarities, namely: smith and non-smith alike speak the same language; adhere (at least nominally) to the same "official religion," albeit with hints of strong indigenous African ritual roles pre-dating Christianity and Islam, respectively; the origins of the smith/artisans are distinct, they are endogamous, they live close to non-smiths, and perform important technical, artistic, and ritual roles in their respective communities.

Apart from work of transforming materials and artistic creations, *m'allemin* smiths also perform social and political services for Bidan. They are sometimes despised and feared, but are also considered people of wisdom who play roles of counselor, informant, and marriage broker. Like the other Saharan smiths, they (are considered) "part magician, partly doctor, pharmacist, surgeon, journalists, and messengers"(Gabus, 1976:19). Male jewelers are also circumcisers, a role also characteristic of smith/artisans among the Mande-speaking groups in Mali (McNaughton, 1988). Others are hairdressers. In marriage brokering, the smith carries gifts from the fiancé to his fiancée. Smiths' workshops are meeting places between young men and young girls. Everyone needs a smith for jewelry, advice, repair, etc.

In history, some *m'allemin* abandoned their profession, and succeeded in changing, not solely their occupation, but also their social status to become warriors by virtue of their political activities as counselors, courtiers, messengers, and tax collector for emir of Trarza region in Mauritania. This stands in stark contrast to the case of Amhara smith/artisans, who, as shown in both historical and ethnographic accounts, retain their stigmatized social status even in changing occupations, and even in the urban setting. Thus in

Mauritanian Bidan society, there is flexibility and a possibility of upward mobility in prestige for smith/artisans through changing occupations.

Like the Tuareg *inaden*, *m'allemin* pay no tribute; they live by payments that their tributaries bring to them and by the portion that is left to them of fines the traditional leader, the emir, entrusts them to recover. In both Tuareg and Bidan societies, smith/artisans are messengers and tax collectors of the emir and sometimes, even the central state government. The point is that great flexibility and mobility have been possible in both pre-colonial and post-colonial Bidan and Tuareg societies. However, in contrast to the Tuareg *inaden*, who in their own mythico-histories emphasized their non-fighting status, some m'allemin have had warrior origins, and became m'allemin as a consequence of social weakening in conquest. Thus in some cases, genealogical origins were irrelevant to statutory promotion or emergence of *m'allemin*. This status has its parallel among the Tuareg in, not *inaden* groups, but rather tributary *(imghad)* groups (Bernus, 1981; Nicolaisen and Nicolaisen, 1997).

Recent transformations in the *m'allemin* position result from structural changes in Bidan society. Some are wealthy and influential, some are academics, journalists, or lawyers, recognized as quasi-aristocratic Bidan who have remote *m'allemin* origins. The majority now live primarily in towns, where they continue to offer their specialized services (Cervello in Berland and Rao, 2004:136). Although as noted, some Tuareg *inaden* also now live in towns in Niger and Mali, many still live in the countryside, and in both settings *inaden* tend to remain known primarily as such, despite changes in profession: for example, a school teacher in Agadez, also a prominent musician, was still known as a smith in terms of reference, although he no longer did work at the forge. He often officiated as a "masters of ceremony" at public events such as political rallies, in his position as both smith and teacher. Hence the stronger social stratum association of smiths in Tuareg society, even today, which remains based upon descent, though this is not an outright stigma, in contrast to the case in Amhara society, and many urban smiths who specialize as jewelers, as noted, prefer to be called *les bijoutiers*, rather than *les forgerons* in French by outsiders; other Tuareg, however, still use the Tamajaq term *inaden* to identify them.

Despite socioeconomic changes in Mauritania, even in the towns, noble families still seek out their traditional smiths (i.e. attached to their descent group and family) in purchase of cushions, mats, utensils in iron or wood, jewelry, domestic services, haircuts, or repair of goods; and in mediation in meetings of young, engagements, negotiation of marriage dowries, in political alliances, and confidential messenger services between politicians (Cervello in Berland and Rao, 2004:137).

Endogamy continues to play an important role in the simultaneous social distinctiveness and "near and distant" status of Bidan smith/artisans. Their familiarity with natural and superhuman worlds also places them within a special sphere. As in a number of African societies, *m'allemin* protect their professional and esoteric knowledge, transmitted through generations, within their own specialized community.

Cervello also offers a hypothesis on the origins and emergence of Mauritanian smiths: in the debut of professional differentiation (between 3400 and 2000 B.P.) in the rise of cities, and in the metallurgy of proto-Berber populations upon their progress into the Sahara (Cervello in Berland and Rao, 2004:138). This specialism became associated with a sedentary mode of life that necessitated luxury products. Once constituted, their knowledge was transmitted within a single, relatively closed, specialized group; the group nevertheless must have been augmented from the outside. Cervello also offers evidence that numerous contemporary *m'allemin*, like Tuareg *imghad* tributaries but unlike *inaden*, derived from Bidan groups who were weakened by wars, famines, or other disasters. This origin applies to numerous peripatetic groups in the world. I would add a caveat here that this does not apply to all of them, and there are varying degrees of clientage and servitude which differ in kind, as well as degree of alterity and abjection, within these groups. Moreover, even in the hierarchical Bidan and Tuareg societies, there is much flexibility and negotiability of roles, in contrast to the Amhara. Recall for example, that Tuareg *inaden* also often escape, to some degree, the nobles' ambivalent attitudes in more urban, national, and global contexts. In these contexts, however, they tend to continue their roles as intermediaries and go-betweens, albeit more in the sense of cross-cultural mediators than as ambassadors for chiefs. For example, many *inaden* who traveled to Europe and the United States extended their roles beyond mere commercial selling of their art works into the realm of cultural knowledge dissemination at ethnic festivals, art museums, and import shops (Rasmussen, 2003). In both Tuareg and Bidan societies, this less official mediation by smith/artisans is regarded by non-smiths, particularly by nobles, with ambivalence. As already observed, some non-smiths gossip resentfully over those allegedly "rich" smith/artisans, who have "abandoned" their nobles for greater financial gain from outside customers. There persists a disdain for working for others for pay, but these reasons appear to run deeper here, in the sense of some veiled envy, not solely contempt as formally expressed in the old system.

The question here is how to account for the fact that those so-called "peripatetics" who are free but non-noble, practicing manual activities judged impure or polluting, may simultaneously play such an important role in domestic and political mediation? Cervello explains this apparent contradiction in terms of the need of society to be able to count on a group who, not being bound to the code of honor of nobles, thereby can negotiate in the name of noble patrons (i.e., by proxy) without noble patrons' losing face (Cervello in Berland and Rao, 2004:136).

The Tuareg case appears on first scrutiny to confirm this view: for many persons of diverse social backgrounds explain that "*inaden* pronounce what others are ashamed to pronounce," and my vignettes and cases encountered earlier offered contextual examples of how this serves to empower *inaden*. But this view does not explain entirely that ambivalence concerning smith/artisans' powers, nor does it completely explain the *inaden's* self perceptions or their perceptions of non-smiths, which are not always "objective" in their own social theories and mythico-histories, any more so than are those of non-smiths, thereby raising questions about Simmel's (1950) notion of the "objectivity" of the stranger.

More relevant here, in my view, is the concept of "weapons of the weak" (Scott, 1992), that smiths in these societies are officially dominated groups who have adopted particular social strategies, in their officially denigrated occupations, which protect them from competition from groups who hold greater official authority and prestige, and also from retaliation from non-smiths from the latters' envy upon smiths' increased material wealth. In other words, there is an uneasy truce or "bargain" here between the occupants of otherwise competitive niches. Its roots and its primary expression are in a complex intersection of religion and property concerns.

M'ALLEMIN, RELIGION, AND POWER

M'allemin, as the possessors of some "magical" (i.e., superhuman) power, have an ambiguous relationship to Islam. Orthodox Islam (i.e., Qur'anic, especially the more reformist Islamist interpretations such as Wahabi Islam) strongly condemns sorcery and magic as impious, although they are practiced by many popular or "para-Islamic" healers. Untangling all these forces requires situating them in wider contexts.

Sorcery practice (*echar*) in Mauritania, in contrast to northern Niger and northern Mali, is not uniquely associated with *m'allemin,* but also with other officially dominated groups, for example, servile groups and women (Cervello in Berland, 2004: 142). Yet importantly, the *m'allemin,* like *inaden* and *buda,* are also felt to have the most direct relations with the *djin* spirits of the earth and metals, and many Bidan, like many Tuareg and Amhara, believe that with the aid of the latter, their acts are the most powerful and direct.

Elsewhere, pioneering works have explored the history of ironworking symbolism in relation to gendered constructs in continental Africa, for example, sexual taboos and reproductive imagery of the smelting furnaces south of the Sahara (Herbert, 1993). In particular, two conditions here stand out as salient in ironworking: its physical danger (smelting furnaces can blow up and kill the smiths, and forges can cause accidents—once I met an elderly Tuareg smith/artisan who had suffered a tragic accident as a child apprenticing at the forge, and was blind in one eye as a consequence, but courageously continued to practice his art—and secondly, its creative reproductive power. Herbert points out, for example, the ironwork symbolism referring to sexuality, reproduction, and the body, as in the furnace designs, which often have decorations depicting female genitalia and the linguistic expressions which make analogies between human and smith creativity, for example, between smithing and midwifery.

Hence the idea that ordering human capacities cannot suffice; there must be something else working here to ensure success—in the indigenous and official religions, which syncretically overlap and interweave, but also conflict and compete in the roles of numerous specialists whose allegiances to the pre-Islamic and pre-Christian spiritual worlds can make them vulnerable to restrictions or even persecution.. In the smith's world, spirits can therefore be significant in both positive and negative ways. Thus there is a certain ambiguity of power in smiths' creativity—this can go awry, can destroy. Also, power from spirits can be misused, particularly if "leaked" or "spilled," so to speak—hence the need for vigilant protectors: smiths themselves. Thus it is not coincidence that where indigenous African religions remain strong, as soon shown among the Kapsiki in Cameroon, smiths are also active in mortuary rituals pre-dating Christianity and Islam in Africa, and are associated with decay, as well as life and fertility. Perhaps the "glass is both half-full and half-empty," in regard to the meanings of smiths' powers; that is, their definition depends upon who is speaking and what their interests are.

Many nobles among the Tuareg, Amhara, and Bidan assert that smiths marry among themselves because they have little social value: their origins are unknown, worse than the status of slaves who have had (in the past) a master and whose origins are known. But nobody knows precisely where each family of *m'allemin* came from (Cervello in Berland, 2004:143). They constantly search for markets to sell works in camps and villages, place themselves under the protection of nobles, but cannot be too numerous at a site because they would compete with one another. A local proverb states, "They work to eat and they eat to work." As among the Amhara, those lacking a historical reference for identity are often stigmatized as strangers, outsiders, or "uncivilized others" unbound by "noble" codes of honor. Yet this view is the "official" viewpoint. From the Tuareg *inaden* narratives earlier analyzed, we know that smiths themselves have their own codes of honor; thus honor is very relative and subjective.

Also significant here, therefore, are prejudices toward those who are different, or suspected to adhere to another religion: whether to lingering "animism" or indigenous African religions, or as Cervello found among the Bidan, hints of anti-Semitism. In Cervello's view, ethnic/religious assignation of *m'allemin* as Jews by some Bidan derives from anti-Semitic prejudices rooted, throughout history, in representations by some Islamized populations. The attitudes of some Amhara nobles, recall, hinted of Christian-based religious prejudice, in mythico-histories linking the *buda* people to the death of Christ.

In Bidan communities, as in Tuareg communities, more revealing are the discourse, narratives, and viewpoints of smiths themselves regarding their origins. Many *m'allemin* consider their origins to be same as those of other Bidan in Mauritania, and claim Arab, Arabo-Berber, or Kwar ancestors (Cervello in Berland and Rao, 2004:144). According to Gabus (1976:8), furthermore, narratives collected at Walata placed the ancestor of *m'allemin* of that town among five legendary persons who came from Baghdad and founded Walata in the second century of the Hijra: Yahya al-Kabir, his son Mohamed, a mason, a muezzin, and an Islamic scholar built the city. In other words, these were culture heroes.

The Walata tradition resonates well with some Tuareg *inaden* traditions in that both mythico-historical motifs emphasize a melding of indigenous African and Abrahamic religious traditions, thereby attempting to reconcile them. But they also hint of tensions and conflicts on the social plane. Ties between smith/artisans and spiritual forces that permit them to subdue and re-shape metal, to found cities, and to mediate between warring parties both distinguish them from others and integrate them into the more "official" organized "orthodox" religious textual and scriptural narratives, and by extension, I argue, act as a kind of "weapon of the weak" socially: in smiths' roles as needed mediators in their skills and knowledge. In effect, smiths need to be viewed as special in their knowledge and skills, but not too special, for fear of envy by others and scapegoating by the officially hegemonic, or at least prestigious, authorities. But it would be an oversimplification to describe smiths as discriminated against or stigmatized, though the Amhara case closely approaches this.

Many *m'allemin* claim Arabo-Berber ancestors who have long devoted themselves to arts and crafts. Other mythico-histories say that *m'allemin* have noble and ancient origins, since they are descendants of Dawud (in Tamajaq, Dauda). It should be emphasized here that Dawud (Dauda, or David) was a Muslim prophet: according to Gabus (1976:19), *m'allemin* themselves claim noble origins since their basic tools in that origin mythico-history—hammer, anvil, tongs, were brought to them by Father Adam when he descended from sky to earth, and the prophet Daoud taught them to shape the stone, knife, flint, mold, and also the preparation of iron. As noted, the Tuareg *inaden* also related a nearly identical story to me, adding the nuance that Dauda was the first blacksmith, as well as their Prophet. In many para-Qur'anic traditions, also, Dauda is described as the first blacksmith who learned his craft from God.

By contrast, the Amhara mythico-history of smiths more oppositionally identifies smiths with the Devil, though also with the earlier acquisition of metalworking skills but here these skills are given a somewhat more negative, destructive twist: allegedly, the smiths, many of whom are alleged to have evil eye they activate in q'alb power, made nails for the crucifixion. These points are intriguing; for taken together, they reveal more broadly the interface and overlap, as well as hints of conflicts, between the indigenous local religions and rituals pre-dating Islam in which smith/artisans were active, and the later conversions to more "official"orthodox Christian and Islamic religions in these ccommunities.

The *m'allemin* narrative is even more fascinating as it goes on to state that, then, following the Daoud teaching, Ehel Balhamar (people of the Devil) taught the smiths magic, without which they could not struggle against the malevolent influence of iron. Thus this tradition collected at Walata brings in another Qur'anic and Biblical character, Adam, father of humans; and also recalls the multiply transformative ties that the *m'allemin* have established with malevolent forces that permit them to subdue iron. Science and art, therefore, can be used in diverse ways, for good or evil. Smiths on their part attempt to gain the trust of their patrons, but patrons for their part fear the sources of power and knowledge that convey this Janus-headed quality, and also, in "real-politik" terms, are concerned to preserve their official religious and economic power.

What needs to be underlined here, a point not sufficiently emphasized by Cervello or Reminick in my view, is that iron is controlled by the spirits, to whom the smiths are in effect, beholden. I regard this aetiological motif of these smith origins and powers as crucially significant. In other words, in worlds now ruled by Muslim and Christian overlords, the smiths represent a hold-over from another spiritual pantheon. Sometimes, this pantheon is integrated into the now-dominant Abrahamic tradition; at other times, particularly in the Ethiopian and Mauritanian cases, it is demonized.

Also at play in all these smiths' origin narratives is pervasive doubt over smiths' devotion to the currently hegemonic mainstream religion—whether Islam or Coptic Christianity. Since many traditions belonging to Saharan artisans in general may have been inspired directly by the Qur'an, they may represent a kind of compromise in collective social memory to facilitate the integration of smith/artisans into official Islam. Several verses in the Qur'an indeed attribute the fathering of working of iron to the Prophet Dawud (Sura 34:10-11; Sura 21:79-80). Adam likewise appears in the Qur'an as the father of men and giver of names, as master of things that being named, are appropriated (Sura 2:31; and 7:11).

Another important point here is that smiths in Africa cannot be considered as a strictly marginal group, but rather as the intermediaries of nobles, specialized and ideally protected. The human rights implications here are profound. Specialists and intermediaries must be protected, but this message is often elided by some scholars in to a false assumption of "inferior" status. I agree with Cervello (in Berland and Rao, 2004) that it was to mark their distance from social roles adopted and accepted by *m'allemin* that noble members of

Bidan society forged ideologies and discourses that emphasized ethnic, moral, and status-related distance between them, and that many nobles' accounts illustrate ideological ambivalence always associated here as elsewhere with the craft of *m'allemin,* But I would add that these discourses, as shown, are not homogeneous or consensual, even within one society, and therefore present at least two simultaneous currents. One always recognizes a double evaluation (negative and positive) of their specialization and of services they provide to non-smiths in their society. But prejudice can also be associated with their "Otherness"—articulated as the ties smiths are believed to have with the superhuman world and their supposed stranger origins, which, as among the Tuareg, are more widespread in the rural milieu. In the urban milieus of these societies, nobles and smiths alike tend to emphasize recent evolution of egalitarian values and new political and social positions acquired by secular education. This contrasts markedly with urban Ethiopia, where Mains (2007) found that these memories persist more. Many Bidan, again by contrast to many Amhara, note and praise their resourcefulness. But Cervello notes a paradox in Mauritania: when smiths there cease to practice the activities of smiths, they become simply "noble Bidan" (Cervello in Berland and Rao, 2004:148). Indeed, this author notes that many smiths in more urban settings among Bidan now resent being called smiths, and call themselves "Bidan" in public in politeness (Cervello in Berland and Rao, 2004:142).

This change contrasts markedly with the Tuareg case, where I found that *inaden* never call themselves *imajeghen* (nobles), either before other Tuareg or before outsiders, in neither rural nor urban nor transcultural contexts, but always—regardless of socioeconomic position—proudly emphasize their identity as smith/artisans. Despite the tendency for those who specialize in silversmithing and goldsmithing in towns to call themselves by the French terms *les forgerons* (smiths) or *les bijoutiers* (jewelers), nonetheless, in Tamajaq, they continue to refer to themselves as *inaden*, and in English, the smith identity remains salient, even in international travel. Most also continue to emphasize their endogamy and unique origin. When I introduced a Tuareg smith/artisan who was visiting me in Houston to an American jeweler, for example, even there, my guest explained proudly, "My father and my grandfather, and my ancestors before them were all *inaden.* So am I."

Smith/artisans have been called "strangers" in Simmel's sense (Simmel, 1950:402) of being simultaneously near and far. His/her position in this group is determined essentially by the fact that he/she has not belonged to it from the beginning, and imports qualities into it which do not stem from the group itself. But are groups always so neatly bounded? Cultural borders are not impermeable to non-smiths, any more than they are to smiths. This concept tends to fix a status and a boundary, as does Douglas's (1966) concept of anomaly, despite its tropes of mobility.

Many smith/artisans have also been called peripatetic since they show a broadly similar characteristic of great flexibility and even literal mobility (Berland and Rao, 2004). But "peripatetic" groups are in both nomadic-pastoralist and also agro-pastoral societies, thereby suggesting not solely commonalities, but also contrasts between these specialists in diverse settings, and that peripatetic is too broad a gloss. My purpose in this cross-cultural comparison is not to suggest universal "laws" or even rigid correlations, but to contextualize the similarities and differences between these powers.

CHAPTER SIX

BESHENGU POWER AND KAPSIKI *RERHE* SMITH/ARTISANS

Many Kapsiki in north Cameroon use scent as social classification in pollution beliefs concerning smiths called *rerhe* and smiths' alleged power called *beshengu*. In Kapsiki cultural classification, the line separating blacksmiths (*rerhe*) and other Kapsiki (*melu*, pl. *melimu*) is drawn by aroma in local belief, with good-smelling *melu* allegedly having distinctly higher status than allegedly malodorous blacksmiths (Van Beek, 1992:39).

Kapsiki in the Cameroon live on the edges of a small plateau, and have primarily a horticultural subsistence economy: they cultivate millet, sorghum, maize, and groundnuts, and raise cattle, sheep, and goats. There is also an emerging group of traders and middlemen. Before colonialism, they migrated to mountain ridges to escape slave raiding, and gradually moved down from the hill slopes. These people are called Kapsiki in Cameroon and Higi in Nigeria; they reside on both sides of the border. The village is the most important level of social aggregation and identity, and is internally divided into wards, clans, and lineages, with descent groups usually scattered over various wards. These groups were important during fighting in the village in the past, but they had little authority beyond those contexts, with limited functions in resource management and marriage arrangement. The smallest social unit, the compound, is inhabited by a monogamous or polygynous family, important in daily life and production. Kapsiki society is also characterized by a pervading sense of privacy and individual autonomy, which according to Van Beek, precludes all close corporate control (Van Beek, 1992:39).

Blacksmiths (the English term for these specialists Van Beek uses) among Kapsiki constitute a 5 % minority within the total population, and as in many other African societies, they are endogamous, and practice specialized, professional occupations. Van Beek reports that their position in village society is characterized by "an ambivalence between difference and belonging, between their substantial contribution to the village economy and the view society in general has of them as a low stratum comprised of 'dirty and dangerous people'" (Van Beek, 1992:40).

There are symbolic, ritual, and social referents to smiths' alleged "dirtiness." *Rerhe,* like *inaden, buda,* and *m'allemin*, perform the most manual and ritual work requiring specialization. But unlike the other cases I have compared thus far, in addition to artisan work of leatherwork, pottery, forging and casting brass, and performing music, divination, "magic," and medicine, the Kapsiki smiths also perform very important roles in funerals. Their role in mortuary rites is crucial to the social construction of the local belief complex concerning their alleged ritual powers and dangers. *Rerhe* have their own organization, which depends partly on their choice of occupation, and partly on the social structure of the village. As in the Tuareg case, they have a chief blacksmith as a central figure, who is closely associated with the village chief. He, in turn, is assisted by helpers for specific functions.

The Kapsiki *rerhe*, despite their endogamy and their separateness based on cultural, occupational, ritual, and aesthetic factors, have no separate clans or descent groups of their own. They are more embedded socially than smiths in the other societies considered here within the mainstream non-smith clans called *melu*, and are widely believed to be similar to other villagers, except, as noted, for their alleged "smelliness," their specialized tasks, and also except that in their origins, these smiths emerged from other Kapsiki (Van Beek, 1992:40). Mythico-histories related that long ago, some Kapsiki turned into smiths. Interestingly, therefore, in contrast to both the Amhara and the Tuareg nobles, the Kapsiki *melu* emphasize smiths' continuity, rather than distinctiveness in originating from others in that society: in other words, Kapsiki smiths' distinctiveness does not depend so much on their separate origins, but rather on the nature of their work. Among the Kapsiki, therefore, the identifies of smiths and non-smiths overlap, and smiths may be called Kapsiki also, although, interestingly, they may not be called *melu*. Thus succinctly phrased: smiths are Kapsiki, but not *melu*, and other Kapsiki are not smiths, thereby suggesting a narrower category of *melu* within Kapsiki more generally, notwithstanding this society's lesser stratification than the Tuareg, Amhara, and Bidan/Moors.

Central to the status of *rerhe* are mortuary rites. Funerals are of prime importance for male Kapsiki smiths, in particular: they are the people of the dead, and non-smiths view smiths primarily as what in English would be called undertakers. The chief smith directs the complicated proceedings of a funeral, seconded by his son to lead in the drumming, and by a representative of another smith's family to dig the grave. As part of this ritual, smiths dress the corpse, dance with it for two consecutive days, provide the musical accompaniment with their drums and flutes, prepare the corpse for burial, direct the digging of the grave, and bury the dead after three days of their intense ritual work (Van Beek, 1992:40). After burial, smiths conduct some minor rituals during construction of the tomb, and terminate proceedings with a final ritual at the tomb site. Funerals constitute an important source of smith income, often paid in goats; musicians, too, receive a substantial reward.

It is during funerals that the Kapsiki smiths' position in their village is at its strongest. Whereas by contrast, among the Tuareg and the Bidan, Islamic scholars and imams, but not smiths, play most important roles at funerals. In these mortuary rituals among the Tuareg, for example, official Islamic rituals, presided over by Islamic scholars, never smiths, place greater emphasis upon memorial feasts held at intervals following the death (Rasmussen, 1997). Tuareg *inaden* play important roles at two other rites of passage: weddings and babies' namedays. But *inaden* never preside at funerals. As I show presently, these differences are illuminating, and key to my general argument in this book, in that they reveal the broader relationships between smiths in these societies and organized religion: smiths in these societies enact, to varying degrees, the social memory of indigenous "traditional" religions in their communities' past, and attitudes toward their powers reflect these preoccupations, which take different specific forms in these different societies, but also display similar common themes more generally. The Kapsiki indigenous religious rituals remain alive and vital, and smiths there continue to occupy important roles in them.

Smiths among the Kapsiki have a monopoly over all instruments played at rites of passage, especially funerals. They routinely serve as praise singers for a village, like Tuareg smiths in northern Niger and griots in the Sahara and Sahel. They also dominate divination; they are intermediaries for any communication with the superhuman world. They dominate "magic" and medicine. Kapsiki medicinal knowledge is esoteric and secret, guarded closely, and is also a considerable source of income. Van Beek argues that this knowledge offers fame for some male and female smiths that offsets their otherwise "low" status (Van Beek, 1992:41).

In my view, the *rerhe*'s dancing with the dead at funerals serves to distance them from other Kapsiki (*melu*) in order to protect their professional knowledge and skills; in effect, the rerhe's alleged "bad smell" and monopoly over dangerous magical power , like the Tuareg inaden's tezma, ritually ward off intrusions, and thus constitutes a weapon of the weak guarding their specialism from appropriation by others. Indeed, Kapsiki smiths' dancing with the dead is approximately analogous to the Tuareg smiths' performing of the *alburusa* mumming protest ritual analyzed earlier, during which the *inaden*, recall, don sandals resembling hyena ears to play up their mediating roles and control their patrons' reputations. Yet there is more at play—property and inheritance—in the Kapsiki smiths' dancing with the dead: These prolonged mortuary rites also allow resolution of potential and actual conflicts among *melu* over the legacy and wealth of the deceased. In this, Kapsiki *rerhe* also perform a social, as well as ritual, mediating role, which is approximated in the Tuareg smiths' roles, as go-betweens, confidantes, and mediators in marriage, albeit within informal social contexts, and with Islamic scholars acting in more "official" public contexts— for example, during bridewealth negotiations inaden work for the woman's family, whereas Islamic scholars work for the man's family. Not coincidentally, furthermore, many *inaden* also perform as curers at the predominantly female Tuareg possession ritual in northern Niger, which though multiple in its meanings, often involves conflicts over love and marriage (Rasmussen, 1995).

In Kapsiki artisan practices, there are gendered divisions of labor. Pottery is reserved for smith women. Kapsiki male smiths practice three types of metalworking: smelting iron; forging iron; and casting brass. Smelting of iron traditionally was not an important feature of smith work among Kapsiki; smiths relied on iron from the North. Instead, Kapsiki smiths concentrate on the forging of iron bars into utensils and ritual implements. Much local leatherworking, which is less exclusively a smith's job, is associated with iron sheaths, quivers, and bags. Brass traditionally was used for bodily adornment, but is now made for the tourist trade.

For a *melu* Kapsiki, the most important identifying characteristic of a *rehre* is in food habits: smiths are "people who eat smith food" (Van Beek, 1992:41). Among the Tuareg, similarly, recall that *inaden* eat the same food as others, but directly out of the pot, i.e., directly from the cooking fire; whereas nobles eat food transferred to dishes, i.e., more refined containers closer to culture than to nature. Thus in both these societies, there is some breaking of the officially dominant group's food taboos by smith/artisans, though among the Tuareg, this takes the form of etiquette style and how one eats, practices at different points along the nature/culture continuum, rather than what one eats. On the other hand, it could also be argued that non-smiths break smith food taboos. Also, more powerful among Tuareg are Islamic food taboos for everyone—the interdiction against pork and alcohol, observed by most persons of diverse social backgrounds. But the Kapsiki smiths do not heed non-smiths' meat taboos: rather, smiths eat horse, donkey, monkey, snake turtles, felines, black birds, and carrion birds, all of which are strictly forbidden to *melu*. These non-smiths often accuse smiths of eating anything, but according to Van Beek, this is "etically untrue," as smiths have their own taboos as well: for example, they abstain from the flesh of dogs and several kinds of birds (Van Beek, 1992:41). In my view, many of the foods forbidden to *melu* are less domesticated (i.e., more "natural" or "bush meats")., though foods forbidden to *rerhe* include both domesticated (dogs) and wild (birds).

Van Beek, in an insightful Levi-Straussian structuralist analysis of symbolism also recalling Edmond Leach's analysis of animal categories and verbal abuse and Mary Douglas's analysis of the "abominations of Leviticus," believes that the Kapsiki definition of what makes a smith may be read as a culinary definition of the position of the *rerhe* within Kapsiki society: smiths consume meat of those animals whose position in the animal realm coincides with that of smiths in the human sphere (Van Beek, 1992:42). The analogy is striking: tabooed animals are not in themselves considered dirty by non-smiths, but smiths eating them are considered dirty. Eating forbidden food pollutes the eater; anything cooked by a *rerhe* will pollute a *melu*, who cannot eat food or drink prepared by a rerhe woman, or eat together from the same bowl or drink from the same cup as a smith. Visitors to *melu* bring along their own bowl.

Recall that Tuareg indicated that *inaden* and *imajeghen* in the past did not eat or drink together, and nowadays in rural communities, I noticed that they still refrain from sitting on the same mat when they do visit, drink tea, or eat together. In both Amhara and Bidan societies, respectively, the data revealed less sociability and commensuality between smiths and non-smiths, most extreme among the Amhara.

On the other hand, in all these cases, smiths play intermediary roles, and therefore visit non-smiths and participate in their social and ritual events. Thus the eating restrictions and food taboos in Kapsiki society stand out for their connection to local notions of pollution, but these notions of pollution differ from notions among the Tuareg, Amhara, and Bidan. Van Beek argues that the local notion of dirt, called *reda,* and what is inedible, is closely associated with the other dominant feature of the relation between smiths and non-smiths: endogamy. So smiths are not dirty because they eat dirty food, but food is dirty because is it is either prepared or eaten by smiths, in the view of non-smiths.

Importantly, as Douglas pointed out long ago (Douglas 1966), the sense of "dirt" is not solely literal, but extends into figurative domains. Relevant here are Kapsiki smiths' and non-smiths' respective definitions of pollution and odors. Dirt and odor belong together. As a category of so-called "dirty people," according to the officially dominant *melu,* smiths "stink" (*zungwu*) Yet significantly, the self-perception of smiths is different from the non-smiths' perceptions and allegations, including their definitions of smell. *Ndaleke* as a lexeme is important: this connotes the smell of rotting meat, any meat. For *melu,* this represents or evokes the smell of a corpse. For *rerhe,* it is different: smith men do not consider the smell of a corpse as at all worth mentioning, while smith women classify it as somewhat *ndaleke*; they also mention the smell of dogmeat in this category, as well as red millet beer, monkey, and burning goat dung, which is used for seasoning (Van Beek, 1992:44). Thus smiths are considered malodorous primarily because of their role as undertakers. Their alleged malodorousness is in turn connected to their relationship to the superhuman world and its powers, via the circuit of death. Kapsiki smiths' own definition of smell is at variance with the non-smith one, with differences following divisions and definitions of edibility, i.e., of established food taboos. Also, this distinction between rerhe and melu is mediated by gender. Women emphasize it less than men. Corpses are considered to be filthy more by one social group than by the other.

In my view, a more positive empowering interpretation is possible here, as well: smiths may well "play up" this malodorousness to keep others at a safe distance from smith powers. In effect, this is a non-verbal mode of saying "keep away," thereby protecting their esoteric knowledge as gate-keepers to the afterlife..

Relevant here are Kapsiki notions of evil. Many Kapsiki distinguish between evil that originates from a non-human source and evil from a human source. Humans who are born evil include witches, born with a deviant shadow. Witchcraft, however, is limited to those who are not smiths or anomalous; rather, witches in Kapsiki cosmology are widely perceived as otherwise normal,

or outwardly conventional. Kapsiki blacksmiths, in contrast to the Tuareg and
Amhara specialists, form an important sector of society as sorcerers whose
powers can be used destructively (in the sense of intentional use of power), but
never witches (in the sense of unintentional activation of power, albeit in anti-
social actions). They fabricate *beshengu,* encased inside harmful magical items,
but do not use it, only sell it to melu (Van Beek, 1992:47).

Kapsiki notions of smell contrasts and transformations seem to evoke things
different from everyday life: among animals, those that stink are non-edible
species. Thus smells associated with the difference between *rerhe* and *melu*
convey the in-between status of the *rerhe*. Like his food taboos, the "smelly"
smith is defined as an ambivalent person, standing between the human and
superhuman worlds. The smith is simultaneously healer and poisoner,
undertaker and musician—neither completely evil nor completely "normal"—
and one who makes it possible to transform bush into farmland, though he
himself does not cultivate (Van Beek, 1992:48).

Hence the idea here of a Janus-headed figure with powers that are
multidirectional, which are actively used as weapons of the weak, by those who
are vulnerable in some contexts and powerful in others. At a smith burial, for
example, no *melu* will venture into the dance, as the smith dance is extremely
dangerous for non-smiths. The point is that the dirtiness of the smith is not
literal, and not evil, which has no smell, but resides in ambivalence, in a kind of
anomalous and liminal position between humans and nature, individual and
gods, beyond distinctions of good and bad.

Thus in contrast to the Tuareg communities where smiths and nobles
reciprocally invert their roles at each other's weddings and namedays, in Kapsiki
communities, there is no such inversion. But notably, in the Tuareg case, again
in contrast to the Kapsiki case, Islamic scholars jealously guard their roles more
closely in mortuary rituals, but allow smiths to preside alongside them in the
otherTuareg rites of passage. Death, then, is an important domain of mediating
figures in African religions pre-dating Christianity and Islam, and in effect,
Kapsiki smiths appear relatively protected from abjection and political violence
and other scapegoating processes by their important connection to the afterlife—
indeed, they are gate-keepers on the threshold between life and death. In my
interpretation, this suggests that *melu* keep greater distance from *rerhe* from a
kind of awe, not simply from a sense of social superiority in dignity or prestige.
Although this distance is articulated in terms of denigration as smelly, and
aroma in many societies has strong social and political implications of hierarchy
and hegemony, nonetheless, this idiom may have an unconscious purpose or
effect of mystifying the power of *rerhe*.

In Kapsiki funerals, there is lack of haste to bury the dead. Since people
from neighboring villages must see the deceased, funerals last for three days,
and the corpse is buried at the end of the third day. There are collective claims
on activities and goods: men defend their autonomy, and resent intrusion by

kinspersons. Here, property is significant. Often, one hides wealth (cattle) from the eyes of agnates and potential heirs, and seeks friends outside the circle of close kin. On the other hand, kinspersons, both agnates and matrilateral kin, are needed. Kapsiki inherit debts, as well as riches. They are competitors. Brothers are seen as equivalent in revenge and in danger. A man thus needs to extend social and economic relationships widely; friends come from inside the village, but most wives come from beyond the village. In-laws are potential enemies whose daughters one has married.

In burial, these ambivalent relationships are replayed. Each of the living has to see the corpse to be convinced. The deceased also has to see people around him or her, to see those who played a part in life. After one generation, the dead are forgotten. However, death is a transition not to an ancestor, but to a non-social person; thus the corpse is something in between living and dead (Van Beek, 1992:50). Thus smiths are to non-smiths what the corpse is to living persons, and each identity centers about the social contradictions in Kapsiki society. There is the need to display the corpse, yet also abhorrence toward it. This contradiction is resolved by a mediator: namely, the smith in the role of undertaker , as a marginal person. Thus the Kapsiki smith is a person out of place, yet also needed. Thus the alleged dangerous powers of smiths in the Kapsiki case are symbolically represented by aroma, in effect a phonemic contrast between the living and the dead.

The Kapsiki material suggests that in some contexts, at least, smiths' powers are less subject to scapegoating, exclusionary projects, or classical witchcraft patterns. I interpret the Kapsiki smith/artian situation as much more open to positive definition of smiths' powers, despite their alleged "smelliness," since Kapsiki traditional religion remains relatively less challenged by Christianity or Islam. Also, there is the property factor here: although there is private property in the form of cattle and other inherited wealth, land does not appear to be an object of great contention between *rerhe* and *melu.* Nor do *rerhe* and *melu* occupy extremely stratified relationships, in contrast to the Tuareg, Amhara, and Bidan cases, whose societies to varying degrees, are characterized by much greater monopoly over land, (or in more nomadic communities, livestock), labor, and/or goods along the lines of a traditional aristocracy than does Kapsiki society, though there are intrafamilial tensions..

In my re-reading of Van Beek's structural analysis in the light of the other cases examined, I am led to wonder if smiths and non-smiths among the Kapsiki ever reciprocally exercise these powers, if so, how and if not, why not. If *melu* consider it too dangerous to dance at *rerhe* funerals, then what actually occurs there? Many qualities are anomalous structurally (Douglas, 1966) and liminal temporally (Turner, 1968), but the question raised here concerns practice, context, and relationships. As Crapanzano (1994) has pointed out in his analysis of Moroccan circumcision as a rite of passage and his critical re-analysis of

Turner and Van Gennep, transformations of identity (e.g. the boy treated as a baby and then a bridegroom during his circumcision celebration) may pertain only in the immediate ritual context, but not more generally in other situations (e.g. thereafter, he returns to ordinary everyday status and is treated as such).

An important point that comes across in the Kapsiki case, less explicitly emphasized by Van Beek, is that smiths facilitate transformations of *melu* into deceased status, in effect, ushering them into the world of the dead—a feat that appears to buffer Kapsiki smiths from some more negative consequences of local typifications concerning their potentially dangerous sorcery and alleged smelliness. Indeed, Kapsiki smiths occupy a status neither "marginal" nor "peripheral" to *melu* non-smiths, but rather, a centrally authoritative status in local ritual: they bridge life and death—a position that may prevent, or at least discourage scapegoating for their *beshengu*. Van Beek does not explore why exactly these specialists sell items containing their potentially destructive power. But they are still the source of this power, and know how to manufacture it; whereas others depend on them for this product. In effect, Kapsiki smiths cannot so easily be excluded socially, for if they are, *melu* may be become excluded and marginalized also (from inheriting property, from *beshengu* transactions, from social ties needed in marriage, and from smooth transition into death). Thus these specialists' practices reveal the finer nuances of marginality and peripherality. There are also hints here that, in the past, smiths among the Tuareg, Amhara, and Bidan fulfilled broader ritual roles than they do today, and that these ritual roles are still fulfilled by some other smiths in Africa where more orthodox Islam and Christianity are less hegemonic, and have not as yet at least, become so entwined with stratified property interests. For further insights into these processes, I now turn to smith/artisans among Mande peoples in southern Mali, where indigenous religion also remains powerful, despite conversions to Christianity and Islam, and where there are also persisting, though modified client-patron relations between stratified, inherited occupational groups based upon descent.

CHAPTER SEVEN

NYAMA POWER AND MANDE *NYAMAKALA* SMITH/ARTISANS

There is a large ethnographic literature on the closely-related Mande-speaking peoples of Mali and neighboring countries, but a rich description of smith/artisans is found primarily in the work of McNaughton (1988) in his study of Mande smiths in southern Mali. This scholar, correctly in my view, is critical of using "witch" or "sorcerer" and related terms to describe Mande smiths and their alleged power called *nyama* (McNaughton, 1988:10-13), and prefers to emphasize concepts of "ambivalence and ambiguity" to describe smiths' roles, others' attitudes toward them, and relationships between smiths and other Mande peoples.

Smiths and non-smiths, particularly non-smiths of aristocratic background, practice joking relationships, characterized by "stylized insolence," (McNaughton, 1988:10), similar to those that I found among the Tuareg and Cervello found among the Bidan. These are social contracts that allow individuals to hurl insults at each other in a benign, often public environment where retribution takes the form of additional insults. These smith/artisans have joking relations with many Mande farming clans, and also with clans of sedentary Fula who live among Mande-speaking peoples. Joking masks aspects of relationships that are of paramount importance; joking relationships are in fact alliances (McNaughton, 1988:10). Participants exchange services, and since they are members of different clans and likely to have different principal occupations, such exchanges are mutually beneficial. Participants also assist each other, and very often are friends. According to McNaughton, these alliances unite and oppose people at the same time. Thus there are positive aspects to relations between smiths and non-smiths, but the connotations of *nyama* power are more ambiguous.

Again, context is key. Undeniably, among Mande, as among some other peoples, a degree of negative stereotyping sometimes targets smiths. These conflictual aspects of relations between parties become more prominent when Mande confront "sorcery" (McNaughton, 1988:11). Since this is a potent power, many are cautious about speaking about it, and buffer sorcery for protection. Specialists and sometimes others as well, protect sorcery itself from the avarice of outsiders (McNaughton, 1988:12). Epics, for example, emphasize the need of leaders to have access to sorcery, as a vital component of their capacity to solve problems, address crises, subdue antagonists, and satisfy their ambitions (McNaughton, 1988:13).

In other words, these descriptions imply that dangerous power is a precious resource, a form of cultural or intellectual property used interactively, rather than an immutable, stable negative "trait" always exercised by a particular group.

Those who use sorcery negatively are believed to be either temporarily or habitually unrestrained by social mores: they are aggressive, egocentric, disruptive; such persons—anyone, regardless of social origin—they have huge appetites for economic or political aggrandizement, in a state called *fadenya* (father-childness), referring to competition for honor and resources that occurs between siblings who have the same father but different mothers. Its counterpart is called *badenya,* or mother-childness, trait of affection and loyalty between siblings born to same father and mother. Everyone is believed capable of either type of behavior, and people shift back and forth according to situations. Some persons, however, incline toward one or the other most of the time; those inclined toward father childness are feared.

Herein resides the specificity of the idiom of smiths' alleged powers. Many Mande consider *nyamakala* clan members (who include "blacksmiths"—the English term McNaughton uses for these specialists who work iron and also serve ritual roles, described presently) to have many of traits associated with "father-childness." Smiths, bards, and leather workers are "highly secretive and protective of the expertise they consider their rightful inheritance" (McNaughton, 1988:14). These specialists possess knowledge, which makes them capable of aggression. Herein resides the uniqueness of the prevalent local typification of smiths, despite the equally prevalent recognition of their potential to use power either for good or evil. As in Kapsiki communities in Cameroon, part of smiths' ritual and performative competence in Mande communities involves exaggeration of this power: this includes behaving dramatically at public festivals, for example, holding red-hot iron bare-handed, and displaying unrestrained ill temper. In McNaughton's view, smiths reinforce other people's opinions of them and encourage ambivalence that insulates and protects them (McNaughton, 1988:15). Recall how smith/artisans among the Kapsiki and among the Tuareg, in their respective rituals and performances, also often play up or exaggerate dramatically others' stereotypes of them, for purposes of protecting their esoteric knowledge. Even smith/artisan "evil eye" people among the Amhara, in their very presence at some cures for the condition they allegedly cause, are involved with dramatically reinforcing popular stereotypes of them.

Yet Mande typifications of smiths do involve a degree of attribution to them of greater "aggression"; thus there is a stereotype in the first place, however skillfully *nyamakala* smiths "play" with it as a "weapon of the weak" to assert their informal influence and to protect their profession. In other words, what needs further analysis here is the need, in the first place, for *nyamakala* specialists to "play up" these stereotypical representations many non-smiths hold of them regarding them. Such representations suggest some threats to, not solely from, smiths. This again, in my view, underlines smiths' vulnerability to potential, if not actual scapegoating and abject status.

Nyama, a concept of cosmic energy that animates the universe, is at the base of broader "sorcery" power. McNaughton (1988:15) calls this a special energy or "occult" (I prefer "superhuman") power. Many Mande see it as both natural and "mystical," and as a source of moral reciprocity. This force is potentially dangerous, even deadly. People can learn to control it through sorcery, however, and thereby harness it to help them carry out their activities. Bird and Karp (1987) call this energy of action; Arens and Karp (1989) call this non-Weberian creative power. These nuanced descriptions reveal *nyama* as not a one-dimensional negative or anti-social practice, but rather, a necessary power source behind every movement, every task; it is a "prerequisite to all action and is emitted as a by-product of every act" (McNaughton, 1988:15).

Yet these findings also show that *nyama* is highly subject to manipulation and redefinition according to context. Thus the question arises, what is this power's connection to smith status more generally? Iron-working demands a great deal of energy of action, lodged in inorganic matter and emitted as part of the extraction and processing enterprise. Iron smelting (Gabus, 1977; Herbert, 1993) was a practice of tremendous difficulty and danger, demanding refined expertise, arduous labor, and great amounts of time. During that process, iron ore was transformed to bloom and enormous amounts of power and energy were given off. The same is true when iron is molded at the forge into useful implements and art; thus smiths command and work with huge stores of energy. McNaughton views *nyama* as a little like electricity, "... unconstrained by insulated wires, but rather set neatly into a vast matrix of deeply interfaced social and natural laws; but is more than energy" (McNaughton, 1988:16). This is an interesting analogy, though not always used exclusively to characterize smith's powers. For example, I found that some Tuareg diviner/healers used this analogy to me in explaining a practice resembling what in the West is called "laying on of hands" (Rasmussen, 2001a).

The point here is the important role, in several African belief complexes surrounding smith/artisans, of powerful non-visual sense modalities relating to these specialists: as shown, these include for example, images of gustatory food taboos, olfactory aroma idioms, and tactile media. Elsewhere, Rasmussen has explored the importance of the tactile in Tuareg healing (Rasmussen, 2006), though *inaden* do not practice laying on of hands methods of healing, but instead are more active in the aural and musical spirit possession rituals (Rasmussen, 1995). More broadly, this multi-sensorial aspect of smiths' power as ritual, artistic, and technical specialists needs greater emphasis by scholars in order to enhance understanding of its positive and regenerative aspects on the cosmological plane. This task is all the more important, since on the sociopolitical and economic plane, as shown, this power can become re-defined negatively by some local residents and outside observers alike, in specific contexts of tension—by the former, over religious and property concerns, and by the latter, in colonial and postcolonial hegemonic knowledge and power structures. From this perspective, Tuareg smiths's protest ritual, *albourousa,* described in the previous sections, emerges as not simple retaliation, but more: a protection of their cultural and intellectual property.

Relevant here is the spirit world. As in the cases of the Bidan *m'allemin*, the Kapsiki *rerhe*, and the Tuareg *inaden*, one of the Mande blacksmiths' strengths generating fear and awe (not simply denigration, though these sentiments can take this form, as with the Amhara *buda/tayb*), resides with the spirits that live in the wild. Most Mande non-smiths consider wilderness spirits too powerful and frightening to be pleasant. Some peoples, such as many Amhara non-smiths, consider them demonic, implicating smiths in a kind of "fall" from an earlier Creation. In Mande cosmology and philosophy, these *jinew* spirits can be beneficial to people, but they are, like the *djinoun* among the Bidan and the *Kel Essuf* among the Tuareg (Rasmussen, 1995,2008), also capricious and dangerous—uncontrollable by most persons. Wilderness spirits are a major reason why most Mande shun the "bush." (those places outside social centers of human habitation). Smiths and spirits are almost "colleagues" in the eyes of other Mande (McNaughton, 1988:18). The Mande smiths' tasks, like those of many smiths elsewhere, send them into the wild space often, for wood and other materials, and, formerly, for iron ore to smelt. Without alliances with spirits believed to be masters of the wilderness, success, even survival, would be difficult. Even the most dangerous, least sociable spirits can only be subdued by smiths or *kule* wood workers. Thus, as McNaughton terms this process, "the bush writ large is brought to town by individuals who themselves have a foot in each domain" (McNaughton, 1988:18).

Thus smiths among the Tuareg, Amhara, Bidan, Kapsiki, and Mande, to varying degrees, negotiate what I term "treaties" with a complex of spirits through ritual mediation, as they do with humans through social mediation, and these alliances with the superhuman world thus created give smiths access to powers of spirits for any task they care to undertake. Yet in each of these societies, importantly, non-smith social responses to this position vary somewhat. In some societies and in certain contexts within each society, smiths alternately become defined as bridging facilitators/mediators, and alternately become defined as "others," even occasionally as abject outsiders—particularly where religious intolerance and/or property-based tensions arise. The pendulum tends to "swing" between two possible poles of identity, depending upon local histories of client-patron relationships, patterns of property including land, and religious hegemony. Again, key here is the relative resilience of indigenous cosmology and philosophy and the relative flexibility and negotiability of stratified social relationships. Among the Mande, as among the Kapsiki, "traditional" African religion (i.e., pre-dating Islam and/or Christianity) remains stronger in cosmological and ritual practice. In the Mande case, smiths' relation to the spirit world pre-dating Islam in the eyes of non-smtihs resembles somewhat the Kapsiki cultural connections between smiths and the ancestors in the world of the dead. Closer attention to the double-face of *nyama* further illuminates this connection, as well as the Mande and Kapsiki similarities in smiths' powers' double aspect, in their common location between the living human world and the world of the dead.

Nyama energy or life force has a homonym meaning feces, trash, garbage, and by extension, bloated, swollen, "literally crawling with nature's products or processes gone out of control" (McNaughton, 1988:18). Feces contain some of the life force of animals that produce it. In my view, there is a connection here (unmentioned by McNaughton) between death and re-generation. What is rotten is also full of creativity in natural and cultural cycles—dung, for example, a waste product, can be used to fertilize fields and make fires. Perhaps this is why, in Mande-speaking communities, McNaughton reports that a town's most powerful devices are hidden beneath garbage piles that surround it. Indeed, many Tuareg, Amhara, and Mande say that spirits occupy spaces such as empty markets, garbage dumps, and abandoned homes and campsites.

This association between creative power and filth—most closely paralleled in the Kapsiki case specifically connecting the *rerhe's* alleged "smelliness" with dancing with corpses at funerals and eating forbidden foods---may imply danger harbored by the power. In other words, the message here is that the world's energy allowed to get out of hand could leave this world in a fetid ruin; like nuclear power, or powerful antibiotics or cancer-treating toxins, therefore, smiths' powers as "too hot to handle" (recall the Tuareg association between *inaden* and the tiny "fire djinn") must be controlled, and trust—not mistrust—is paramount toward those specialists who possess it or know how to control it. As among the Kapsiki, therefore, life, death, decay, and regeneration are interwoven in mutually reconstituted powers still vital in Mande cosmology and philosophy that pre-date some residents' conversion to Christianity or Islam later introduced into these communities. Moreover, official, organized scriptural religions in Kapsiki and Mande communities are not powerfully intertwined with the stratified social order involving overlords monopolizing land, livesstock, and/or other property and military control over client or servile peoples, as they are in the Amhara and Bidan/Moor and in someTuareg communities.

Thus smiths' ritual powers in Mande and Kapsiki communities are somewhat less threatening, since the collective memory of their positive regenerative role tends to be less submerged; but still, as in the other ethnographic and cross-cultural cases, these powers must be carefully guarded and harnessed properly to fight evil. Still, these powers may be socially constructed, for political purposes, as threatening. Thus power is very relative, situational, and subjective.

Other findings on the Mande smith/artisans reinforce my argument here. Control is the idea behind another etymology for *nyamakala*; *kala* is the term for "handle;" *nyamakala* clans are, poetically stated, "metaphorical handles of power, points of access to energy that animates the universe" (McNaughton, 1988:19). Nonetheless, there is also some hostility toward smiths. McNaughton attributes this negative aspect to competition, important in Mande society. Smiths produce valuable resources and provide access through sorcery to the world's energy. This gives them tremendous power, and other citizens can neutralize this with less flattering ideas and restrictions about smiths (McNaughton ,1988:19). Here, again, as in the Tuareg case, envy is significant in scapegoating and exclusionary projects. But in the Tuareg case, the envy stems more from smiths' adaptation to socioeconomic transformations in Tuareg society, whereas according to Bird (in Arens and Karp, 1987) and McNaughton (1988), in the Mande case, this sentiment stems more from the longstanding cultural value of a tension between fadenya and badenya.

Yet the spiritual power of Mande smiths, when viewed comparatively, opens up additional perspectives. *Nyamakala* hold a power akin to that of the Kapsiki smiths, in their mediating roles on the borders of, not solely the living social person transformations at birth and marriage (as with Tuareg smiths), but in Mande communities, also their mediation between life and death. *Nyamakala* inflict dramatic social and spiritual changes on young persons, and expose them temporarily to dangerous levels of *nyama:* for example, as surgeons who circumcise boys in their rite of passage during the *ntomo* initiation association ritual (McNaughton, 1988:19).

In this, there is, if not literal dancing with the dead as among the Kapsiki, at least figurative dancing with death, among the Mande, in the *nyamakala* presiding over the perilous boundary between life and death. This role is another reason for some Mande hostility toward *nyama* power in local mythico-history. Many Mande believe a legendary smith named Ndomajjiri created the *ntomo* association and its arduous program of socialization. The smiths of the *nyamakala* social category still control this, particularly in the countryside, despite the influence of Islam and Christianity among some Mande. *Ntomo* makes irresponsible male children into responsible male adults. As part of this process, neophytes are at certain point led to the wild and forced to confront a horrifying, monstrous horizontal mask, which belongs to one of most powerful secret Mande initiation associations, the *komo*. This mask, as vividly described and photographed by McNaughton, has jaws, horns, organic matter, and a generally filthy appearance (McNaughton, 1988:19). The mask is intended as a didactic moralistic device, iconically warning youths of the problems antisocial persons are likely to encounter. Youths know that the mask and its association are the property of blacksmiths, who will circumcise them and then protect them from the operation's hazards, and who will fashion needed tools for them, but possibly also fail to protect them, and even visit sorcery upon them.

Revealed here is smiths' power in another, more creative light, as mentor-like: smiths test, support, and protect the novice, but also like mentors, may alternatively turn against and discipline the novice. There may be ruptures in these relationships.

By contrast, in Tuareg communities, male circumcision has become subsumed under the official organized religion of Islam. For example, when I inquired whether *inaden* circumcise boys in Tuareg communities, many insisted emphatically, "No! Never *inaden.* Only an Islamic scholar /marabout, or a barber specialist called a *wanzam* (derived from the Hausa term for "barber") does this." It is difficult to ascertain whether or not *inaden* performed circumcision in the distant past, before Tuareg converted to Islam over a thousand years ago, since data on male circumcision prior to that time is unavailable. Yet there are hints that, prior to their conversion, some Tuareg did not circumcise boys: a circumciser described how long ago, a small group of Tuareg near the far northern town of Arlit were not circumcized (for reasons unknown), and when others discovered this, they felt ashamed (Rasmussen, 1997).

The important point here is that Tuareg tend to distance *inaden* from, not solely morturary rituals, but also the more dangerous genital surgery of male circumcision. Van Beek does not report smiths' roles in circumcision in Kapsiki communities. There is strong evidence that, in the Tuareg case, the closer to danger of death one approaches, the ritual roles of inaden become more attenuated than in the Kapsiki and Mande cases; and that, in Tuareg death-focused rituals, the roles of smiths tend to become appropriated by the Islamic clergy. Although the Mande in Mali include many Muslims, significantly, their Islamic scholars have thus far, at least, interfered less with the ritual practices of the blacksmiths in southern Mali. [This situation contrasts markedly with some other neighboring regions where Islamist-reformist groups have recently sought to minimize religious pluralism.] In the Amhara case, data on a different, but related topic is instructive. In the past, some operations making captive slaves in East Africa eunuchs were performed not by smiths, but by Coptic priests. The implications here are interesting, for this detail still suggests the same general pattern of circumcision specialisms. In other words, dangerous procedures of cutting in which humans approach death are entrusted to specialists in either the indigenous or the dominant orthodox religion, depending upon which tradition asserts greater hegemony.

McNaughton reports that many Mande blacksmiths actually do become *somaw,* powerful and aggressive sorcerers (McNaughton 1988:49). In this, smiths often become antagonists of malevolent sorcerers, quite frequently overwhelming them with their own super-sorcery. *Somaw* often aspire to heroic fame. Consequently, their characters become full of unconstrained ferocity called *karo* that makes them very tough. But these *nyamakala* sorcerers aren't prevented from behaving malevolently among themselves. Sometimes, furthermore, smiths are rumored to secretly create problems, with the goal of being asked afterward to solve them and thereby become heroes a la "Munchausen by proxy." Mande say "a hero is welcome only on troubled days." (McNaughton, 1988:49). These findings suggest that competition has taken place, but primarily between smiths and sorcerers, rather than between these specialists and non-smiths who are not sorcerers. Mande blacksmiths are also reputed to invent and possess vast collections of poisons called *korotiw*. Some of these recipes for poison are sent to their victims on the wings of insects. Others ride the wind currents. Others are slipped into a victim's food or drink. All of them are asserted to be potent, deadly devices that provoke much fear among non-smiths.

"Witch-like" power is therefore not always negative or anti-social, and is valued positively or negatively according to the wider religious and sociopolitical contexts and the social interactions of the parties involved. It is true that power acquires character as licit or illicit, harmful or protective, by virtue of the intentions of the individual user. Jealousy, desire for revenge, or quests for fame or political authority frequently lead people to illicit use of knowledge. But fundamental to understanding these processes is analysis of the directions of accusation and of a confluence of forces that lead accusers to target smiths as "witch-like."

CONCLUSIONS

FROM CULTURE HERO TO WITCH AND BACK AGAIN

Many smith/artisans, as shown, self-identify as smiths but also as jewelers, and also buy, sell, and trade their art objects and other wares. But as also shown, even in the urban and global contexts, many of these specialists continue to fulfill mediating social roles, albeit on a larger cultural scale. Simmel's (Simmel in Levine, 1971:144) early use of the "trader" as the prototype for his "stranger" construct because a trader is required only to mediate for goods produced outside the group, assumes that there is no opportunity for anyone else at it (Simmel in Levine, 1971:144). Yet all peoples who survive in culturally and economically threatened situations are prone to social categorization—itself a highly hegemonic process. The problem here is the diversity of possible consequences in representation—by both local official authorities and outside observers.

I favor a shift away from simply identifying and defining "peripatetics" or specialists and their patrons and customers, or for that matter, "witches" and their accusers, toward a better understanding of the emergence and endurance of those situations that support them. How vulnerable and how empowered are they, and when? Berland and Rao (2004) constructively argue for nearness and remoteness at the same time, and favor greater flexibility and positive interaction in overall findings on this topic. Yet I believe one must address an important issue raised here: What shapes either outcome, of negative and positive definitions of power to emerge at given times and places?

Historical archives, as noted, consist of almost entirely dominant voices, and tend to exclude or distort or minimize peripatetics' own voices (Berland and Rao, 2004:11). For example, police records and other official discourses in Europe criminalized peripatetics, as they continue to do today to immigrant labor migrants. Aristocrats in many African and Middle Eastern societies also tend to disparage them. Indeed, even in Italy in 2008, a law was enacted requiring all Roma to be fingerprinted. These policies and attitudes are neither new, nor limited to one group. By the 19th century, nomadism in Europe became equated with vagrancy. There has been widespread criminalization of poverty, also.

Yet trends are problematic if over-generalized or de-contextualized. In the Tuareg case, some trends of nomadism noted for other peripatetics are reversed: smiths follow nobles, and until recently the latter, not the former, have been more nomadic, and some smith/artisans are now wealthier than some nobles in Tuareg society. Yet nomadism—whether by smiths or nobles in Tuareg society—has generally been defined as a "problem' by colonial and post-colonial nation state governments, not specific social statuses (Claudot-Hawad,

1993,1996). Itinerant lifestyles were sometimes assumed to consist of "wandering" without positive goals or definite destinations; yet in a sociological self-fulfilling prophecy, the Roma in Europe were forced to "wander," rather than settle down, to escape persecution. Moreover, among Tuareg, there are varying degress of "nomadism" and different social categories historically have been involved in it—not solely smith/artisans. Social subordinates such as former slaves were often sedentarized on oases, whereas nobles, as already observed, came in to the oases only to collect tribute (Bernus, 1981; Nicolaisen and Nicolaisen, 1997). Rather than levying this tribute on *inaden*, *inaden* assisted the nobles in collecting it. Finally, nomadism can be taken too literally.

While qualities of nearness and remoteness, landlessness and rootlessness, powerlessness, mobility, objectivity, flexibility, and resourcefulness may positively enable the position of stranger, these same characteristics may also engender negative, detrimental, even dangerous consequences in their relationships with "client" communities. There is both mutual dependence and asymmetric tension to these relationships, historically and cross-culturally, and both dimensions need to be accounted for. Among the Tuareg, as already observed, relationships between smiths and non-smiths are not fixed; their relationships are changing, with some symmetric and some asymmetric elements, and in the latter, smiths and nobles both sometimes assert power and sometimes lack power—the outcome depends on the context. Although smith praise-songs are widely considered to be less powerful than Islamic scholars' *al baraka* blessing or benediction, a smith's *tezma* power can have an active effect if nobles bypass smiths at their weddings; hence the potential social consequential power of praise songs, as well as *tezma,* even if they are not officially classified by Tuareg as equally effective as the Islamic *al baraka.* Similarly, although among the Amhara, *buda* smiths of the "evil eye"are usually portrayed as malevolent and destructive, their presence and role in at least one method of curing this affliction are essential. In effect, they immunize against evil.

Moreover, as noted, the old social dyad of noble/smith client/patron has become de-stabilized and there is interference from "third parties" in many contexts, particularly in urban, state and NGO-related settings, and in cultural encounters. What happens to *inaden* powers in these circumstances is interesting, for they begin to mediate between diverse, cultural agents, farther afield than the old noble patron modeled on fictive kinship and gender tropes. Yet cultural pluralism does not guarantee relativism in attitudes, let alone equality in statuses. In India, strangers were and are integrated either as rulers or as untouchables, or as both; does such structural integration take place in all host societies? Is it easier in some than in others? How far and why do humans need a concept of "the strange" in the first place?

Here I offer a framework that retains the analytical strengths of the Simmelian "stranger" concept, but corrects its limitations. This requires an analysis juxtaposing envy and blame with more positive and integrative creative power in cultural reproduction.

BLAME AND ENVY: THE "EVIL TWINS" OF ADMIRATION

What is the relation between a transgression of norms, guilt feelings, ensuing punishment, and reversal of this process in mythico-histories? There is often the tendency to attribute or transfer blame to others as a mechanism for preserving one's own self-esteem. Self-protection is important here; recall, for example, the meaning of Tuareg smiths' alleged lack of shame or reserve to themselves. There is also a reversal here: in myths, as shown, the transformation of their "original niche of high status and /or prosperity, to their present niche, of low or ambiguous status and/or poverty" does not always convey self-perceptions, but can also convey perceptions by official voices to validate oppression by the latter. Or alternatively, myths may serve as a consolation since they assure a respectable genealogy, and as evidence that contemporary peripatetics not responsible for their present situation, to the extent they interpret their position as oppressive. On the other hand, myths may serve as enabling tools, to maximize the benefits of their interactions with host communities, for example, to show remorse. For example, in the 15th century in western Europe, Roma explained that they were going on pilgrimage to expiate their sins, and they were well received by local authorities. But even this appears to be the product of the official viewpoint—did the Roma, in fact, really believe in this "guilt" and "sin" themselves?

What is the difference between discriminated against, pariah, low caste, holy, taboo, marginal, and mediator? In my view, anthropologists need to revise concepts of Simmelian strangeness, Turnerian liminality, and Douglasian anomaly to interpret diverse forms of otherness. Social and collective transformations of personal sentiments are pertinent here. For one common sentiment evoked throughout many encounters with smith/artisans and other specialists in client-patron relationships, as shown, is in fact a sentiment close to admiration: its "evil twin," envy.

As Epstein (2003) points out, envy is far from innocuous. It is, moreover, neither completely idiocyncratic nor completely shared collectively. According to Epstein (2003:1), in the Websterian English language definition, envy is ill-will occasioned by contemplation of superior advantages possessed by another. This author suggests that envy is also a Rorschach test: "tell what you envy, and you reveal a great deal about yourself" (Epstein, 2003:2). Aristotle in *The Rhetoric* writes of emulation as good envy, or envy ending in admiration, in the attempt to imitate qualities one began by envying. What determines this outcome, or the opposite outcome, of hatred and oppression? To Epstein, jealousy is not always pejorative, whereas envy always is pejorative (Epstein, 2003:4). Envy is bent on destruction. Envy is also distinct from open conflict: envy is almost never out in open; is secretive, plotting, behind the scenes (Epstein, 2003:7). In western philosophy and Abrahamic traditions, envy is one of the so-called cold-blooded sins, proceeding from not physical passion, but from a state of mind; envy is the cruelest of all (Epstein, 2003:9).

Among the Tuareg, there are elaborate and complex philosophical efforts to control envy and protect against its destructive consequences, in the numerous Tamajaq terms for coveting, resentment, and jealousy-based anti-social tensions, for example, *tehot, awal, togerchet*, terms for approximately evil eye and evil mouth in English (Casajus, 2000; Nicolaisen, 1961; Rasmussen, 2004). Often, misfortune is attributed to not solely the Islamic God Allah or chance, but also to human frailties. In local concepts of speech, there are direct connections between speech, power, and envy. Tuareg concepts of sin (*ibakaden*) tend to hold in check the more destructive effects of envy by emphasizing lack of generosity as a grave sin: prosperous and successful persons should give alms and share wealth; they strong should care for and support the weak. In other words, although as in any society, humans covet, there are efforts to prevent this through cultural ideals of reciprocity, which are said to protect one from natural and human adversities, much more than hoarding does. For example, if one is suffering from *togerchet* (the jealous gossip of others) one should give alms to a small child who cannot yet speak, ideally on Friday, the Muslim holy day. Other generosity should be directed toward subordinates in the pre-colonial social hierarchy, for example, giving food to former slaves, which prevents human-activated disasters such as sorcery and evil eye, and protects from natural disasters such as lightning. Still, even if one is generous, some persons remain jealous and continue to covet; indeed, many insisted to me that malevolent powers can strike precisely those persons "who are very nice" (Rasmussen, 2001a).

Envy comes in varying degrees. Real envy may reserved not for the great or the greatly gifted, however, but for those whose situation seems only slightly better than ours, for example, many accused witches in Europe tended to be those with not great wealth, but only a little wealth. The point is that many beliefs can be found to derive from particular anxiety about envy, and may be interpreted as a system of ritual environmental control directed against envy (Epstein, 2003:34).

Envy becomes political when it becomes generalized (Epstein, 2003:53), as in class resentments; Evil eye representations tend to luxuriate around contradictions, especially: for example, between an asserted equality and objective conditions which make its realization impossible or in the Tuareg case, the opposite: an asserted inequality and objective conditions which make the prestige of the old hierarchy impossible to realize: for nobles, in their poverty; for smiths, in their newfound relative wealth.

Often, envy involves not solely coveting, but also blame. Much anthropological literature has analyzed the way blame takes the form of witchcraft, but few connections have been made between witchcraft, more general exclusionary projects such as racism, sexism, homophobia, and religious intolerance, and superhuman ritual powers. I agree with ter Haar (2007) who points out the challenges of problems represented by witchcraft accusations: it is not beliefs in witchcraft per se, but actions taken against alleged witches that cause scapegoating, persecution, and other suffering—this is a distinction that merits greater emphasis in anthropology. One needs to consider the extremes to which retribution against supposed witches has been taken recently, as human rights violations and "hate crimes," not just "leveling mechanisms;" for the latter theory—traditionally more favored in anthropology, and relevant in some contexts—tends to more often blame the victims of political or physical violence and implicitly condone witch-hunts. Walter van Beek in ter Haar (2007) argues that some anthropologists have been prevented by their relativist stance from investigating or understanding an important aspect of subject of witchcraft: intra- and intersociety variability in consequences to those accused of witchcraft has been described, but not explained. Understanding why violence does or does not ensue, and the forms it takes, is therefore essential if its modern manifestations and approximations, if not exact equivalents, are to be halted.

In a recent work, Pamela Stewart and Andrew Strathern (2003) productively combine studies of witchcraft and sorcery and rumor and gossip. They reveal the importance of rumor and gossip as catalysts for accusations of witchcraft and sorcery, and demonstrate their role in the genesis of social and political violence, as seen in peasant rebellions, as well as witch-hunts.

Yet gossip and rumor can also be marshaled in protecting from violence, in certain circumstances. As observed, in Tuareg communities, particularly in the countryside, although everyone participates in gossip, *inaden* tend to control this more, since they interact in visiting with a wider range of persons from more diverse backgrounds, and tend to be more far-reaching in the effects of their gossip; for in effect, *inaden* disseminate news more widely than some others. Thus there is malleability of local typifications of power, social identity, and relatedness. Yet witchcraft accusations have, over the years, been usually analyzed functionally and structurally: as a social strain-gauge (Marwick, 1964), linked to social control and change (Moore and Sanders, 2001:7), as resistance to such change (Comaroff and Comaroff ,2000); and as anomaly (Douglas, 1966,1992). Hopefully, consideration of more positive cultural reproduction by smiths offers additional perspectives of how and why their ambiguous powers are alternately reviled and celebrated.

SMITHS AND CULTURAL REPRODUCTION

Smith/artisans, although surrounded by imagery suggesting "strangeness," are often very much insiders cosmologically, philosophically, and socially in several cultural settings, even as they stand apart in some sense, to mediate. I now conclude by pondering issues of belonging, relatedness, identity, and distinctiveness. Specifically, two questions arise here: first, why despite their vital and central (not always peripheral or peripatetic) roles, are smiths in some contexts—particularly socio-political domains of struggle—simultaneously constructed as "outsiders," and why, if neither women nor smiths are always associated invariably with nature, are there frequent symbolic analogies between smiths and women and nature? These questions are puzzling in light of smiths' centrality to culture, but also their ambiguity in society and ritual.

In many smelting and forging rituals, particularly in Africa south of the Sahara, anthropologists have observed widespread anthropomorphism, especially genderization, of smith's powers. Among the Mafa, for example, men are to women as Vavai are to smelters; the smelter as a transformer and converter, and thus this "outsider" status, Herbert argues, may be seen as "a situational female" (Herbert,1993:84). Hadza smelters in Tanzania formerly wore women's raffia skirts (Herbert, 1993:84). Similarly, I have described how Tuareg smiths are sometimes said, by both themselves and non-smiths, to be "like women...you (in principle) never argue with them."

But why must this status be read as "outside" or marginal? Interpreting females as outsiders to culture is now recognized as problematic (MacCormack and Strathern, 1988). Instructive here is the close association, pervasive in Africa, between fire and birth. A child, like a pot, is the product of a successful firing which must be followed by a ritual cooking and then a gradual cooling down as it is integrated into the lineage (Herbert, 1993:87). Reproductive processes are frequently surrounded by taboos. For example, among the Luba in the Congo, no ironworker was allowed to have anything to do with preparation or food. Each type of cooking must therefore be kept separate.

Here the identification of smelting and cooking and danger is metaphorical, of like to like, somewhat recalling the Beng need for separation of human and forest fertility in Cote-d'Ivoire (Gottlieb, 2004). In the symbolism of female reproduction in smelting and furnaces of smiths in a number of societies in Africa, there are frequently taboos against sexual relations and menstruating women near these activities. Thus these different channels of fertilityand reproduction are analogous, but cannot be mixed if they are to remain effective.

In other words, there are symbolic analogical relationships, in cosmology, philosophy, and symbolism, between smiths' and women's reproduction in many of these societies, but—importantly—their social roles are not equivalent.

In some other social contexts, more is at play. In the Tuareg case, as noted, smiths are compared to women, but this analogy is not salient solely on the cosmological level; for *inaden* men, it should be recalled, traditionally act in the interest of women in spirit-related healing rituals and in the interests of the woman's family during marriage bridewealth negotiations. *Inaden* manufacture the jewelry given the new bride by her groom and by her mother. In general, *inaden* are viewed as more sympathetic to women's interests, and make better confidantes, than Islamic scholars, in delicate matters such as marital discord. In divorce and ensuring property division, for example, Islamic scholars in rural areas often rule in favor of the husband (Rasmussen, 1995,2006).

The point is that social practices and cosmological configurations are fundamental to understanding the "feminine" imagery surrounding many smith/artisans. Yet this role as women's confidante, as also shown earlier in the Tuareg case of alleged adultery, can be fraught with potential conflicts of interest: as when, for example, smiths are feared by some male non-smiths to morph from "women's friend" into "women's lover." Thus in my view, the anthropomorphism and genderization in smiths' symbolic representation can make them vulnerable to social conflicts in some situations. As Jackson observes, vicarious mastery of the world entails ironically also a separation from it, in "clandestine gains at the cost of social integration" (Jackson in Arens and Karp, 1990:69). The power to shape-shift condemns the specialist to periodic scapegoating and exclusionary projects. Local residents sometimes call on stereotypes to comprehend and cope with the crisis which erodes self-control and subverts identity. This observation holds true, but to varying degrees, and with diverse situational consequences, for smith/artisan powers.

SMITHS, SOCIAL CLASS, AND ETHNICITY

Thus a situational approach to these processes suggests both uses and limitations to "peripatetic" (Berland and Rao, 2004) as a literal cover-term for somewhat diverse specialists who are minorities in societies where they work. This usage can be too broad; for some smiths and griots, for example, are only partially peripatetic. In many parts of Africa, furthermore, there has been shown to be a fluidity to the boundaries between, not only so-called "peripatetics" and those for whom they work, but also among these specialists themselves, as well as transformations over time. Many frequently combine artisan and other work; recall, for example, Tuareg smiths' recent taking up of oasis gardening, competing for land with their traditional noble patrons in some sedentarized communities, and becoming additional rivals over increasingly scarce garden plots since freed slaves took over some oasis gardens. Anthropologists need to accept these groups' fluid identities, and analyze them in terms of relatedness, practice, and process.

As shown, often, specialists are mentioned in some older literature, in ways that were often racist, ethnocentric, or at least denigrating, for example, early authors used such terms as "rabble" and "refuse," out of context. Hence the issue, raised earlier, of how far apparently abject status derives from local typifications and how far this arises from ethnocentric portrayals by outside colonial administrators, travelers, and missionaries. The point here is that "abjectness" (Butler, 1990,1992,1993) attributed to these specialists in some accounts derives, not entirely from the host society, but rather as much or more from some historical portrayals in the literatures.

Yet this critical insight does not resolve the problem of very real prejudice coming from a few local residents. More broadly, the smith/artisan material reminds us that labels such as "caste" and "ethnic group," as used in much ethnohistorical and anthropological literature elsewhere—for example, in Burundi and Rwanda (Mamdani, 2001), are Euroamerican cultural and linguistic categories, constructed and often "frozen" into rigidities by colonial or colonial-impacted accounts, and this insight needs to be considered in analyzing the roles of smith/artisans and their relationships to non-smiths. In social practice, the picture is far more dynamic. On the other hand, the salience and uniqueness of smith/artisans' identities and powers are partly constructed from local stratified social systems, albeit to varying degrees.

The rich spiritual and socially integrative side to their powers can be obscured in peripatetic and even Simmelian stranger concepts, which tend to emphasize structural status and etic nomenclature, and also to ignore the importance of intention, practice, and consequence. Among the Bidan (Moors), the Tuareg, and the Mande, as shown, some local non-smiths do represent *m'allemin, inaden,* and *nyamakala* smiths respectively as using powers malevolently. But as also shown, there are believed to be varying degrees of intentionality in exercising malevolence; *echar,* for example, approximates the classic anthropological concept of sorcery, as this is intentional; whereas by contrast, *tezma* approaches more closely the classic idea of "witchcraft," as this is often unintentional, but this is complex, since its sentiment, anger, is very real, but its effect—of flying from the heart of the offended smith to the offender or to their kin or property—is often beyond control. Thus neither of these powers is exactly equivalent to these classic anthropological concepts of "malevolent" power.

On the surface, these specialists' roles in religion appear paradoxical. They are often surrounded by symbolic imagery of fertility, life, and regeneration, on the one hand, and on the other, also death, decay, and danger. Yet if one examines these powers in context, their meaning becomes clearer, independently of whether or not these specialists "belong" to a specific category. Relevant here in my view is the reason given for a smallpox goddess in India: in effect, one must appease this power over disaster, as a source of potential disaster or a source of repelling disaster, as in the biomedical "vaccination." This idea is, in effect, a spiritual innoculation. One must receive a small portion of the power, with its malevolent potential, in order to derive its positive protective benefits, though there are also very real conflicts in some other contexts of assertion of these powers. In fact, some Tuareg stated that *inaden* "give injections to women," suggesting a power over them but also protection of them. Herbert's (1993) explanation of smiths' powers, that they straddle the boundary between culture and the wilderness, are placed outside, yet confronting their client communities, while compelling on one level, emerges here as on another level as somewhat misleading. For nature and culture are not everywhere considered separate domains in the first place. The synergy of these specialists enables them to act dynamically, but not solely in terms of strange or wild status; rather, in starting up the powers of the universe and mediating between human and superhuman powers. Thus my own interpretation does not refute their position out of hand, but rather offers, hopefully, an additional nuance to ritual specialists' powers.

Many aetiological mythico-histories of these smith/artisans, as I have shown, appear to emphasize their otherness and explain their apparently "subordinate" position. The first motif is found among the *inaden* and the *buda*. The second motif, also, was found among the *inaden*, and also among the *m'allemin*. According to Bollig (in Berland and Rao, 2004:221), the first motif is found in myths mainly in stratified societies, and the second motifs in myths are found primarily in societies with minimal stratification . More distant examples include the mythico-history of the origins of the "Gypsies" of the Nile Valley, very similar to those Reminick (1974) recorded among the Amhara pertaining to the *buda* people, relating how they were smiths who produced nails for the crucifixion of Jesus, and then they were cursed and damned to roam the world eternally. These general motifs, mostly not identified as to their tellers (were these accounts from the "peripatetics" themselves or from the "hosts" or patrons?) or their contexts of telling, seemingly present a picture of self-induced marginal positions, guilt, and atonement. Yet as shown in my Tuareg data, the voices of the marginal group often elaborate further that, in their own viewpoint, finer nuances are involved suggesting a re-reading of these meanings situationally. For the second motif, as well as the first motif, also occurs among the Tuareg: recall how the *inaden* related how they were once wealthy, but when they divulged the secret of their wealth, God withdrew it, and they became poor. Thus both motifs can be present within the same society—whether more or less stratified, perhaps reflecting social transformations over time such as those occurring in Tuareg society more broadly, particularly changes in noble-servile and noble-client relationships. The important point is that these aetiological myths about ritual specialists portray their origins in terms of reflections on the moral and political ambiguity of the social relationships between patrons and clients, who are fraught with concerns to control unchannelled and unchecked powers—not solely those of smiths, but also those of others. All parties to these relationships must continually reassure each other that they are neighbors and culture-heroes, not witches.

BIBLIOGRAPHY

Achebe, Chinua. *Things Fall Apart*. New York: Fawcett Press, 1959.

Agg-Alawjeli, Ghubayd. *Histoire de Kel-Denneg avant l'arrivee des Francais*. Copenhagen: Akademisk Forlag, 1975.

Ardener, Edwin and Shirley Ardener. *Perceiving Women*. Cambridge: Cambridge University Press, 1977.

Arens, William and Ivan Karp. *The Creativity of Power*. Washington D.C.: Smithsonian Institution Press, 1989.

Asad, Talal. "The Translation of Culture." In *Writing Culture*, edited by Marcus, George and James Clifford, 141-65. Berkeley: University of California Press, 1986.

Auslander, Mark. "Open the Wombs!" In *Modernity and its Malcontents*. edited by Jean and John Comaroff, 167--93. Chicago: University of Chicago Press, 1993.

Baier, Steven and Paul Lovejoy. "The Desert-Side Economy of the Central Sudan." In *The Politics of Natural Disaster: The Case of the Sahel Drought*, edited by M. H. Glantz, 144-75. .New York: Praeger, 1977.

Bakhtin, Mikhail. *Rabelais and His World*. Bloomington: Indiana University Press, 1986.

Baudrillard, Jean. *Simulacres et Simulation*. Paris: Galilee, 1981.

Beidelman, Thomas. O. *The Translation of Cultures: Essays to E.E. Evans-Pritchard*. London: Travistock, 1971.

Berland, Joseph and Aparna Rao. *Customary Strangers: New Perspectives on Peripatetic Peoples in the Middle East, Africa, and Asia*. Westport, Ct. and London: Praeger, 2004.

Benhazera, Maurice. *Six mois chez les Touareg du Ahaggar*. Algiers: Adolphe Jourdan, 1908.

Bernus, Edmond. *Touaregs Nigeriens: Unite culturelle et diversite regionale d'un people Pasteur*. Paris: Editions ORSTOM, [1981], 1993.

————"The Tuareg Artisan: From Technician to Mediator." In *The Art of Being Tuareg*, edited by Loughran, Kristyne and Thomas Seligman, 75-90. Palo Alto and Los Angeles: Iris B. Cantor Center for the Arts and UCLA Fowler Museum, 2006.

Bird, Charles. 1987. "The Mande Hero." In *Explorations in African Systems of Thought*, edited by Bird, Charles and Ivan Karp, 13-27. Bloomington: Indiana University Press.

Bollig, Michael. "Hunters, Foragers, and Singing Smiths: The Metamorphoses of Peripatetic Peoples in Africa." In *Customary Strangers*. edited by Berland, Joseph and Aparna Rao, 196-231.Westport and London: Praeger, 2004.

Bonte, Pierre. "Structure de classe et structures sociales chez les Kel Gress." *Revue de l'Occident musulman et de la Mediterranee*, 21(1976): 141-162.

Briggs, Lloyd Cabot. "European Blades in Tuareg Swords and Daggers." *Journal of the Arms and Armour Society*, 5 (2) (1965): 37-55.

Bunzl, Matti. "Between anti-Semitism and Islamophobia: Some Thoughts on the New Europe." *American Ethnologist*, 32 (4) (2005): 499-509.

Butler, Judith. *Gender Trouble*. NY: Routledge, 1990.

———*Feminists Theorize the Political*. NY: Routledge, 1992.

———*Erotic Warfare: Sexual Theory and Politics in the Age of Epidemic*. NY: Routledge, 1993.

Carrier, James. *Occidentalism*. Cambridge: Cambridge University Press, 1995.

Casajus, Dominique. *La Tente dans l'Essuf*. Cambridge and New York: Cambridge University Press, Editions de la maison des sciences de l'homme, 1989.

———*Gens de la Parole: Langage, poesie, et politique en pays Touareg*. Paris: Editions la decouverte texts a l'appui/anthropologie, 2000.

Cervello, Mariella Villasante. "They Work to Eat and They Eat to Work: *M'Allemin* Craftsmen, Classification, and Discourse among the Bidan Nobility of Mauritania." In *Customary Strangers,* edited by Berland, Joseph and Aparna Rao, 123-55. Westport and London: Praeger, 2004.

Ciekawy, D. and Peter Geschiere. "Containing Witchcraft: Conflicting scenarios in Postcolonial Africa." *African Studies Review* 41 (3) (1998): 1-15.

Claudot-Hawad, Helene. *Touaregs: Portraits en fragments*. Aix-en-Provence: Edusud, 1993.

———*Touaregs: Voix Solitaires sous l'Horizon Confisque*. Paris: Ethnies, 1996.

Comaroff, Jean and John Comaroff. *Modernity and its Malcontents*. Chicago: University of Chicago Press, 1993.

Crapanzano, Vincent. *Hermes's Message and Hamlet's Desire*. Cambridge, MA: Harvard University Press, 1992.

Crick, Malcolm. *Explorations in Language and Meaning*. New York: John Wiley and Sons, 1976.

Donham, Donald. *The Southern Marshes of Imperial Ethiopia: Essays in History and Social Anthropology*. Cambridge: Cambridge University Press, 1986.

———*Marxist Modern*. Berkeley: University of California Press, 1999.

Douglas, Mary. *Purity and Danger*. London: Routledge Kegan Paul, 1966.

———1975. *Implicit Meanings*. London: Routledge.

Douglas, Mary and Aaron Wildavsky. *Risk and Culture*. Berkeley: University of California Press, 1992.

Englund, H. Witchcraft, Modernity, and the Person: The Morality of Accumulation in Central Malawi. *Critique of Anthropology,* 16(3) (1986): 257-79.

Epstein, Joseph. *Envy*. New York: Oxford, 2003.

Evans-Pritchard, E.E. *Witchcraft, Magic, and Oracles among the Azande.* Oxford: Clarendon Press, 1937.
————*Nuer Religion.* Oxford: Clarendon Press, 1950.
Fabian, Johannes. *Time and the Other.* Cambridge: Cambridge University Press, ————1981.
Foster, George. *Traditional Societies and Technological Change.* NY: Harper and Row, 1973.
Foucauld, Charles (Pere) de. *Dictionnaire touareg-francais: Dialecte de l'Ahaggar.* Paris: Imprimerie nationale, 1951-52.
Freeman, Dena and Alula Plankhurst. *Initiating Change in Highland Ethiopia: The Causes and Consequences of Cultural Transformation.* Cambridge: Cambridge University Press, 2003.
Gabus, Jean. *Au Sahara: Arts et Symbols.* Neuchatel: Editions de la Baconniere, [1958], 1970.
Gardi, Rene. *Sahara.* Bern: Kummerly and Frey, 1970.
Gottlieb, Alma. *The Afterlife Is Where We Come From.* Chicago: University of Chicago Press, 2004.
Greschiere, Peter. *The Modernity of Witchcraft: Politics and the Occult in Postcolonial Africa.* Charlottesville: University Press of Virginia, 1997
Grinker, Roy Richard and Christopher Steiner. *The Experience of Africa.* Malden and Oxford: Wiley Blackwell Press, 1997.
Hale, Thomas. *Griots and Griottes.* Bloomington: Indiana University Press, 1999.
Herbert, Eugenia *Iron, Gender, and Power.* Bloomington: Indiana University Press, 1993.
Herzfeld, Michael. *Cultural Intimacy.* NY: Routledge, 2004.
Jackson, Michael. *Paths Toward a Clearing.* Bloomington: Indiana University Press, 1990.
Keenan, Jeremy. *The Tuareg: People of Ahaggar.* London: Allen Lane.
Kohl, Ines. *Beautiful Modern Nomads.* Berlin: Reimer Verlag, 2009.
Leinhardt, Godfrey. *Divinity and Experience.* NY and Oxford: Oxford University Press, 1961.
Levine, Donald. *Georg Simmel: On Individuality and Social Forms.* Chicago: University of Chicago, 1971.
————*Greater Ethiopia: The Evolution of a Multiethnic Society.* Chicago: University of Chicago Press, 1974.
Lhote, Henri. *Les Touaregs du Hoggar.* Paris: Hachette, 1955.
Loughran, Kristyne. *Tuareg Jewelry: Continuity and Change.* Ph.D. dissertation, Bloomington: Indiana University, 1996.
Loughran, Kristyne and Thomas Seligman. *The Art of Being Tuareg.* Palo Alto and Los Angeles: Ida B. Cantor Center for the Arts and UCLA Fowler Museum, 2006.

Mains, Daniel. "Neoliberal Times: Progress, Boredom, and Shame among Young Men in Urban Ethiopia." *American Ethnologist* 34 (4) (2007): 659-74.

Malkki, Liisa. *Purity and Exile.* Berkeley: University of California Press, 1995.

Mamdani, Mahmood. *When Victims Become Killers.* Princeton: Princeton University Press, 2000.

Marwick, Max. *Witchcraft and Sorcery.* Harmondsworth: St. Martins Press, 1964.

Masquelier, Adeline. *Prayer Has Spoiled Everything.* Durham, NC: Duke University Press, 2001.

MacFarlane, Alan. "The Root of All Evil." In *The Anthropology of Evil,* edited by Parkin, David, 57-77. NY: Basil Blackwell, 1985.

McNaughton, Patrick. *The Mande Blacksmiths: Knowledge, Power, and Art in West Africa.* Bloomington: Indiana University Press, 1988.

Middleton, John. *Lugbara Religion.* London: Oxford University Press, 1960.

Moore, Henrietta and Todd Sanders. *Magical Interpretations, Material Realities.* London: Routledge, 2001.

Mudimbe, V.Y. *The Invention of Africa.* Bloomington: Indiana University Press, 1986.

——*Parables and Fables.* Madison: University of Wisconsin Press, 1992.

Murphy, Robert. "Social Distance and the Veil."*American Anthropologist* 66(1964): 1257-74.

N'Diaye, N. *Les Castes au Mali.* Bamako: Editions populaires, 1970.

Nicolas, Francis. *Tamesna: Les Ioullimmedan d l'Est, ou Tuareg Kel Dinnik, cercle de Tahoua, colonie du Niger.* Paris: Imprimerie nationale, 1950.

Nicolaisen, Ida and Johannes Nicolaisen. *The Pastoral Tuareg.* Copenhagen: Rhodos, 1997.

Nicolaisen, Johannes. "Essai sur la religion et la magie touaregues." *Folk* 3(1961):113-60.

Norris, H.T. *The Tuareg: their Islamic Legacy and its Diffusion in the Sahel.* London: Fryson, 1975.

——*Sufi Mystics of the Niger Desert.* Oxford: Clarendon Press, 1990.

Parkin, David. *The Anthropology of Evil.* New York: Basil Blackwell, 1985.

——*The Sacred Void.* Cambridge: Cambridge University Press, 1991.

Pratt, Mary Louise. *Imperial Eyes.* Berkeley: University of California Press, 1992.

Rasmussen, Susan. *Spirit Possession and Personhood among the Kel Ewey Tuareg.* Cambridge: Cambridge University Press, 1995.

——*The Poetics and Politics of Tuareg Aging: Life Course and Personal Destiny in Niger.* DeKalb: Northern Illinois University Press, 1997.

——"Ritual Powers and Social Tensions as Moral Discourse among the Tuareg." *American Ethnologist* 100(2) (1998): 458-68.

————*Healing in Community: Medicine, Contested Terrains, and Cultural Encounters among the Tuareg.* Westport, Ct.: Bergin & Garvey, 2001a.

————"Betrayal or Affirmation? Transformations in Witchcraft Technologies of Power, Danger, and Agency among the Tuareg." In *Magical Interpretations, Material Realities,* edited by Moore, Henrietta and Todd Sanders, 136-160. London: Routledge, 2001b.

————"When the Field Space Comes to the Home Space." *Anthropological Quarterly* 76(1) (2003): 7-33.

————"These Are Dirty Times! Transformations of Gendered Spaces and Islamic Ritual Protection in Tuareg Herbalists' and Marabouts' *Al Baraka* Blessing Powers." *Journal of Ritual Studies* 18(2) (2004): 43-60.

————*Those Who Touch: Tuareg Medicine Women in Anthropological Perspective.* DeKalb: Northern Illinois University Press, 2006.

————"The People of Solitude: Recalling and Reinventing *Essuf,* (the Wild) in Traditional and Emergent Tuareg Cultural Spaces." *Journal of the Royal Anthropological Institute,* 14 (2008): 609-627.

Reminick, Ronald. "The Evil Eye Belief among the Amhara of Ethiopia." *Ethnology,* 13 (1974): 279-291.

Rodd, Lord of Rennell. *People of the Veil.* London: MacMillan, 1926.

Saenz, Candelario. *They Have Eaten Our Grandfathers!* Ph.D. dissertation. Morningside Heights: Columbia University, 1991.

Said, Edward. *Orientalism.* NY: Pantheon Press, 1978.

Salifou, A. *Kaoussan ou la revolte senoussiste.* Etudes Nigeriennes numero 33, CNRSH: Niamey, Niger, 1973.

Scott, James. *Domination and the Arts of Resistance.* New Haven: Yale University Press, 1990.

Simmel, Georg. [1908] 1950. "The Stranger." In *The Sociology of Georg Simmel,* edited by K.H. Wolf, 402-408. New York: Free Press, [1908] 1950.

————In *Georg Simmel: On Individuality and Social Forms,* edited by Donald Levine. Chicago: University of Chicago Press, 1971.

Smith, Andrea. "Heteroglossia, Common Sense, and Social Memory." *American Ethnologist* 3(2) (2004):251-70.

Sperber, Dan. *Rethinking Symbolism.* Cambridge: Cambridge University Press, 1979.

Spooner, Brian. *Population Growth: Anthropological Implications. Cambridge.* MA.: MIT Press, 1970.

Stewart, Pamela and Andrew Strathern. *Witchcraft, Sorcery, Rumors and Gossip.* Cambridge: Cambridge University Press, 2003.

Stoller, Paul. *The Taste of Ethnographic Things.* Philadelphia: University of Pennsylvania Press, 1989.

Stoller, Paul and Rosemary Coombs. "X Marks the Spot." *Popular Culture* 7 (1994): 249-74.

Stoller, Paul and Cheryl Olkes. *In Sorcery's Shadow*. Chicago: University of Chicago Press, 1987.

Ter Haar, Gerrie. *Imagining Evil: Witchcraft Beliefs and Accusations in Contemporary Africa*. Trenton, NJ: Africa World Press, 2007.

Turner, Victor. *The Forest of Symbols*. Ithaca: Cornell University Press, 1968.

Van Beek, Walter. "The Dirty Smith." *Journal of the Royal Anthropological Institute* (1992): 38-58.

————In *Imagining Evil: Witchcraft Beliefs and Accusations in Contemporary Africa,* edited by Ter Haar, Gerrie. Trenton, NJ: Africa World Press, 2007.

Van Gennep, Arnold. *Les Rites de passage*. Chicago: University of Chicago Press, 1960.

West, Harry. *Ethnographic Sorcery*. Chicago: University of Chicago Press, 2007.

Wood, John. *When Men Are Women*. Madison: University of Wisconsin Press, 1999.